# FECKIT

# FECKIT

BY
LITTLE BRIAN

A Memoir
By
BRIAN O'DONOGHUE

Dedicated to my brother 'Raymin'
who sadly passed away
four weeks before completion.


Published by Brian O'Donoghue



ISBN: 978-1-3999-0958-7

# *Acknowledgements*

Thanks to my family for reminders and corrections.

Thanks to my dear friend Grace McNulty for typing my first manuscript and pushing me forward many years ago.

Many thanks to Anna and Lucy at Carnegie Scotforth Books.

And thank you to my dear wife Marcia who brought stability into my life 30 years ago.

# *Introduction*

## Limerick City, 1995

Myself and my wife Marcia are on holiday in Ireland. I'm showing her the row of cottages my family had lived in nearly forty years before, when I was aged six. We were evicted after my father lost his very good job as a radio officer at Shannon Airport, due to his heavy drinking and absenteeism.

As I point to Number 4, a lady comes out of number Number 3 and asks if she can help. I explain why we are here and tell her about my family connections with Number 4. She looks at me for a short time and then says, 'You'll be little Brian then.'

Her name is Carmel Ryan and, standing in the warm summer sunshine, she tells us stories of what went on in my family in the early nineteen fifties, some of them good, some bad, but all very interesting to myself and Marcia. It amazes me to find out that in the row of six cottages there is only one change of family name in nearly four decades.

After a twenty-minute chat we say our goodbyes and, following Carmel's recommendation, make our way to O'Connell Street in the city where we find a nice coffee shop at the front of one of the big stores. Marcia wants to know more about my childhood in Ireland (she is a 'Yorkshire rose'). I start to tell her about the turbulent times of family life when we lived at Number 4 Crosbie Row, behind King John's castle on King's Island.

After the second cup of coffee she stops me talking and says she wants me to tell her in the way that Carmel Ryan talks.

"Did your mother call you Little Brian? And what were the words that people would use back then in Limerick?"

I tell her that my mother called me Little Brian or Young Brian, which in Gaelic is Brian Óg and sounds like Brian Ogue, as in vogue, and that the word 'liten', that she used a lot, means dirty. Yes, Marcia says, that's what I mean.

"OK, but let's get out of here, these coffees are getting a bit expensive." She gives me one of her looks. "Typical you!"

Right, here we go, I'll do my best. I hope you like it. I'll tell you the story from the child's point of view, in a child's words. Some of the names will have been changed, and some might be spelled wrongly, mostly 'cos I can't remember them all.

# *Chapter 1*

## Limerick City, 1955/56

Mammy tells us all to go out into the backyard and play with the little chicks while she's scraping Daddy's dinner off the wall in the front room where he threw it last night when he was drunk and being a liten bastard. She uses the cursing words all the time when she's been fighting with Daddy. It's not me using the cursing words, I'm only telling you what Mammy says.

She's at the back window now, leaning over the big white sink, with the new glass washboard in her hand doing the washing. I'm playing near the coal shed trying to catch the little yellow chicks and the hens. The big radio is on in the front room and it's been playing happy songs, but Mammy hasn't been singing along with the radio today. I'm thinking it's because she's sad, 'cos of Daddy being a liten bastard.

Daddy has gone to work at Shannon Airport where his job is to listen to pilots in aeroplanes with his headphones on and tell them which way they have to come in to land their planes so they don't crash into things, while he twiddles the radio aerial on the roof of his shed in the middle of a field.

Mammy and Daddy have been fighting since last week when Daddy's mammy came to visit from Dublin, and when she went home, my oldest sister Marie who is eight went to Dublin to live with her and Grandad and Uncle Colm and Uncle Fintan in their big house that has apple trees in the back garden. Marie used to live with them before and she wanted to go back and Nana said that Marie looked neglected. Now there's just Raymin, Helen, me and Louise and the chickens here, but Mammy says there might be another baby coming soon, from Holy God.

When Nana was here Daddy kept telling Mammy to stop cursing and saying words like 'feck' in front of her. He also told Mammy to get dressed better when she meets him off the bus from work and stop wearing that old brown dress and the green knee-high socks that don't stay up. He said that Nana and Grandad don't go around saying feck and things like that. Mammy told him not to worry about the cursing thing. She says that sure if Nana stayed with us a bit longer, she'd soon pick it up. Daddy said that Nana wouldn't want to pick up the cursing words. Then he gave Mammy one of his looks, like I've seen him look at her when he's drunk, just before he thinks about who he wants to have a fight with.

Sometimes when Daddy is shouting at Mammy I go out onto the spare ground at the corner of the street, between the end house and Saint Mary's, the big grey Protestant church. Then I'm far enough away and I can't hear them fighting. I keep away from the Protestants too 'cos Mammy says they'll never go to Heaven and it's not good to talk to people who won't get in. I pick dandelions and collect little golden shiny beetles to feed to the little yellow chicks. At the same time I keep a watch out for Mr Penny Halfpenny, the rag and bone man, who Mammy says will take me away if I'm being bad. And I have to watch out for the man called 'Split the wind' too. He's called that because he walks so fast that he splits the wind. He goes around the houses and gets paid for telling stories. She says he's not a kidnapper or anything like that but he could hurt you if he knocked you down in his hurry.

One day Mammy tells us a new baby will be coming to stay with us. She says Surgeon O'Regan will be bringing the baby soon, when God has decided if it will be a boy or a girl we'll be getting. She says when it's time for the baby to come Daddy will be paying a home-helper girl to do some of the washing and things.

*

Daddy is at work, and Raymin and me are playing out on the street. Helen and Louise are playing in the house. The helper girl is in the house today with Mammy, waiting for the new baby to come. I'm asking Raymin if the new baby will be sleeping in the bed with us, so we can all keep warm together. I'm thinking the baby can sleep at the top of the bed with Helen and Louise to keep our feet warm, so then on a cold night Mammy won't have to warm the old clothes iron on the gas stove and wrap it in a blanket in our bed, so it keeps us from the cold. Raymin says I'm being stupid. He says babies aren't that warm anyway, not until they're about two or three years old. Up 'til then, he says, they sleep in the drawer in the bottom of their Mammy's wardrobe at night.

The helper girl comes running out of the house. She says the baby is about to come and she's off to get the doctor. In a while she's coming back up the street with a man, who must be the doctor 'cos his shoes are all shiny and he has a black bag with him.

He goes into the house and starts doing his job by talking to Mammy and throwing Helen and Louise out into the garden. Helen says they must be having a cup of tea 'cos the doctor told the helper girl to put the kettle on the gas stove. I'm thinking that Mammy is going to read the tea leaves for the doctor. Then she'll know if it will be a boy or a girl that's coming. We're taking it in turns to look in the letter box, now that the front room curtains have been pulled closed to stop us looking in.

It seems ages to when the doctor comes out of the house. He tells us that we have a new baby sister. He says we have to wait outside 'til Mammy calls us in. I'm asking Raymin how the baby got into the house without us seeing her. He says not to be so stupid, the baby was in the doctor's bag. In the doctor's bag all the time! I'd have never figured that out all on my own. Now we're all laughing about the baby being in the black bag while we were waiting for her to come from Holy God and the angels.

The front room curtains are pulled back and the front door is opened by the helper girl. We all dash in to the front room where Mammy is lying down on the long armchair with a tiny baby that's crying. Mammy tells us all, "This is baby Deirdre." I'm asking why the baby is all red and wrinkly, and why I couldn't hear her crying when she was in the black bag. Helen says the baby must have been a bit big for the bag and the doctor probably had to squeeze her in. Louise says that it'll be a special quiet bag for carrying new babies. "OK," I say, "I know the baby came in the doctor's bag, but where did the doctor get it?"

"From Holy God", says Mammy, "now shurrup the lot of you and hould yer whisht!

I'm feeling really happy, 'cos now I know all about babies and doctors and when Daddy gets home from Durty Nelly's pub, after being to work, I can tell him all about it.

Daddy comes home early. He hasn't been to Durty Nelly's. He says he didn't think baby Deirdre would be here so soon. He says her face looks red and she looks very small, but when I explain how she was squashed into the bag he understands why, and now he's smiling and happy.

Soon baby Deirdre is fatter and she isn't as ugly and wrinkly and squashed-looking anymore. Surgeon O'Regan has stopped coming to see Mammy. Mammy says he stopped coming because we all wanted to look inside his black bag and wouldn't give him a minute's peace.

It's good having a new baby and a helper girl. When Mammy's friends come to see baby Deirdre they sometimes give us pennies and sweets. And we get more visits, with ice cream, and not just on Sundays, to the People's Park where we play on the grass at the bottom of the big stone pillar with a stone man on top who Mammy says built the park for the people of Limerick. Mammy says he built it for all of us and baby Deirdre in the pram too.

After the walks we go home and have samiches or one-sided toast. Then we drink tea out of jam jars so we don't break the good cups from the front room. Sometimes baby Deirdre needs cleaning after doing yellow skitters in her nappy. When that happens and I can see it and smell it, it makes me want to be sick, but the others don't bother about it and just laugh when I'm trying to be sick outside the back door. Then I'm trying to be sick again when I see the chicks eating the first sick. Mammy scrapes the skitters off the pieces of torn sheets or pillowcases that she uses to make the nappy, then she washes them in the sink and hangs them out to dry. If it's raining she hangs them around the coal fire in the front room. If it's not raining Mammy sometimes lets us play in the front garden with baby Deirdre as long we don't talk to strangers. She says we must never go down Newgate Street to the tiny little harbour, where the poor little Kelly boy drowned after going down the steps to the river.

*

After school one day, Helen tells Mammy about Raymin.

"Mammy, Raymin is playing down in the water by the fisherman's cottages, and the tide is coming up."

Raymin is 8 years old now, sneaking out a lot to play with Pat Minogue and 'Dreamer' Eagan. When you've seen Mammy in one of her rages you know what he'll be in for if he goes down to the river after so many warnings.

The rain is lashing down as Mammy runs out in her brown dress and green knee-high socks to find him. She doesn't put on a coat 'cos she's in a hurry, but not such a hurry that she forgets the rubber off the handle of the pram that she wants to beat him with. She sees him coming up Newgate from the river. Raymin can see what he's in for and makes a run for it past her to the house, but she's running faster now, with her long socks sliding down her legs into a clump that stops at her ankles.

Mammy catches him as he gets to the front door. She belts him all around his legs as hard as she can, shouting at him, "How many times, God help me, do I have to tell you to keep away from the river! Get inside that house now. I'm going to tell your father when he comes home." Raymin gets it on his hands as well, as he tries to stop her beating him. Red marks stick out from his white skin where the rubber has landed on his bare legs. Me and Louise are standing back from the doorway wondering why Raymin should be getting this awful beating, just for playing down by the river steps.

He breaks away from Mammy's grip and dashes through the hall, into the kitchen where he slides on the concrete floor, wet from rain. He crashes into the big white pot sink, before getting back on his legs and running out the back door, right through the little golden chicks and hens pecking around the garden. He tries to jump onto the upside down tin rubbish bin by the coal shed so he can get over the wall and escape onto the back lane, but he doesn't make it. His legs go through the rusty bin and he falls flat on the ground. His legs are in the bin he's knocked over and the sharp edges are sticking into him. There's blood running down over the red swelled up skin, and all the way down the bin 'til it drips into the black rain puddle outside the coal shed. The chicks are looking at him on the ground in the mud. They're probably thinking he's a bit too big to eat.

*

Raymin is back from the hospital, with the stitches in his legs covered with plasters and a stitch in his little finger with a plaster on it. He has been given some sweets from the nurse to help him get better. Louise helps Raymin into the front room and onto the long armchair. I do my best to help him with the sweet eating. Mammy tells him that he got walloped for his own good, but when Daddy comes home from work she won't tell him about playing down by the river and getting walloped. She'll just tell him about the fall through the rubbish bin, going to hospital to be stitched up and mended, and he'll not have to go to school on Monday because of his damaged legs. Helen says to him that she's sorry for telling on him and getting him a beating and can she have a sweet. She only wanted to save his life she says. Raymin tells me I can eat the sweet that could have been hers. I'm not sure if I should eat Helen's sweet. I'm trying to feel sorry for her, but I can't, not if I might lose the sweet. Mammy says Daddy won't be late home from the airport 'cos it's Friday night and they will be going to the Stella Ballroom where she'll be wearing her fancy dress that makes a swishing noise when she moves.

*

The helper girl looks after us and baby Dierdre while Mammy and Daddy are out dancing. We have all been playing with baby and her new rattle that makes her laugh a lot. When Baby goes to sleep in the drawer from Mammy's wardrobe the helper girl hangs the rattle on the iron frame of Mammy's bed and sends us off to bed in the back room. Helen and Louise sleep at the top of the bed, me and Raymin at the bottom.

Mammy and Daddy are home and the helper girl is gone. Baby Deirdre is asleep in the drawer. Me and Raymin and Helen and Louise are in bed listening to Mammy and Daddy singing and dancing in their room. They must like Baby's new rattle too because we can hear them playing with it when they stop singing.

On Monday Daddy is back at work at the airport and Raymin is staying in bed with his bad legs, and I don't want to go to school on my own. I hide my shoes behind the curtains in the front room. Mammy is going mad looking for them and she won't give up. When she finds them she gives me a good wallop across my ear, with one of the shoes. Now I'm crying 'cos my ear is sore and there's a ringing in it and I still don't want to go to school. Mammy says I have to take a note for Raymin's teacher to explain about his damaged legs. She tells the teacher that he fell off the chicken shed roof when he shouldn't have been up there at all in the first place. So now I'm wanting a note for my teacher 'cos I might get the stick or the leather strap for being late. Mammy calms down and begins to hould her whisht.

So off to school I go with my samiches and Mammy shouting after me, 'And watch the traffic across Nicholas Street, them mad horses and carts could kill you stone dead!'

I give the two notes to my teacher and put my samiches wrapped in brown paper into the box in the corner of the classroom with all the other samiches, mostly wrapped in brown paper. At dinner time I'm last to get my samiches from the box, but they're not mine, they're only marge with sugar on. I want my own samiches like I always have, the ones with jam on the marge. I'm eating the marge and sugar samiches when the nun comes up to me and asks how Raymin is doing. So I tell her all about Mammy beating him for going near the river, and about him cutting his legs on the rusty old bin. Then she asks me why Marie hasn't been to school for a long time. So I tell her about Nana coming to visit us and Mammy wanting to teach her how to curse, even if she didn't want to learn, and about Nana taking Marie to live in Dublin so there's more room for us now that baby Deirdre has been sent to us from Holy God and the angels. And how Nana said that Marie looked sad and neglected. Now the nun is asking how baby Deirdre is doing and I'm wanting to eat my samiches. I tell her that Baby is a lot better now that she's not as ugly as she was when she came out of the doctor's bag all squashed up, and she'll soon be big enough to sleep at the top of our bed to keep our feet warm. The nun is looking at me and saying nothing. So I take my chance to stuff a big bite of samich into my mouth. Then before I can start to chew it she asks me, "Did you hide your shoes behind the curtain this morning?" Now I'm standing here with a mouth full of samich, trying to figure out how she can know about the hiding of the shoes thing! Then she asks me, "Did you get a wallop on your ear this morning?" But before I have time to move the bit of samich in my mouth to one side so I can answer her, she says that Mammy told her she can wallop the other ear for me if she wants to. Then she walks away. The first bite of samich has finally reached my belly. I'm thinking that's an awful bad thing for a Mammy to say. I better eat my samich while I'm trying to figure out how Mammy came to tell the nun what happened without me seeing her.

# *Chapter 2*

## From riches to rags

Daddy is late coming home from the airport. Mammy says he will have called at Durty Nelly's pub near Bunratty Castle for a drink with his friends again. It's getting late and Mammy is acting nervous because his dinner is in the oven and the peas are like bullets and stuck in the hard Bisto gravy. She says he's promised to get a bicycle for Raymin's birthday that's not far off now, maybe that's why he's late today. Maybe he's not in Durty Nelly's after all.

I can tell Mammy is jumpy. She's smoking a lot and she's been reading the Halpin's tea leaves to see if there's any sign of trouble in the cup. If Daddy comes in drunk, Mammy will be calling him 'Bren' and 'a ghrá' (love) and trying to please him so he won't want to fight with her. The last time Daddy was drunk, she was trying to please him and asking him if his dinner was fine and did he want anything else. Did he want some fresh butter she got for him or would he like a nice cup of tea and things like that. But the dinner still bounced off the wall that time and he started shouting about having cheap cod for his dinner again.

Mammy sends Helen to the front gate to watch for Daddy coming round the corner between the church and the women's jail. When she sees him coming round the corner she runs to tell Mammy.

"Is he walking slow or fast?" asks Mammy. "Slow," says Helen. "Has he got his left hand in his trouser pocket?" "Yes,' says Helen. "Is his left shoulder higher than his right?" "Yes" says Helen. "Oh Christ," says Mammy, "he's really drunk tonight!"

Mammy sends us all to bed quickly. Me and Raymin are at the top of the stairs listening to see if there's any talk about his birthday bicycle. I'm thinking Daddy might even remember about Mrs Sexton next door taking him to court for walloping her son Tony on his bad ear. Then he might take some furniture upstairs, like he did before, more than one time, to throw it down again making noise so that the Sextons can't sleep. Mr Sexton has to be up early in the mornings to go to work at Shannon Airport where he works in a different department to Daddy. And it's just as well he does work in a different department 'cos they don't talk to each other anymore. But Mrs Sexton still says 'Hello there' to me with a smile when she sees me.

Me and Raymin are still listening on the landing. We can hear Daddy singing. He's singing 'Bimbo Bimbo where're you gonna go-e-o'. Now Mammy says to Daddy, "For feck sake will you stop dancing and eat your dinner!" an' Raymin says to me "It's OK, they're not fighting tonight."

Mammy's asking Daddy if he's looked for a bicycle for Raymin's birthday.

"No," he says, "the shop was closed."

Now Mammy is talking loud to Daddy, she must think he's not wanting to fight tonight. Now she's shouting at him! I'm thinking it must be her turn to shout tonight.

"I suppose you went looking for a hoor instead!" she says.

"There's no hoors in Durty Nelly's, they're all ladies that go in there!" Daddy is shouting back.

"I'm sure they are!" she says.

Now I'm asking Raymin what a 'hoor' is.

"I'm not sure," he says.

"Has it got wheels?" I'm asking him.

"I don't know," he says, trying to shout at me in a loud whisper. "Shurrup an' let me listen to see if it has!"

There's a loud crash from downstairs and me and Raymin run off into bed – I'm thinking Daddy's fallen over again 'cos of the drink. Raymin is quiet for a while, and says, "I bet ..." then he's quiet for another while and says, "I bet the dinner is on the fireplace wall." So I bet him that Daddy fell over. Right, he says, a square of Cleeves toffee on it. Right I tell him, two squares of Cleeves toffee on it, if we get any.

Baby Deirdre is big enough now to be pushed around in the old push chair that used to be for Louise. But we don't go to the People's Park much now, or have ice creams on Sundays anymore. Mammy doesn't sing along with the radio much, like she used to sing about Mrs Sera Sera, who's first name is Kay. And she doesn't go dancing with Daddy and come home happy and singing and play with Baby's rattle like before.

I heard Mammy telling her friends that Daddy has been warned about having time off work due to the drink. She told them that even Sean, who works with him at the airport, came to see if he could help him sort himself out. Then she said she found lipstick on his shirt collar again and asked them, "Christ, can things get any worse?"

*

Mammy is shouting up at Helen to get out of bed for school. Helen says she can't. Mammy says if she doesn't get up now she'll throw a bucket of cold water over her. Mammy is upstairs now, shouting. Helen is crying, she says she can't move her legs, she can't get out of bed, she's frightened. Mammy calms down. She's looking worried. Helen is pushed in the baby's pram to Barrington's Hospital, where Surgeon O'Regan tells Mammy that Helen has romantic fever. He says she'll have to stay in the hospital. If she doesn't, it will damage her heart.

While Helen is in hospital, Mammy takes us one by one to see her, so we can help her eat her sweets. When it was Louise's turn to visit, on Helen's birthday, she said she had a great time helping her to eat her birthday cake. Mrs Ryan next door to us took her daughter Carmel to see Helen as well. Carmel said she'd rather stay at home and play, but her mother told her you have to visit the neighbour's sick children when they are in hospital.

At the same time Helen is in hospital with her fever, Mammy has to take Raymin in there too, to have his fork circumcised because of him having trouble weeing. On the way to the hospital walking over Mathew Bridge, Raymin has the house key in his hand and is pretending to whizz it over the bridge into the river. Mammy is telling him to stop acting the goat, but he takes no notice of her. He keeps swinging the key out over the bridge. Just as his hand is right the way out, Mammy gives him a wallop across his ear and the shock makes him drop the key into the river. Now Mammy is calling him all the stupid little feckers going, but Raymin is just laughing, thinking it's all very funny. Mammy tells him he'll be staying in the hospital for a while. But don't worry, she says, I'll be saving a good walloping for you when you come home. While they are in hospital cousin Johnny Murphy goes to see them with Mammy. Me and Louise are at home trying to look after the chicks and sometimes Baby Deirdre.

It's early in the morning. I'm looking out of the bedroom window at the chicks running around the back garden. I open the bedroom door quietly and sneak down the stairs in my vest. I want to go out to the backyard to see the chicks, but when I get to the kitchen door, I see water flowing over the big white sink. The floor is covered with water and the kitchen is filling up. I scream with fright, holding onto the door handle. I think we're all going to be drowned. Mammy comes running down the stairs to see what's happening. She lifts me up and pulls my hand off the door handle, telling me that the water won't drown me as she turns off the tap. She sits me on the window sill in the front room. Then she gets a brush to sweep the water off the concrete floor and out the back door, where the chicks are standing looking in.

Now Mammy's talking to herself about "That feckin' Johnny Murphy," our twenty-year-old cousin who stayed the night after visiting Helen and Raymin in hospital, 'cos she says he was the last one in the kitchen the night before. Daddy comes down the stairs. He is cursing about Johnny Murphy too, "Him upstairs sleeping, and the water all over the house."

Mammy gives me a piece of one-sided toast and jam, and tea in a jam jar. She sits me on a chair in the front room. Daddy is drinking his tea out of a good cup and is arguing with Mammy about Johnny. I am crying again 'cos they are fighting and I don't want to eat my toast and Daddy shouts at me to shut feckin' up and that makes me cry more. I feel a bang over my eye and I see something like a flash, then my eye hurts and I cry out more. Daddy's cup has bounced off my head and hit the wall and now there's tea running down the picture of the sacred heart that's covering the old stains on the wall. Something wet is running down my face from my eye, I put my hand up and it comes down covered in blood and I'm crying even more. Mammy runs over and picks me up from the chair and turns to Daddy and calls him a lousy liten bastard.

I'm in Baby Deirdre's pram being pushed to the hospital by Mammy, who is talking to herself about liten bastards and feckers and things like that. But I'm not taking much notice of Mammy or my cut head that's not hurting much now. I'm too busy trying to figure out how I can have a cousin that's twenty years old. I'm sure cousins should be the same age as me.

While I'm in the hospital with my cut head, Mammy leaves me with the nurse, who gives me a sweet and some stitches, and goes off to collect Helen. Raymin will be coming home tomorrow.

*

We're all back home again. I have the stitches over my eye covered with a plaster, and there's no Johnny. Raymin and Louise bring me sweets from the Lent box upstairs, where the sweets are supposed to be kept safe until Easter. I shouldn't really have the sweets 'cos it's still Lent time and we all promised to give up sweets for Lent as a sacrifice to show our love for Jesus on the cross who will soon have a sore head, just like mine. But Mammy says this is a special occasion, as I have a cut head and stitches and I told her that the hospital nurse says that sweets would help me get better. During the daytime, Mammy and the others sometimes talk about the stitches in my head, and the stains on the wall, but no one talks about them when Daddy is home.

Sometimes the cruelty man comes to the house to check on us. Mostly he calls after Daddy has been drinking at the bars and has come home to have a fight.

She shows the man the marks on the walls and on the stairs where the chair was thrown down to annoy next door and she shows him the stitches in my head, that wouldn't have happened if Johnny Murphy hadn't left the tap running all night. "And sure, what else would you expect from someone who's always rushing around with nowhere to go, an' jumps over the garden gate 'cos he won't take the time to open the feckin' thing," says Mammy.

She tells the cruelty man she doesn't know what to do, and her nerves can't stand it much longer. Then the cruelty man goes away and Mammy is talking to herself in the kitchen saying that the useless fecker of a cruelty man probably won't do anything anyway.

Other times when Daddy is late, especially on payday, and Mammy is bad with her nerves in case there's going to be trouble, she gets us all dressed in our going out coats, and with Baby Deirdre in the pram we go out walking the streets of the city 'cos she is afraid to stay at home, especially when he is very late, with his left hand in his pocket and his shoulder up in the air. Mammy says that lately things have been getting worse at home due to Daddy drinking more and more.

*

It's evening time and we are walking down O'Connell Street from the city. Then across Ennis Road Bridge, along Clancy's Strand by the river wall towards the treaty stone beside Thomond Bridge. There's Mammy, Raymin with his fixed fork that's still a bit sore, he says, Helen who is better now after being in hospital with romantic fever, but still being huffy, me, Louise and Baby Deirdre in the pram. We're not all in the pram, just Baby Deirdre. We are on our second walk down this way, the rain is lashing down, it's dark and we are all tired, but Mammy won't take us home. She's heard today that Daddy lost his job at the airport and he has been drinking all day. "Christ," she says to herself, "things ARE getting worse."

I can see Mammy is frightened and bad with her nerves. She's telling us all to keep away from the river wall in case a big wave comes over and washes us all away. Raymin is wanting a wee and saying that his fork is hurting, so Mammy tells him to go behind a tree and pull his fork out and be quick.

As we walk along the road, Mammy is talking to herself and God. She's asking God almighty what she can do. Then she says to us, "Things will be all right children. Ah, God is good. God is good." She is quiet for a while before she says again, "Yes God is good, God is good. It won't always be like this, things will get better, God is good." Then she shouts, "And for God's sake keep away from that wall!" Then she goes quiet for a while, worrying to herself again with her bad nerves. I can see tears in her eyes. Now I feel like crying too. It's awful hard to see tears in your Mammy's eyes and not feel like crying.

She takes us into the Garda station front hall where there's a long wood bench against a wood wall with glass along the top half. On another wall there's a window in the middle that slides to the side to do your talking through. The floorboards are bare and haven't been swept for a long time. Cigarette butts are lying all over the place. I pick up a butt and pretend to smoke it. Then the others join in. Mammy looks too weary to tell us to stop, like she usually does when we fool around. We sit on the wood benches, in the middle, on the clean bits away from the dusty ends that haven't been cleaned by bums.

A guard slides back the glass window. I can see through into the other room where there's two green lampshades hanging in a cloud of cigarette smoke under the ceiling.

"What can I do for you, missus?" the guard asks Mammy, while his eyes are running around the big hallway squinting at us all. Mammy tells him about being too frightened to go home because Daddy might want a fight and throw things about the house, and down the stairs to annoy next door. She tells him about her struggle to look after us all, with Helen just getting over romantic fever, Raymin with his sore fork, me with my stitch on my eye, Louise who is as thin as a rake, and a newish baby that's always hungry. And no one to help us at all, and soon there will be no money now that daddy has lost his good job as a radio officer at the airport, and hardly a plate left in the house.

Mammy starts crying again and the guard gives her a Woodbine to calm her nerves. She asks the guard to come home with us in case Daddy wants a fight. The guard says he doesn't think it's a good idea. And anyway, he can do nothing 'cos nothing is threatening the law at the minute, and if they went places all the time about things that might happen there would be no one left to sort out the things that do happen. He says the best thing to do is to go home and get us children off the streets on this cold wet night. Then if anything does happen when she gets home, she can come back and he will see what can be done, maybe call in the cruelty man again.

*

All the lights are on in the house, so that means that Daddy is at home. We stay outside and listen through the letterbox 'til we can hear snoring sounds from upstairs. Then we all sneak in and stay downstairs in the front room with the chair wedged under the handle of the door to keep Daddy from getting in to fight us all if he wakes up. When I want to wee, I have to creep through the kitchen to the toilet and make sure not to flush it or make any noise so I don't wake Daddy who is still snoring.

In the morning, Mammy goes upstairs with a cup of tea for Daddy and calls him 'Bren' instead of Brendan, 'cos she's still bad with the nerves and is trying to please him and see if he has any money left for food. Daddy is still in bed when Mammy takes me out shopping with her. She leaves Raymin in charge of Helen, Louise and Baby Deirdre and tells Daddy we won't be long.

I'm with Mammy in Woolworths up in the city. One minute she's there, the next she's gone. I can't find her anywhere. I run to the big wood-framed glass doors, push them open and look down O'Connell Street. I can't see her. I run back inside Woolworths to where she was before she got lost. I look round the corners of the counters 'cos I'm too small to see over them. Mammy is gone. Just disappeared.

I push the big doors open again. I run outside again and looking down O'Connell Street I see her. I run down shouting "Mammy, Mammy!" and grab her hand, but she pulls away. It's the wrong mammy – she's talking to me but I don't hear what she says 'cos I'm running back up to Woolworths to find the right mammy. I push the doors open again and I can't see her anywhere. I'm thinking she must have gone home without me. I'm running back down O'Connell Street where I see the wrong mammy again. I run past her but I look back to make sure it IS the wrong mammy, and I'm right, she isn't the right one, she's the wrong one. She's looking at me, now she's running after me and shouting for me to stop, and be careful of the traffic. Other grownups are looking at me and wondering why I'm running away from my mammy – they don't know she isn't, and I'm looking for the right one. I'm not stopping for anyone, 'cos my mammy tells me not to talk to strangers. Other grownups are trying to grab me for her, but I dodge past them. I'm panting for breath and I can feel my curly hair getting wet with sweat. But it's OK now 'cos I'm past the crowd. I'm running over Mathew Bridge where Raymin lost the door key, down Merchants Quay, past the courthouse and the women's jail, along Crosbie Row and up the garden path. I push the front door open and run in.

Mammy's not there. I'm shouting upstairs to Daddy, "I lost Mammy in Woolworths and I can't find her anywhere!" I run upstairs and tell him about running all the way home and not talking to strangers. He looks at me, turns away and tries to go back to sleep.

Soon the front door opens and Mammy runs in crying. She doesn't see me. She runs upstairs to tell Daddy she's in an awful state, bad with her nerves and weak at the knees. She tells Daddy that she lost Brian Óg in Woolworths and all the guards in Limerick are out on their bicycles looking for me. I shout up and tell her I'm here. She runs down, sees me and picks me up and kisses me. She's happy and still crying. She says "Thanks be to God and Saint Anthony" for finding me. She puts me down. Now I'm happy 'cos Mammy isn't lost anymore. I'm dancing in front of the coal fire. I'm singing 'Bimbo Bimbo where you gonna go-e-o' and lifting my legs side to side. Just when I have one leg in the air I get a great wallop on the side of my head that knocks me to the floor. When I look up, Mammy is looking down at me. She's calling me a stupid little fecker for running away like that and making her worried. She says she was there in Woolworths all the time. She said she went weak at the knees and nearly fainted when she realised I was missing. Now she has to go out to tell the guards that she's found me. "So stay there like your arse is nailed to that floor 'til I get back," she says. When Mammy goes out, Raymin calls at me "Brian lost his mammy, Brian lost his mammy!" and calls me stupid.

*

Mammy is talking to Mrs Ryan, she's telling her about me being lost in Woolworths and that Daddy has finally lost his good job at the airport because of the drink, and that's why he's at home more these days. She says he is looking for another job and they're not easy to find, "Especially if you're particular, and won't take a labouring job, like he won't." Mrs Ryan says a job is a job and he should take anything that's offered. Mammy agrees with her and says that she's been feckin' telling him that for weeks, but he doesn't listen to a word she says. Mammy goes quiet for a minute, smokes her cigarette and stares at nothing. Then she says, "I should have married McInnery the farmer from Hospital village when he asked me."

Other times when Daddy is out, Mammy's friend Claire Power comes around to the house to talk with her. She helps her read the Halpin's tea leaves in the cups to see if things are ever going to be better than they are now, with us being short of money all the time. Mammy sends us all into the kitchen out of the way. Raymin is listening at the door and telling us what they are saying. Mrs Power is telling Mammy that she can see travels across water in the tea leaves. Raymin says it probably means that Mammy is going shopping across Mathew Bridge again, then he looks at me and says, "But you won't be going with her!" Now I'm thinking, who's going to look after her then? Mammy reads Mrs Power's cup, but there's no mention of going across water in that. I'm asking Raymin if that means Mrs Power won't be going shopping up in the city, but he's too busy listening to them to answer me. Now I'm asking him "Why would Daddy put lipstick on his collar when he's drunk?" but he's still not answering me.

When Mrs Power has gone Mammy sends me out to search the shed and the back garden for eggs from the big chickens, but there's none there. She says have you looked to see if there's an egg coming and I'm telling her I don't know what she means. So out she comes and grabs one of the hens, holding it upside down. She's telling me about when she was a young girl living in Hospital village and she had to check to see if there was an egg coming by pressing the hen's bum. Now she's showing me how, and I'm feeling like I'm wanting to be sick, like when she was cleaning the new baby's bum. Then Mammy says that there'll be an egg out soon, and she says that I'll never make a good farmer.

It's a long time since we went to the People's Park up in the city to play and have ice creams, like we did when Daddy had his job at the airport and Baby Deirdre was new. It's now nearly Easter Sunday and the sun is shining today. A good ice cream day, if we could get some. It's seems a long time too since we had any sweets, except when Raymin got some Lent sweets for his cut legs and I got some for my cut head. The time before that when we got sweets was Christmas. We all got some sweets, an orange and two balloons in our stockings from Santa Claus, who was also short of money and a week late getting to our house, "Because of the weather," Mammy said, "and it doesn't help when Daddy's spending all his money in the Limerick bars."

*

Mammy tells me and Raymin we can go out playing with Mrs Minogue's son Pat, while she's having a talk again with Mrs Ryan. But we're hanging around the house being nosy parkers. Mrs Ryan is asking how Helen is doing after being in hospital with her romantic fever, and telling Mammy how her daughter Carmel, who goes to the same school as us, was locked in a dark cupboard by one of the nuns for messing about in class. Mrs Ryan says she's just got back from the school, where she told the nun exactly what she thought of her. Mammy is telling Mrs Ryan that she'll be ready for a nice cup of tea and she agrees. The kettle is on the gas. She tells me and Raymin to get off out to play before it rains and warns us "Don't go near the river. And if that Pat Minogue wants you to make loud bangs up people's drainpipes with tins of carabine powder you come straight back here!"

There's no sign of rain or Pat Minogue, so me and Raymin go round to King John's Castle, on Castle Street by Thomond Bridge. We're going to play on the big stone at the other end of the bridge, that Mammy calls the treaty stone. It's a stone that people lean on when they sign agreements, she says.

It's a sunny day and there're lots of people around the castle. They tell us that some people are making a film that's going to be called 'The rising of the moon' and they are going to use big hose pipes to make rain, 'cos of it being dry today.

The filming has to stop for a while, because of a farmer bringing lots of sheep over the bridge from the 'big stone' side to the fields behind the school. The film men turn off the rain to let the sheep through. I run across the road in front of the sheep to go home to tell Mammy about the film making and the crowds. I slip and fall in the middle of the wet road where the sheep are coming. I think I'm going to be trampled to death, like the cowboys in the films when the American cows run at them. Just as the first sheep comes at me, ready to start killing me, Raymin runs over and helps me to get up off the road and pulls me over to the doorway of the Thomond picture house, until the sheep have gone.

I run home to tell Mammy about the filming, the hose pipes making the rain, the crowds of people, the sheep running up the road to get me and how Raymin saved my life. But Mammy isn't listening to me. She looks like she's busy being nervous and worrying again. She has caught all the hens and golden chicks from the back garden. She's pulling their necks and putting them in the gas oven, with the gas turned on, but not lit. She's killing them dead. I'm telling her not to, but she still does it.

Now the chicks are just lying on the floor, flopped flat, stone dead. I'm crying for the chicks. I feel sad for them. I'm shouting for Raymin, who has just come in, to tell him about Mammy killing the chicks.

Mammy's having a cigarette to calm her nerves. She's telling us she's sorry, but the chicks had to go because we are moving out of the house quickly and we can't take them with us. We have to leave by tomorrow due to the rent not being paid. Due to Daddy losing his job. Due to his bad timekeeping. Due to him drinking. Due to him not having another job. Due to him being too fussy. Due to him being a liten bastard. "And where is he now? He's out looking for a job. In some bar."

She says the hens and chicks will go to Heaven and everything will be alright, please God. Because God is good and she's said a prayer to Saint Anthony to find us somewhere to live and find Daddy a job too.

The chicks are in Heaven and Mammy is in the kitchen washing clothes in the big white sink. She's rubbing the clothes up and down on the wrinkled green glass washboard that has a wood frame that has changed colour from when it was new. Now it's worn and hairy looking, "from overwork," she says.

Every now and then she stares out of the window into the back garden where the chicks used to be. She taps her soapy knuckles against the top edge of the sink, and chomps her teeth in time with the tapping. She pushes her hair out of her eyes with the back of her hand, whispering to herself, "The liten bastard." She's in deep thinking again and doesn't notice me watching her. She suddenly stops the washing and wipes her hands on her apron. She's going out, saying she'll be back soon to finish it. She leaves Raymin in charge.

It's late when the clothes are washed and dried out in the garden. Mammy's putting them into old tea chests and orange boxes that she brought back from the shops on Nicholas Street, ready for the flit tomorrow.

*

Soon it's tomorrow and the tea chests and orange boxes are on the grass in the front garden waiting for the moving man. There's furniture, cardboard boxes not so full of cups, plates, jam jars and things. Other things are wrapped up in blankets with knots tied in the tops to stop them from falling out. We play in the street while we're waiting. Daddy has set off early with Baby Deirdre in the pram. In the middle of the afternoon, the moving man comes with his horse and cart. The man says he's sorry he's late. He's been washing the cart down after his morning's work collecting rags and scrap iron. He fitted in a delivery of coal too, he says.

The beds, chairs and other bits of furniture are put onto the cart. Then the boxes and the things tied up in the blankets. The mop and brush and the hairy glass washboard are loaded up. Last of all there's Mammy, Raymin, Helen, me and Louise lifted onto the cart. We all think it's great fun, except Mammy, who doesn't look too happy. Mammy's telling the moving man that Daddy set off early with Baby Deirdre in the pram. She says he is fussy about everything, and didn't want to be seen with us on the horse and cart, traipsing through Limerick city on our way to Ballinacurra Weston. We are going there to stay with Mrs Movita and her family, who are helping us out, she tells him. Mammy says that Daddy probably didn't want his drinking pals to see him with us on the horse and cart.

We set off past the women's jail. Some of the neighbours are looking at us out of their windows. Mammy brushes her hair back, lights up a cigarette for her nerves and tells us all to sit up straight and hold our heads high. I'm thinking that Mrs Movita, who we are going to stay with, must be a friend of Saint Anthony's, 'cos that's who Mammy said her prayers to, for us to find somewhere to live.

# *Chapter 3*

## Living on charity of others

Mrs Movita lives in a council house not far from the house in Hyde Road where Mammy says we used to live before we moved to Crosbie Row. When we get to the house, we want to play in the fields where we can see the railway line and the river. Mammy warns us not to go near the river or the railway line in case a train comes off the tracks and runs over us and "kills you stone dead." She warns us to keep away from the dump by the railway, with all the grey clay dumped there that smells awful and might give us typhoid fever. So off we go to play by the railway line and to see what that grey clay smells like, before we go and play by the river.

Later, I'm in the house rooting around and asking Mrs Movita where my bed is. She says there's not room for all our beds but don't worry about it, some of us might have to sleep on the floor, but we'll be covered up and warm. One of the Movita girls comes dashing into the house, running straight upstairs, and then two fishermen are by the door and they say they have chased her all the way from the river. They're saying she stole a fish from them, but she's saying she didn't, even when her mammy said she'd call the guards. The men go away, cursing their way down the road.

In the evening it's early to bed. Helen, Louise and one of the Movita girls are in one bed in the back bedroom where me and Raymin are sleeping on the floor with blankets for a mattress and more on top. Baby Deirdre is nice and warm in the same room inside the long drawer from the bottom of the wardrobe that came on the horse and cart. Just the drawer came, not the whole wardrobe. Mammy and Daddy will be sleeping downstairs on two armchairs that have been pushed up to the long armchair. Mammy checks Baby in the drawer and says there's a funny smell, but Baby is clean. Raymin blames me for the smell, and says I blew off a fart. I blame Deirdre. Mammy tells us to hould our whisht and go to sleep.

It's all quiet now but I can't get to sleep. I'm worrying what's going to happen to us all, and if Raymin will ever pay me the two squares of Cleeves toffee he still owes me from the bet about Daddy falling on the floor.

In the morning I'm woken up by the others, all laughing at Baby Deirdre who is walking around the room slapping them all with a smelly fish. We all think it's great fun, except Mammy and Mrs Movita who is calling her daughter downstairs to have words with her. We can hear Mrs Movita saying she's going to send her daughter to the nuns in the orphan's home at Mount Saint Vincent Convent for stealing the fish.

*

Not long after we move to Ballinacurra Weston, Daddy leaves us and goes to Dublin, to Grandad's. Mammy says that he has gone to look for a job, 'cos there is very little work in Limerick, and if he was lucky enough to be offered a job here it would probably be a mucky job. But he is still being picky about jobs like that. Mammy says that he might get a job in Dublin, where he'll fit in better with all them fussy feckers up there. After he has gone, Mammy goes to the welfare office to claim home assistance, 'cos of us being left on our own and with no money. She says that what they give her wouldn't feed us for a day, never mind a week.

Some days we all go with Mammy and Baby Deirdre in the pram, walking on the country lanes. We call at the farms and ask the farmers for a few spuds and any vegetables they can spare. She tells them that Daddy has left us and we have no money for food. Most of the time the farmers are kind and give us something. Sometimes they even fill baby Deirdre's bottle, the old HP sauce bottle with a tit on it, full of milk. Mammy tells us that if the farmers ask our names, we have to tell them it's Murphy, 'cos there's a lot more Murphys around than O'Donoghues, so they won't know who we really are.

We're out walking in the country lanes. It's getting dark and it's starting to rain. Baby Deirdre is in the pram with the spuds and vegetables and the sauce bottle full of milk. With all the miles we have walked over bumpy roads, the stuff from farmers, and us taking turns to ride on the pram, one of the wheels gets wobbly. Mammy says it's getting hard to push the pram with the broken wheel. So now we can't sit on the pram anymore and we are all tired and getting wet.

There's a road works sign that says the traffic must slow up. I think it means they have to slow down. There's a big hole in the road that has orange oil lamps all around it, and it looks a bit like Christmas time. There's a hut with a fire outside and a roadworks man sitting on the doorstep. It's raining heavier now and Mammy tells us to run down the road to the hut. When we get there the man says "Come inside out of the rain." It's a tight squeeze in the hut, but at least it's warm and dry. Baby is lifted out of the pram, 'cos there's not room inside the hut for all of us and the pram.

It's dark now. It's raining very hard and it's getting late. The man boils a kettle over the fire and makes a big mug of tea that he shares with all of us. Mammy puts some potatoes on the fire, enough for us and the workman. Her and the workman have more tea and share his cigarettes while our spuds are cooking in their skins on the fire outside. It doesn't take long 'til the spuds are burnt nearly black on the outside. The man sharpens a long twig with a small penknife and sticks it into the spuds to see if they are cooked on the inside. He says they're done. Mammy says "Dinner's ready". By now we're all starving with the hunger. The man picks up the potatoes with the stick and leans over to the corner of the hut, where he puts them on top of an old dressing table, that he calls his workbench, next to some rusty tools. He cuts each spud into small pieces, sprinkles salt on them, and warns us to let them cool down a bit before we share them. The spuds are steaming from the inside. The flickering flame from the fire is lighting up the steam from the spuds and making shadows onto the back wall of the hut. The spuds are sitting there now, just waiting to be gobbled up as soon as they are cold enough.

Now we're eating them. They taste lovely. Mammy says they always taste better when you're starving with the hunger. "A lump of butter now and wouldn't this be a grand dinner," she says. "I bet that liten bastard in Dublin isn't eating burnt spuds out in the rain." I'm thinking she's talking about Daddy again.

The rain isn't stopping, so the man says we can stay there for the night if we want to. He tells Mammy that we can sleep on the clean sacks lying by the old dressing table. Then he pulls out the bottom drawer, puts a couple of sacks in it and tells Mammy to "Stick the baby in there." Mammy puts Baby into the drawer. Then she looks at the man and says "Thank God for drawers" and now the man and Mammy are laughing and he is laughing so much that he coughs his cigarette out into a rain puddle. He picks it up and puts it by the fire to dry out.

*

It's morning. It's stopped raining and the sun is trying to look through the fast clouds. The workman shares his tea with us again and puts some of it into the sauce bottle for the baby. Baby Deirdre is put into the damp pram sitting on two dry sacks from the hut and we set off down the road towards the city. Mammy turns and thanks the workman. She tells him, "God bless you mister for your kindness". He says he hopes things will work out all right for us and he thinks it's a shame for us to have to walk the country roads looking for food for our little bellies. Mammy says things will work out all right, "For God is good." Then she waves goodbye to the man who is now sitting by his fire smoking his dried out cigarette, looking at us and scratching his head.

The wheel on the pram is wobbling more now and we've walked no more than a mile down the road when it falls off altogether. Mammy shoves the wheel back where it should be, but it's still loose. She says it looks like there's something missing that should keep it on. Another few yards and the wheel is off again. Mammy says "Feck it!" and drags the pram onto the grass at the side of the road and says it's no good to us now. "You children take out the spuds and things and put them in your pockets or carry them." Raymin asks if he can throw the pram over the hedge into a field, but Mammy says "No, leave it there, the tinkers might find it and fix it and get a few shillings for it."

Off we go walking down the road again carrying our load of spuds, cabbages, carrots, cauliflowers, and parsnips. The ones with the most pockets have the heaviest loads and Mammy is left carrying Baby Deirdre. Raymin is telling me he's glad Mammy dumped the pram with the rubber cover on the handle. I think he's remembering the beating he got for playing down by the river at Crosbie Row. I'm looking at Mammy being tired carrying Baby Deirdre and soon Mammy is looking at the baby's bottle with no tea in it, and Baby sucking air.

It's nearly the middle of the day and we are back with Mrs Movita. She's listening to Mammy's tales of losing track of time, the kind workman cooking potatoes on the outside fire and us losing the wheel off the pram. Mammy says her feet are paining her and her corns are aching and that's a sure sign that there's more rain coming. Mrs Movita says it must have been an awful night and Mammy agrees, "It was feckin, feckin awful." Mammy is laughing and telling Mrs Movita that the roads are so bad and full of holes that if you saw a pair of ears sticking up out of them you wouldn't know if it was a rabbit or a donkey down there. Now they are both laughing. I can see tears in Mammy's eyes. They're not sad tears like she had in her eyes when we were walking around the streets, being afraid of Daddy who was being drunk and wanting to fight with her. Now I'm wondering what Daddy is doing in Dublin and if he's got a job and what would a donkey be doing down a hole in the road anyway.

Weeks have passed since Daddy went to Dublin to get a job that's good enough for him. Mammy is talking to Mrs Movita about not getting any letters or money from Dublin like he promised. Then Mammy tells us that although Mrs Movita is very kind to us and has never moaned about the overcrowding, we can't carry on like this. So Mammy's going to sell the bit of furniture we have and also her wedding ring that she says has been in a pawn shop more than once before now, to scrape together enough money to take us all to Dublin to help Daddy find a job.

"God forgive me, it's the only way," she says. "If only he would agree to move to England like Auntie Mary and Uncle John did. At least he could get a job, even if it is the Devil's Country."

I'm thinking it would be a great idea, 'cos we could all have sweets and ice cream again. Then she says to herself, "Things won't always be this bad, God is good, things will get better."

Mammy sends me and Raymin to the Mount Saint Vincent Convent on O'Connell Avenue in the city to ask the nuns for a loaf of bread. "Tell them we have no food and no money and I can't come down myself 'cos I'm weak at the knees and my varicose veins are killing me."

We go to the back door of the convent where we can smell something cooking and tell the nuns about Daddy leaving and us being starving with the hunger. The nuns give us a big loaf of bread. Then they tell Raymin that they can't just keep giving bread to anyone who knocks at their door. Raymin thanks them for the loaf. One of the nuns asks him "What's your name anyway?"

"Raymin, sister, Raymin Murphy."

"And where do you live?"

"Shannon Airport, sister, Shannon Airport."

Mammy is at the sink again. In between rubbing the clothes up and down on the hairy washboard, she stops. She's knocking her knuckles on the washboard and the sink again, and chomping her teeth in time to the knocking. She doesn't know I'm watching her. Then she says in a quiet voice, "The liten bastard." Now there's tears in her eyes again. Not like the laughing tears when she was joking with Mrs Movita. These are sad tears. Sad tears that make her call Daddy a liten bastard again and again. She sees me and wipes her eyes with the back of her soapy hands. "Go on out and play with the others," she says, "and don't go near the railway line!"

# Chapter 4

## Mammy runs away to the Devil's Country

It's a rainy evening and we're on the platform at Limerick Colbert railway station. I'm looking at the big steam engine. There's a man shovelling coal into the hot burning red fire to make the steam. He grins at me, showing me the tooth hanging down in the middle of his big smile, shining white against his black face and dirty clothes. There's streaks of clean skin on his face where the sweat is running down from his flat cap that is wet around the edge. I'm shouting at him, asking if he cooks potatoes in their skins on his fire. I don't think he can hear me.

Mammy shouts at me through the noise to come away from the platform edge in case I fall under the train and be "kilt stone dead", and she drags me away from the edge where I'm trying to figure out how the man on the engine gets the coal to turn into steam. My ear is being twisted and I'm being pulled across the platform to where the others are waiting to get on the train. And now I'm sad 'cos I can't see the fire and the engine man smiling anymore.

*

Mammy, Raymin, Helen, me, Louise and Baby Deirdre are getting on the train to Dublin. We're going to see Daddy and Marie who are living at Grandad's house. Raymin asks Mammy if Daddy knows we are going to see him. Mammy says, "No, it'll be a nice surprise for him."

On the train we are all happy. Mammy says that Nana and Grandad have a lovely big house and garden and "Please God, everything will be fine and soon all our troubles will be over." She looks happy, and Baby Deirdre has a sauce bottle full of milk and she is making happy noises. We all fit into the one carriage by ourselves. Just as the train starts to move very slowly, Mammy calls us all over to the window. She's pointing to a woman on the platform.

"See that woman in the grey two-piece costume and hat?" she says. "That's that 'Craig' one, your father's girlfriend, the one with the painted face that your father spent his money on in the Limerick bars, while we were at home with no rent paid at Crosbie Row. That feckin horizontal trollop there."

We're all sat down and the train is moving faster now out of the station. It's heading for Dublin and Grandad's house and his big garden and apple trees, where things are going to get better for us. Mammy is smoking and looking out of the window. I'm looking over and whispering to Raymin, but he won't answer my question. Now I'm asking him again and this time he shouts at me. "I don't know what a horizontal trollop is!" he shouts at me. Now they're all looking at me and

I can feel my face going red, so I'm saying nothing, I'm just looking out of the window and houlding my whisht.

The train is getting faster. I'm leaning against the steamy window listening to the rattle of the wheels coming up the side of the train and into my ear. The tracks are sending me messages: 'Clickety click, clickety click.' Then it changes from saying 'Clickety click, clickety click' to saying 'We-are-leaving-Limerick, we-are-leaving-Limerick.' Now I'm saying it out loud, in time with the rattle of the wheels.

I'm pretending that I'm the train. I'm running around the carriage shouting, "Clickety click, clickety-click, we are leaving Limerick!" I'm excited 'cos I've never been on a train before. Now the others are laughing at me. Mammy's shouting at me.

"Hould your whisht or I'll clatter some sense into your thick head and nail your arse to the floor!"

The others are still laughing at me and calling at me, "Brian the train, Brian the train, lost his Mammy out in the rain!" Mammy is telling me to sit down and telling everyone "Hould your whisht too!" I'm back at the window listening to the tracks, looking out at the telegraph poles swishing past the clouds, quietly houlding my whisht. I'm thinking about the little golden chicks. Are they really up there in Heaven with God 'who is good'?

Raymin is still laughing at me. He's asking me questions but I'm not answering him. He's asking why my face is all screwed up as if I've just had a good walloping. But I'm not telling him in case they all laugh at me again. I'm telling you though, 'cos I know you won't laugh at me. I'm wondering how much it would hurt if you really had your arse nailed to the floor.

*

People are walking up and down the passage past our compartment. Some look in as they pass, some smile at us and some don't. Mammy says the ones that don't smile are probably snobs from the rich Protestant families who look down on us. I ask her if they are snobs like the Queen of England. She says the Queen isn't a snob, "She just has to act like one 'cos its part of her job, and she has to keep the Prime Minister happy." She says that if you met the Queen and Mr Edinburgh out on their own shopping they would probably be ordinary just like us and invite us into their house in London for a cup of tea. Then when we were finished with the tea Mammy says she could read the Queen's tea leaves for her, and give her advice on running the country and things like that. I'm thinking that they might even have some old shoes to fit me instead of the ones I have that have holes in them. Mammy says the Queen is just doing a hard job and she's probably fed up with things, like all of us poor woman, but at least she has a bit of help from her husband.

Some people in the train grab the door handle as if they're coming in and when they look around and see all of us, they smile as they walk past. Mammy is feeding Baby from the sauce bottle, I am eating my jam and bread samiches and drinking water from the big glass lemonade bottle we brought with us. Raymin, Helen and Louise say I'm greedy 'cos they're saving their samiches for later. Mammy says she would give anything for another cigarette and Raymin says he'll have a walk up the train to look for any big cigarette butts the snobs have thrown away. Mammy says, "No thanks, I'm not that desperate yet, I'll die of the want first!" Raymin says he was only codding but Mammy says she doesn't think so.

*

It's late when we get to Dublin and Raymin is pushing me to wake up. Mammy's looking out the window and points to a small man standing on the platform.

"Look children," she says, "that's a foreigner man. He's a Chinaman, from the other side of the world. You'll see lots of foreigners in Dublin, but you mustn't stare. It's bad manners. Come on now, off the train and hold onto each other and me, there's lots of kidnappers in Dublin, especially at this time of night and this time of the year, so stay close to me now."

We're on the platform and making our way to the waiting room. It's very late now and the station man tells us the buses have stopped running for the night. I trip over the handle of a luggage cart and my knee is scratched on the floor. Mammy helps me up, saying

"You're a clumsy fecker, watch where you're going!" I don't tell her I fell 'cos I was busy watching the man from China and being bad with my manners.

There's a coal fire in the waiting room. Mammy asks the porter man to put some more coal on the fire 'cos it's starting to die down.

"Surely I will missus," he says, "but I'm supposed to lock up soon. I'll make it nice and warm for you and them children. I'll be back before you can say up the rebels."

The porter man is soon back with a bucket full of coal.

"It'll soon be hot enough to scald the legs off you, missus," and then he says to Mammy, when he thinks I can't hear him, "I nearly said scald your arse but that wouldn't be right saying a thing like that in front of the little ones, missus." Mammy is laughing now.

The station man fills the fire to the top and then fills up the coal bucket again. He's back again with a cup of milky tea, trying to fill the baby's bottle without spilling any. I'm watching him and I can smell the drink on him, like Daddy smells when he's been to the bars looking for a job. Now we're all watching him trying not to spill the tea. He gives the tea to Mammy so she can fill the bottle herself and tells her to lock the door with the Yale latch when we leave. She thanks him for his kindness and off he goes down the platform, swaying from side to side. Mammy says it's too late to walk the streets to Grandad's house. She says we might as well stop the rest of the night in the waiting room by the nice, warm coal fire while she thinks about what she's going to say to Daddy in the morning.

I'm trying to sleep on the long wood bench away from the fire. Louise is lying on another and Raymin and Helen are sitting on the benches at each side of the fire. It's hard to sleep on a wood bench, so I take a look out onto the platform. It's quiet and there's a cold wind blowing through the station moving bits of paper around. I pick up a Woodbine packet, fold it and put it inside my shoe to cover up the hole to stop it hurting when I walk on the hard ground. Mammy calls me back into the waiting room, telling me to watch out for the foreigners and kidnappers.

A woman comes into the waiting room. She's wearing posh clothes. I know she's not a snob 'cos she's wearing too much paint on her face, what Mammy calls lipstick. She's probably a trollop or a horizontal like Mammy called the Craig woman in Limerick. She's talking to Mammy and gives her a cigarette. Mammy tells her all about Daddy leaving and us and now we're here in Dublin to see him. "That's a terrible thing to happen," says the trollop. "I had a husband once myself that took to the drink.

God, that drink has a lot to answer for."

Mammy agrees and they're talking for a long time and she takes another cigarette from the woman. They're talking and talking, telling jokes and laughing in between. Mammy says she's sorry she can't give the woman any cigarettes back, as she only has the money for the bus fare to Grandad's house.

"It's alright missus, here, you can have the rest of the packet, I'll get some more. I have to go now and start work. Good luck missus and God bless you and the children, and if you want a job, I'm here most nights, but not Sundays, that's the Lords day."

Now she's laughing as she checks the paint on her lips in the mirror above the fire and powders her cheeks. Mammy says "Goodbye and God bless you." The woman walks off down the station and I listen to the click-click of her heels on the platform, till they go into the wind and the blowing bits of paper.

*

It's early in the morning, daylight has been out a while and even with the fire still burning we're all cold and shivering, ready to go outside for the first bus of the day. It's a foggy frosty morning. Mammy leaves the waiting room door open for the people who will be getting on the trains soon. She says it's too cold to stand at the bus stop and we'd be better walking to warm us up. Then she calls into a shop to buy some Sweet Afton cigarettes with the bus money, to calm her nerves. With the cigarettes calming her nerves and a lollypop keeping Baby Deirdre quiet we're on our way up South Circular Road, to Dolphin's Barn past the cigarette factory that you can smell a mile away and past the Boy's Brigade ground next to some houses.

Mammy knocks at number 314. The door is opened by Marie. She looks surprised to see us. She opens the door wide to let us all in then runs past us, past a bicycle leaning against a big coat stand, and down three steps and into the kitchen to tell Daddy and Nana and Grandad. "Look who's here, it's Mammy and Baby Deirdre, and Raymin, Helen, Brian and Louise. They've come to see us."

Mammy goes into the kitchen first and stands by the fire range holding Baby Deirdre. The rest of us follow and slide along a wood bench to sit between the big table and the wall. I'm wondering why Daddy isn't fussing over us, after not seeing us for so long. Nana and Grandad are looking surprised to see us too. Mammy was right when she said it will be a surprise for Daddy. Grandad says he'll put the kettle on. Then he stands by the big gas cooker at the other side of the fire from Mammy. Someone comes down the stairs in a hurry, grabs a bit of fried bread from the kitchen table. He looks around at us, says "Jasus," then he says "Hello," then runs back up the three steps to the hall, grabs the bicycle and rushes out the door. "That was your Uncle Colm," Marie tells us. "He's always late for his job at the post office."

Nana is round, with a flowery apron on over her flowery dress and has streaky grey hair. Grandad is long, needs a shave and has white-grey hair. He looks like he's in charge of the kitchen. Marie is standing by Grandad in her flowery dress and she has pigtails in her hair. I'm thinking Marie is the only one who looks happy to see us.

"Take the children out into the back garden for a while now that the sun is trying to come out, so the grownups can have a cup of tea and a talk," Grandad tells Marie.

Up to now no one has been talking much, not even Mammy and Daddy. There's a knock at the front door. Marie says that'll be Chrissy her friend from school.

Marie's gone to school with her friend. We're all out in the garden. It's big, with lots of apple trees and pear trees. The apples and pears are very small. There's sheds leaning against the wall, some broken and some with ivy growing all over them and the walls. There's lots of snails about. One of the sheds has Bunty the dog in it. He's barking at us but I can't tell if he's saying hello or go away. Bunty is black and white and looks like a sheepdog. On the other side of the garden there's a long brick wall. There's a gate in the garden wall that goes onto the lane and there's an old wood garage at the end, with the doors hanging off. It's just the best place for hiding or exploring and looking over the wall to the Boys' Brigade ground where I can see the Protestant boys' band, marching and playing.

Back in the garden, I sit on the white two-seat, iron chair. It's a good place to think about eating an apple or a pear – which one first? Grandad comes out with a big plate of sausage samiches.

"They're Donnelly's sausages, the best in all Ireland," he says. When he comes out for the empty plates, he tells us, "Don't make too much noise and have Bunty barking, the dog's not used to having lots of children here."

"You're right, Grandad, they are the best sausages in Ireland!"

The sun is shining and we're out in the garden all day. Raymin and me have been listening, trying to hear what the grownups have been saying. Helen has been looking after Deirdre and being huffy when anyone tries to speak to her. Louise has been playing with the dog 'cos the dog likes everybody. He's not a bit like Helen.

When Marie comes home she takes us back into the house, past the kitchen where the grownups are still talking and Daddy is talking the loudest. We follow Marie upstairs where she shows us the four bedrooms. Three of the bedrooms smell of mothballs. The fourth bedroom is locked and the bathroom smells of carbolic soap like Mammy uses. We go back down the stairs into the dining room which is only used as a dining room at weekends. She says it's used more for reading and listening to the big radio that has a round glass on it that glows bright green when you tune into a loud station. Beside the radio is a tall wardrobe with glass windows at the top and it's full of books.

There's a big wood door that can slide back to join the dining room and the parlour together when it's open. The front parlour has fancy chairs and a piano, but the door is locked today and we can only see them through the keyhole. Marie takes us down to the kitchen, where the talking stops when we go in. We go past the fire range and down the passage leading to the room used to store the apples and pears for the winter. There is a scullery at the end of the passage with a stone sink and a cold-water tap sticking out of the wall by the window, where I can look through to see the dog's hut with Bunty in it. We go back to the garden and the grownups in the kitchen start talking loud again.

*

In the morning I wake up to see the sunshine on the wall and the ceiling. I don't know where I am 'cos I'm sure this isn't the room I fell asleep in last night. I can smell something cooking. I don't know what it is, but it sure smells good. Soon Grandad is calling us down for breakfast.

"Is there no one getting up at all this marning?" is how he calls us. "No one wants to go to bed at noit and no one wants to get up in the marning, God help us all. If you don't get up, oil eat all the sausages meself!"

We're all down in the kitchen with Mammy, Daddy and Baby Deirdre, quicker than the man at the railway station said 'Up the rebels.' There's sausages, black pudding, fried bread and a cup of tea. Lovely. And no jam jars – except the one with jam in it. Nana is in the kitchen but Grandad seems to be still in charge, dishing out the breakfasts. We can have bread and butter and two-sided toast as well if we want. The radio is playing and an advert for Donnelly's sausages comes on. "That's what you're having now," says Grandad. I start cheering for Grandad and Donnelly's. Everyone joins in and we all think it's great fun. Except Mammy and Daddy.

After breakfast the sun is shining again so we play in the back garden. I can see Mammy, Daddy and Baby Deirdre through the kitchen window. Mammy is having a cigarette and Baby is having a bowl of bread and warm milk. Daddy doesn't look very happy so I stop looking in the window and go back to the others who are playing with Bunty the dog. Marie tells us not to eat too many apples in case they make us sick but I do, and then I am.

It's early afternoon and Mammy calls us into the kitchen for some dinner with Daddy. There's bacon and cabbage and parsnips that she has cooked. I don't like parsnips and I won't eat them. She says they're not parsnips, they're new potatoes.

"They're not feckin potatoes and I don't like them!"

Now my ear is ringing and sore. Daddy has walloped the side of my head and told me not to use the cursing words. Mammy says they really are new potatoes and mashes them up in the bacon water. They taste better, but they're still not as good as real spuds. Anyway, real spuds don't look like white carrots.

Later on, Mammy comes out to the garden, talking to Raymin, and gives Baby Deirdre to Helen to look after for a while. She says she is going to see her sister Delia down Gray Street and then she's going to get some milk of magnesia for Baby's upset tummy, and that we have to behave ourselves while she is gone. She says she won't be long. Now Helen and Marie are looking after Baby Deirdre. I'm thinking I shouldn't have shared the small apples and pears with her . . .

Raymin is hitting a ball with an old hurley stick he found in one of the sheds. He's running round the garden tapping the ball on the stick pretending he is Christy Ring, the great Irish hurling champ, and doing a fast radio talk in a high voice like Michael O'Hehir, the radio man. Louise and me are both feeling sick with eating too many small apples.

Later on Daddy comes out and asks Helen where Mammy went. She tells him "Mammy's gone for some milk of magnesia for Baby Deirdre and if she's a long time she might have called to see Auntie Delia." Daddy goes into the kitchen and is talking loud again with Nana and Grandad. Marie asks Raymin why Mammy is so long at the shops and he says he doesn't know and carries on being Christy Ring and Michael O'Hehir.

Grandad calls us in for tea. Uncle Colm, who looks about the same age as Cousin Johnny Murphy, is home from his job at the Post Office, where he goes early every morning on Grandad's bicycle. Marie says Uncle Fintan will be up in his bedroom reading like he always is. We haven't seen him yet. And Mammy isn't back from the shops yet. We are all sat around the table except Uncle Colm who is eating standing up 'cos he is in a hurry to go out he says, "To see a man about a dog." Nana is talking to Uncle Colm about something and with his answer he says "shit."

"That's not very nice in front of the children is it?" Nana says. Uncle Colm looks at me.

"It's nothing they haven't heard before, Ma. Have you heard 'shit' before Brian, have you?"

I'm looking at the others, trying not to laugh, and they're trying not to laugh back. I've heard shit lots of times before but I can't say yes in front of Nana.

"That's disgraceful talk in front of the children."

Grandad is getting annoyed and squeezing his lips flat together. Uncle Colm walks out the door mumbling, "I'm sure they've heard shit before Ma."

Now we're all sitting quietly at the table trying not to laugh at what Uncle Colm has been saying. And I'm trying to work out how a cousin can be as old as an uncle and why Uncle Colm is looking for another dog.

*

It's late now, but it's not dark yet. We're in the dining room, the radio is on and Mrs Sera Sera is playing, and I'm trying to sing along with it, but it's hard to keep in time with them. I'm sure the radio is getting some of the words wrong. I'm wishing Mammy was back from the shops 'cos she would sing along with me with the right ones. And she'd be happy, now that we are all living with Daddy, and Nana and Grandad are looking after us. I'm happy too, 'cos I get Donnelly's sausages for breakfast. When Mammy comes back I'll tell her about the song on the radio and ask her if she heard it and sang it, like me.

The grownups are in the kitchen talking and Mammy isn't back yet. It's getting dark and Daddy is shouting again. I'm thinking there's going to be some trouble like before. There's something serious going on. There must be, with all the loud talking and now the shouting again, and they haven't even been out to the bars drinking. Marie is listening near the door. She is nearly caught when Grandad comes out to ask her to get us ready for bed. It's nearly nine o'clock when Daddy comes into the dining room.

"Are you sure your mother didn't say anything else when she went out today?"

We all look at each other for answers. There is a silence. Nobody knows. Grandad walks into the room again.

"Is there no one going to bed at all tenoit? It's nearly nine o'clock. No one wants to go to bed at noit an' yous won't want to get up in the marning, God help us all!"

Raymin pulls a letter from his pocket and gives it to Grandad. It's from Mammy, he says. Grandad opens it and reads it with Daddy looking over his shoulder. Daddy looks angry at Raymin and starts to move at him, but Marie and Grandad can see that Daddy isn't happy and they both move in front of him. Grandad tells Marie to put us all to bed and turns to Daddy to tell him to calm down. There's two single beds in the room above the dining room. Helen and Louise are in one bed and me and Raymin are in the other. Baby Deirdre is in Nana's bedroom above the parlour and there's still lots of noisy talking going on downstairs.

Marie is on the landing, she's telling us that she's been listening down the stairs. The letter says that Mammy has left us all with Daddy. By nine o'clock she will be on the boat to England and Daddy can look after us, like she had to, with no money. Marie says Daddy is mad with Raymin for keeping the letter 'til nine o'clock. Raymin says that's what Mammy told him to do, and anyway he didn't know what was in it. Then he says that Auntie Delia must have helped Mammy to go to England, 'cos he saw Mammy with money in her handbag today, when she had no money yesterday. Auntie Delia must have known that Mammy was coming to Dublin he says. Marie tells us that yesterday she heard Mammy asking Daddy to take us all to England where there's lots of labouring jobs and we could all stay with her brother Paddy and his family in Yorkshire 'til we got 'sorted out'. But Grandad said that no son of his was going to England to be a labourer for her.

Now we're all crying 'cos our Mammy has run away to England looking for a labouring job for Daddy, and Helen is crying 'cos Baby Deirdre, who is just over one year old, has no Mammy to look after her. Marie is crying 'cos Mammy has left us.

Marie stops crying and tells us not to cry. She says we will be alright 'cos Nana and Grandad will look after us. Grandad shouts up, "Is there no one going to sleep at all tenoit?" Marie tells us we have to kneel down and say one of Nana's prayers:

Holy St Jude, patron saint of hopeless causes,

please look after Mammy and Daddy.

Amen.

# *Chapter 5*

## I love living at Grandad's

The smell of Donnelly's sausages is coming up the stairs at the same time as Grandad shouts up "Is there no one getting up at all this marning?" I jump out of bed and run around the other rooms to see if Mammy is really gone. She is.

Grandad is in charge of the kitchen and the breakfast again. Sausages, black pudding, fried bread and two-sided toast with the cup of tea, but this morning there's no singing along with the radio. Daddy comes down and asks Raymin about the letter and if he knew Mammy was leaving. Raymin says he didn't know, and only did what she told him to do, and he wishes she was still here with us.

During the days we play in the garden if it's not raining. In the evenings we play in the dining room. We are not allowed into the parlour. Marie keeps listening at doors when she can and after a couple of weeks she says it looks like Mammy's not coming back. Baby Deirdre cries for her Mammy and clings onto Helen most of the time. Grandad looks after us more than Daddy does. On Sundays the aunties and uncles come to the house and we can hear them talking about what is to be done about us.

I like it at Grandad's. I like the beds with the crispy sheets and blankets on and no coats on top, like we had to have in Limerick. The beds are much better than floorboards and drawers for sleeping in. I like the garden and the dog and the apple trees, and Grandad and Marie looking after us. The sausages, black pudding and fried bread are much better than bread and jam. I love living here. It feels good being with Grandad. I never feel frightened here. But I still miss my Mammy a lot, 'specially when her songs are on the big radio. I hope she's safe from the Devil, over there, across the water.

It's a good summer with lots of sunny days. On weekends the uncles with cars sometimes take us out for drives to places like Bray at the seaside or up to the Wicklow Mountains. We have picnics in Wicklow Gap and sing songs like 'The Whistling Gipsy' around a fire. On Sunday mornings we all go to Mass at the big church (Our Lady of Dolours) at Dolphin's Barn up the road. Nana tells us to light candles and pray to God for Mammy to come back from England. We have been praying every week and most nights and I think maybe England is too far away for God to reach with his messages. Mammy always said that England is the Devil's country and no one goes to Mass there. People who go there, she says, "Lose their religion and it's not even worth praying to Saint Anthony to find it for them once they cross the water." I'm wondering why Mammy would want to go to the Devil's country. I think I'll have to say stronger prayers for her.

We spend the whole summer at Grandad's and there's still no sign of Mammy coming back from England where the Devil is, and God isn't. Marie has been listening at keyholes again. She tells us that there is no news from Mammy, only regular letters for Grandad with government stamps on them. She says they're probably from his friend de Valera. Grandad and the aunties and uncles have been talking about sharing us out among them. Marie says "Grandad and Nana are too old to look after us all the time."

*

It's nearly September and school will start soon. Grandad keeps saying to Nana that something needs to be done. Marie is getting so good at keyhole listening now that we call her Keyhole Kate. She says she overheard talks about Raymin and me staying with Uncle Denis and Auntie Josie. They live on Maxwell Street, not far away. Grandad also said that Helen and Louise might be taken by Uncle Declan and Auntie Peggy who live out at Bray. Baby Deirdre might be looked after by Uncle Nial and Auntie Evelyn, but this wasn't sorted out yet. They all said they would only take us if they could adopt us forever. Marie says we mustn't say anything about what she tells us, and not to call her Keyhole Kate in front of the grownups.

In September Raymin starts at St Joseph's Convent School at Weavers Square with Marie and her friend

Chrissy, who calls for her every morning. Helen, me, Louise and Baby Deirdre stay at home with Daddy, Nana, Grandad and Uncle Fintan, who is still in his room reading, and Uncle Colm who still says shit now and again and never did get the dog he went to see about. And he can't go to work on Grandad's bicycle anymore 'cos of the frame being broken. But he soon will, because he says that Mr Raleigh has sent him a brand-new frame to cover the lifetime guarantee as the bicycle is only fifteen years old. Helen looks after Baby Deirdre most of the time. Baby Deirdre calls her 'Mammy Helen' all the time now 'cos it's so long since she saw her real mammy.

Marie and Raymin are at school and Helen, Louise and Baby Deirdre are at home with Nana. Me and Grandad are walking halfway into Dublin to Mount Street Bridge and Grand Canal Street Bridge, where he did his fighting in the Easter Rising in 1916. He's showing me the bullet holes still in the walls of the houses by the bridges, and telling me how him and his friend Eamon de Valera, who he calls Dev, were fighting the English soldiers. He says that after a lot of shooting across the Grand Canal, wounding the English, they would stop shooting for a while so the ambulance soldiers could pick up the injured. Sometimes he would fire warning shots above their heads, but if they kept coming he would then shoot to kill. He says that every shot had to count for something because at three pennies for each bullet they didn't want to waste any. Grandad says that Dev nearly shot him one night on his way back to basecamp at Boland's Mill, when Dev couldn't make out who was coming along the railway lines. Grandad had to shout 'volunteer, volunteer,' after two shots fired at him bounced off the railway lines. And then he said that Dev's eyesight wasn't much better in the day.

As soon as me and Grandad are home I'm out in the garden using a hurley stick as a rifle, looking over the brick wall behind the old garage to see if there's any English soldiers in the Boys' Brigade ground. There's some boys at the far side of the field. They could be English spies! My rifle is aimed at the biggest boy, using the tip of the wood handle as a sight. I pull the trigger but he doesn't fall. The sights must be wrong, so I chip a bit of wood off the top of the sights with the help of a piece of brick. When I look down the field again, there's nobody there. The first shot must have frightened them away. I'm thinking today they have had a lucky escape, I'll be back tomorrow!

In the morning Grandad is surprised to see me getting up before he shouts us for the breakfast. When I tell him that I'm going on duty with my rifle, he says it's OK to go. I ask him if I can have two carrots from the back storeroom and he asks me what I want them for. I tell him I want them for the 'cause'. He says if they'll help fight for the cause I can have as many as I want. So I'm out on the wall again keeping a look out for soldiers and spies. It's bright sunshine, it's cold and there's no one to be seen anywhere. After about half an hour I hear a noise and I turn around.

"Halt! Who goes there?"

"It's Louise. Your breakfast is ready and Grandad says you've to come in now."

"Are you a volunteer?" I ask her.

"Yes," she says.

"But I'm doing a very important job here, and I can't leave my post. Is it an order?"

"Yes," she says.

"I have to do something first," I tell her, and I point my rifle at the Protestant boys and a dog, and I get ready to practise marching. I hand her my carrot binoculars and ask her to tell me if anyone goes down. She looks at me and then at the binoculars and then at me again. I tell her they'll be fine, they don't need adjusting. Right I'm ready. Louise is looking through the binoculars. She says they don't magnify much. I explain to her that she's got them the wrong way round. I'm aiming at the leader boy at the front who's twiddling his stick. Bang, and the bullet has gone.

"Did I get him," I ask her. She's looking at me as if she doesn't know what to say.

"Did I get him?"

She says no.

So I missed, that's bad. I'm not happy.

"Are you coming in for your breakfast? Louise asks.

"I'm not hungry."

"Grandad has ordered you to come in for your two-sided toast, fried bread, black pudding, Donnelly's sausages and a nice mug of hot tea, on this cold morning. I did see the dog limping away," Louise tells me.

"I never meant to shoot the dog!"

"It's OK 'cos it's only a Protestant dog."

Even so, I'm thinking, you should never hurt an animal no matter what religion it is.

The cold is making me think that Grandad is right and an order is an order and every good soldier should obey an order without question. I suppose I'll have to go into the warm kitchen and do my duty by eating one of Grandad's lovely breakfasts.

*

Now that Marie and Raymin are going to school every day, the spying at keyholes is left to Helen and me. When they come home we have no secret news for them 'cos we're just no good at spying. One day, I'm listening at the inside of the dining room keyhole, and I get an awful wallop on the head from the door handle when Grandad walks in with a stranger man who is wearing a long coat, and has a flat cap rolled up in his hands. The man looks at us but says nothing. Then Grandad takes him down to the kitchen where Nana is and they're talking for a while. They go out into the garden where we can see them but we can't hear them. I can see their sad faces and I'm not as happy as I have been and I don't feel safe anymore.

When Marie and Raymin come home from school I tell them about the man. I tell them he might be the cruelty man from the NSPCC or a policeman looking for Mammy. Now Marie and Raymin have sad faces on them but Marie tells us not to worry. I tell them that when the man came to the front door, Daddy went upstairs and stayed there 'til he left. Marie says that it must have been the cruelty man that called, 'cos Daddy doesn't like him and won't want to meet him.

Marie hasn't heard anymore talking about us being shared out amongst the aunties and uncles. But she did hear Grandad complaining about the price of everything going up all the time. And the price of coal for heating the house and the hot water has gone up too, and Grandad only has his pension from the government, that's not a big pension to live on, like some. She says it will be good if we can go to live with the aunties and uncles 'cos they all have nice houses and plenty of proper beds and they seem to be kind.

I hope we all stay at Grandad's house. This is the best place ever. None of the other uncles or aunties have apple and pear trees in their gardens or a dog called Bunty. It's easy to get up in the morning here, with the smell of breakfast cooking, drifting up the stairs, and Grandad calling to me, "There's Donnelly's sausages for breakfast again."

*

Chrissie calls for Marie to go to school. Nana tells Raymin that he can stay at home today 'cos someone is coming to see us. He asks who is coming and Nana says it's the cruelty man from the NSPCC office. He wants to see us all together to have a talk with us.

It's not long after Marie has gone to school when the cruelty man comes. Daddy is still in bed. Nana gets our coats and we are all in the dining room waiting for the man to ask us questions. Helen is holding Baby Deirdre who is sucking milk from a new bottle that Nana bought for her. We know something is going on 'cos we don't usually wear our 'going out' coats in the dining room. I tell Raymin we might be shared out today, to the uncles and aunties, but Raymin says he doesn't think so and he looks sad.

Grandad tells us that we're going with the cruelty man. He says he and Nana can't look after us anymore and our Mammy won't agree to let us be adopted, even if she won't come back herself. We say we don't want to go. I run to the bottom of the stairs.

"Daddy, Daddy, the cruelty man is taking us away!"

But Daddy doesn't answer me. Helen is holding Baby Deirdre and hands her over to Nana, but Nana says no, Baby is going too. Grandad takes us along the hall and outside to a black car at the front of the house. I can see tears in Grandad's eyes. He tells us that we will be looked after by the cruelty man, and he and Nana will come and see us every week.

I'm sad because we're leaving the place where we have been all summer, where I have been feeling happy and safe. Now the man who made me feel happy and safe has tears in his eyes and I don't understand why we have to leave. My Grandad, who didn't even cry when his friend Davey Lera tried to shoot him in the war, has tears running down his cheeks. And now Nana is crying too. And Daddy doesn't even come to say goodbye to us. He lets the stranger man take us away.

We're in the car. Helen and Baby are crying. Raymin and Louise are looking sad. I am looking at my Grandad, with his cheeks pulled back, his lips tight and straight and tears running down his face as he tries to say goodbye. I wish Mammy would come back and we all could live at Grandad's. If she was here to look after us, Grandad wouldn't have to be crying, and the man from NSPCC wouldn't have to be bad to us, and say it's for our own good.

We are all taken to Saint Kevin's hospital in Dublin where they deal with homeless children and the NSPCC have an office. We stay there for a week until the courts send us back to Limerick. I must have been right when I thought England was too far away for God to reach with his messages for Mammy. The Dublin council don't want to take care of us 'cos we're from Limerick and the Limerick council don't want to look after us because we were dumped in Dublin.

In Limerick, Raymin and me are taken to stay in the women's ward at the City Home Fever Hospital because there's nowhere else to put us until we go to the Limerick courts. Helen, Louise and Baby Deirdre are sent to stay with the nuns at Mount Saint Vincent Convent. The NSPCC man says this will give the council time to argue to send us back to Dublin 'cos they don't want to keep us either.

*

It's night time on All Saints Day and at the fever hospital Raymin wakes up having a nightmare and screaming that he has seen a ghost at the bottom of his bed. The nursing nuns come running to see about the noise. The women are complaining that us children shouldn't be here anyway. They tell the nuns that we should be sent to an orphanage. Raymin goes back to sleep and he wets the bed.

The nuns wake us up at seven in the morning to make us go to Mass. We are back at the ward before eight, when Raymin is told by the nun in charge to carry his sheets down to the laundry. He's warned that if he wets the bed again he will have to sit outside in the little square between the wards, under the sycamore tree with the wet sheets over his head until they dry out. Raymin doesn't look too happy. One of the women patients tells Raymin not to worry about wetting the bed, "cos some of the grownups do it all the time," she says quietly. The woman is talking to us more, and asking where Mammy and Daddy are. I tell her Daddy is in Dublin hiding from the cruelty man, and Mammy is in England looking for a labouring job in a town called Yorkshire and hiding from Daddy. Then she asks us if we like it here in the city home hospital, and we say no, 'cos we have to get up too early and go to Mass too much. I tell her I'd like it more if I got Donnelly's sausages for my breakfast. Raymin asks her if she likes being here.

"Oh yes, of course I do!" she says. "I love it here. Sure, where else could I go to Mass every day in my slippers?"

At eight o'clock another nun comes in and takes us off to another Mass that we don't want to go to. She says you can never go to Mass too often and that it will do us good. She says Raymin can pray that he is forgiven for wetting the bed, and I can pray to God to find our Mammy. I tell the nun that we've been praying all summer for God to find Mammy and he can't, and Mammy is in England and that's the Devil's country, and God's not there 'cos most of them are Protestants anyway. Now she's twisting my ear and telling me, "God is everywhere child, God is everywhere." I'm thinking that's good, God will be able to see what she's doing to me now.

We're back at the ward at a quarter to nine and me and Raymin are feeling very hungry and very holy with all the Masses and prayers. There's an older nun that comes to the ward, she asks us if we have been to Mass yet. We tell her we've been twice already and she says "That's very good, good for your soul. Would you like to . . .?" And that's it, we're off down the corridor faster than lightening before she finishes the question. Raymin is pulling me by my jumper to make me go faster. We're heading for the kitchen. He says we've fed our souls enough for today and it's time we fed our bellies.

We go into the kitchen to see the cook, like we do each day for breakfast. The smell of the cooking reminds me of Grandad's, except there's no sausages for us. I ask Raymin if we will be sent back to Grandad's in Dublin, he says he doesn't think so. I miss my Grandad and my sisters and my Mammy. Now I'm not that hungry anymore.

*

Outside Limerick city courthouse Raymin, Helen, me, Louise and Baby Deirdre are playing on the steps. Raymin tells the girls about the hospital where we're staying. Helen tells us about Mount Saint Vincent Convent, and how the nuns wouldn't let her look after Baby Deirdre, and how the nuns took Baby Deirdre away from her and how Baby screamed out for 'Mammy Helen' as they carried her off.

After a long time playing on the steps, the cruelty man comes out of the court and tells us that Helen, Louise and Deirdre have to go back to the convent for another week, "To give the judge time to consider the case further." Me and Raymin are to be taken to stay at the Christian Brothers Industrial School in Glin (which is a school for 'bad boys'), outside Limerick, as the judge is not happy that we have been kept at the women's ward in the city hospital. I'm thinking it's the women that aren't happy to have us staying there.

After a week with the Christian Brothers in Glin, we're back at the courthouse again. Today the judge decides to 'commit' us back to the industrial school. Helen, Louise and Deirdre are committed to stay with the nuns at the Mount.

Me and Raymin don't want to go back to Glin where they shout at us and the beds are cold. The infirmary nurse won't even wrap up a warm clothes iron in a towel for my bed like Mammy used to do to keep our feet warm on cold nights, and one of the brothers said things to us like, "It isn't the Ritz, boy."

All last week there wasn't one sausage at breakfast time, just porridge. And now at the courthouse there's crying and sad faces. We are outside waiting, holding on to each other, trying to stay together. The cruelty man is pulling me and Raymin away from our sisters. I'm thinking to myself that this wouldn't be happening if Daddy hadn't been a liten bastard and Mammy hadn't run away to the Devil's Country. And if I'd eaten the parsnips and not said the cursing word, Mammy might still be here. And Grandad might have been able to look after us all if the price of coal hadn't gone up in Dublin.

# *Chapter 6*

## Christian Brothers who are not so Christian

The sky's been dark for a while when we turn off the main road near the school. We go through the village, turn left up the lane and drive past the dark grey walls of Glin Industrial School. We pass lots of windows before we get to the big brown doors with an arch on top. The cruelty man stops his black car in front of them. This is the school for bad boys where the cruelty man Mr Foley says we'll be living from now on. We go in the door and stand by a statue of Saint Joseph, while Mr Foley goes looking for the brothers to tell them that we're back to stay. Soon he's back with one of the brothers, who takes me and Raymin to the office beside the infirmary room where we stayed all last week.

The nurse gives us some warm cocoa and bread and complains that the infirmary room is full up with sick boys today. Raymin has to sleep in one of the big boys' dormitories in the main block. I will be sleeping in the room under the hall stairs again. The nurse takes me past the sick boys in the infirmary room and through the hallway with the wet concrete floor to the room where I slept all last week on my own.

The bedroom walls are painted dark green up to my head, and the top walls have a dirty cream colour. There's no lino on the concrete floor. The nurse says

I'm sleeping here again with the infirmary room being full, and I'm too young for the dormitory in the big building. I ask if Raymin can sleep with me, 'cos I'm not used to being in a room on my own, but she grunts "No." She says she'll be in her room at the other end of the infirmary by the office if I need her, so there's no need to be frightened, as long as I say my prayers to Saint Joseph, because he's the one in charge here. But I'm thinking it's her that's in charge. She can't find any pyjamas for me. She says she'll find some tomorrow. So I'll have to sleep in my vest tonight. I take my clothes off and put my new shoes that the brothers gave me this morning under the bed. I keep my vest on to sleep in. It's a bit big for me but it's alright for sleeping in 'cos it keeps my knees warm. I put my jumper on too, 'cos it's cold. The nurse is gone now. I kneel down, pulling my vest under my knees. I hold the rosary beads that Grandad gave to me in Dublin and say my prayers, like I do every night.

*Please God and Saint Joseph, bless my Mammy and Daddy and my brothers and sisters. Please Saint Anthony find my Mammy who is somewhere in the Devil's Country that's across the water from here. And please St Jude, don't forget to help the hopeless cases, Mammy and Daddy.*

I'm still holding the rosary beads, but I don't say the rosary prayer 'cos I've never said it all on my own. Anyway, it's too long. I kiss the little cross with Jesus on it, like I've seen the priest doing at Mass. I look under the bed for ghosts or devils or scrapmen or foreigners from Dublin who might kidnap me. I jump onto the bed and put the rosary beads under my pillow. I'm feeling frightened.

I'm sitting on my pillow leaning into the corner of the wall. The bulb hanging down from the middle of the roof isn't very bright. I hear some noises so I jump out of the bed to check the hallway, but there's no one there. The outside door keeps banging in the wind. I jump up to see through the glass on the top half of the door to the big infirmary room. It's dark but I can still see the sick boys sleeping in their beds. I go back to my own bed where I sit in the corner again, watching the door for ghosts and kidnappers. I'm remembering the story one of the big boys told me last week about this room being haunted. He said that a boy was kneeling at his bedside, saying the rosary prayers, when a hand came through the wall and took the beads from him.

I hear the door bang again. I'm out of the bed and into the hall. I run across the cold wet concrete floor, through the infirmary door, past the sick boys, and I'm banging on the nurses' room door. I can see her inside if I jump high enough to see through the glass.

"Please nurse, the ghost might come through the wall and get my rosary beads!"

The nurse comes out, pulling me back past the sick boys, who are so sick that they're making ghost noises and pulling faces at me.

"There's no such thing as ghosts in this school, child."

So I'm telling her what the boys said about the ghost and the beads.

"I'm thinking they're only trying to frighten you, take no notice of them."

But it's too late to take no notice of them. I've already been looking out for devils, scrapmen and foreigners from Dublin. Now I've got to watch the wall for the ghost hand, as well as checking under the bed and outside the door. She dumps me on the bed.

"Now you see? No ghosts at all. I'll leave the lights on for you. You know I'm not far away. Be good now and go to sleep."

I'm looking at the wall now and under the bed again.

"What's wrong now child?"she shouts.

"I'm cold and if my brother could sleep with me I'd be alright."

"He can't and that's that."

"At home in Crosbie Row we slept two in a bed and sometimes five if it was really cold."

She walks off, talking to herself and almighty God, a bit like Mammy used to do.

I squeeze into the corner of the room for a long time, watching the middle of the wall. I'm thinking that if a hand comes through a wall it's always in the middle, never in the corners or from the roof. I'm getting more frightened now. Any minute the hand is going to come through the middle of the wall, moving around like a snake looking for my rosary beads, so I'm off again! I jump off the bed, run out and across the hall. I pull at the infirmary room door, but it's stuck. I pull harder and harder, but it's locked. I jump up and look through the glass part, and there's a boy looking over to the door, he can see my head bobbing up and down. He shouts at me to go back to bed, back to the haunted room. I stop jumping up and down 'cos now I'm out of breath and panting. I push open the door leading outside. It's pitch black and it's raining. I'm running out into the rain in my bare feet as fast as I can, past the big room windows. I find the door at the far end and run in to find the nurses' room. It's empty and locked. I pull the handle on the other door to the big room and that's locked too. The nurse is nowhere. She told me lies. She said she would be here.

Now the sick boy is looking through this glass door top at me. He doesn't have to jump up 'cos he's much bigger than me. He's shouting for me to go back to my bed before the night watchman, who carries a big cane and wouldn't think twice about giving me a good clatter with it, finds me running around. I look out the door into the darkness and the rain shouting, "Nurse, nurse!" There's no answer. In the distance I can hear noises, like when you're standing outside a picture house and hear people laughing inside. There's no one close by. I call the nurse again, but she's not there. Now I'm calling "Raymin, Raymin!" 'cos I want my brother, but there's no answer. Now I have another worry to worry about, thinking about the night watchman wanting to clatter me twice with his cane. I run out into the rain and back to the other hallway and peep inside my room and look under the bed. I jump onto the bed and make sure the rosary beads are still under my pillow. I take the beads and hang them on the iron frame at the bottom of the bed near the middle of the wall, where the hand will find them easily if it wants to.

I'm leaning into the corner again crying, with my cheeks wet from my tears and the rain. I'm frightened, I'm sobbing, my chest is jumping when I'm breathing in and my face is sticking to the mucky cream colour paint on the wall. I've got one eye on the wall and the other on the open door to the hallway. Now I'm wishing I knew how to get eyes in my arse, like Mammy used to say she needed sometimes. Now I'm thinking to myself about all my worries, like Mammy used to do. I'm thinking I'm getting bad with my nerves like her. The picture house noises are still in the distance. After a long time, I fall asleep sat up. The wind banging the outside door makes me jump lots of times. Now I'm being frightened again and trying to stay awake, still watching the wall and the door for ghosts and kidnappers and the night watchman.

When the nurse wakes me up in the morning, the first thing I do is look to see if the beads have been taken. They're still there. I tell her that I was looking for her last night, but she says she was in her room all the time. Now I'm thinking why is it that grownups lie to me all the time, when they tell me it's a sin to tell lies.

"Look, your beads are still there," she says, "I told you there's no ghost here at all."

I look under the bed.

"Yes nurse, my beads are there but my new shoes are gone and there's some old ones instead."

"Oh I suppose the ghost is a small one, and takes the same size shoes as you, does he?"

Now she's looking up in the air and blessing herself with the cross sign and saying something about God almighty and patience.

*

One of the brothers walks in with some old clothes for me to wear. He says the clothes I had on yesterday were good clothes for going outside the school, and they are too good to wear every day. The short pants he gives me are too big and when I walk around they bounce up and down on my elastic braces. I'm dressed and I have put on my new old shoes, while at the same time I'm smelling the air. I can't smell any cooking so it must be porridge for breakfast again. I hope it's a bit burnt this morning. It makes it taste better.

Back in the infirmary room I hear the nurse telling the brothers about me being upset last night. She says I kept the sick boys awake and it would be better if I was with the big boys in the dormitories and will they take me up near my brother. I'm thinking she wants me out of the way, so she can sneak off at night after telling lies. She doesn't want me there to call out for her when I think the ghost is coming.

I hear one of the brothers telling her about the reports about me and Raymin and our sisters in the *Limerick Leader*. The brother says there's photographs of us all in one of the Dublin papers. Then I'm thinking that Daddy must still be in Dublin and must be giving away photos of us all. Maybe Mammy and Daddy are in the papers too, but I can't ask 'cos the brother will know I've been listening. Another one of the brothers is saying that on the front page of the *Leader* a woman has written in offering a home to refugees from the war in Hungary. The first brother says it's a pity they can't offer homes for our own. Now I'm thinking about what the second brother said and wondering where Raymin is, and when I see him I can ask him what a refugee is.

I'm taken to one of the dormitories on the first floor of the big building where the brother tells me is where the 'wet-the-beds' sleep. It's the biggest bedroom I've ever seen. Three rows of iron beds reaching the length of twenty-five hurley sticks. The brother says I'll be in this room with Raymin, and if our beds stay dry we can move to one of the other dormitories. He says if the 'wet-the-beds' room is full, then the 'pissy beds' in the other dormitories have to tie a sock on the foot of their beds so the night watchman knows who to wake up to go to the toilet. I'm happy that I'll be sleeping in the same room as Raymin. The brother shows me the wash room and the toilet near the stairs, where there's a row of white sinks with a cold water tap sticking out of the wall over each one. He shows me how to make my bed nice and neat. I have to fold the sheet back over the blankets at the pillow end. Then I need to fold the blankets at the bottom and under the mattress with the side folded down straight at the corner and tucked under the mattress. He says it's the way nurses in the hospitals do it and I'll have to do it like that every morning.

There's a boy with all his hair shaved off, cleaning the dormitory floor. The brother says he had his head shaved when he tried to run away from the school. Then he shows me a leather strap, and says that the baldy boy got a good beating with it. The boy can hear the brother, but he doesn't look up, he keeps his head down, looking at the floor.

I'm taken down across the yard into a classroom with boys of my own age. I'm handed over to the teacher brother as the 'new boy'. The room has high windows, too high to see out of. I'm sitting at a wooden desk with a black iron frame holding the chair and the desk together. There's a black square slate on the desk and a piece of chalk next to it. A boy in the corner with very short hair is looking at me and making faces.

"Now boys, we have a new boy in the class today."

He looks at me and says, "This is young Donoghue. What's your first name child?"

"Brian, sir, my Mammy calls me Brian O'G. She used to call me Brian but now she calls me Brian O'G for short. That's if she was here. But now she doesn't call me anything at all 'cos she's gone away to the Devil's Country in England and no one can find her."

"Where's your father then?" the brother asks.

I tell him that Daddy's probably still in the bars in Dublin looking for a job.

"Count yourself lucky, child. Some of the children here have no mothers or fathers so you're one of the lucky ones, aren't you?'

I say "Yes, sir" but I don't really mean it. I only say yes 'cos that's what I think I'm supposed to say.

The brother asks the boys what they want to be when they grow up. Some say they want to be farmers, others want to be doctors, bus drivers. Some say telegram boys 'cos there's a bike with the job. The boy with the short hair and spotty face in the corner says he wants to be a Christian Brother, and that pleases the teacher very much. I'm thinking that Baldy Spot Face is trying to be teacher's pet.

The brother asks me what I want to be.

"I want money, sir."

"Goody? You want baby food?"

"No, sir, I said money."

He looks over at Spot Face.

"Did you hear young Donoghue say goody?"

"Yes, sir, he said goody alright, sir," Spot Face says.

Now all the boys are laughing and making fun of me. I don't understand why, and I don't like the brother, or this place, and I hate Spot Face the teacher's pet. Now I'm wishing I was back in the haunted room under the stairs with only a ghost and kidnappers to worry about.

*

Me and Raymin are soon moved up into the 'dry' dormitory away from the pissy beds. At night I'm not frightened anymore 'cos my big brother is in the bed next to mine. After prayers and lights out we can whisper to each other, as long as the brothers or the night watchman don't hear us. I ask Raymin about Mammy and Daddy but he says that there's no news from them. He says we'll have to wait and see if the cruelty man can find them.

The watchman wakes me up to go to the toilet in the middle of the night. I'm half asleep and I try to tell him that I'm dry, but he won't listen to me. He drags me to the end of the dormitory to make me go to the toilet. I'm trying my best to pee and telling him that I'm dry but he says if there's a sock tied to the end of my bed it's his job to get me up. I tell him it's the other boys codding around and he still doesn't believe me.

I stagger back to my bed. I'm cold and I'm tired. I take the sock off the end of the bed post and get the other one from the floor. I put them both on to keep my feet warm and hide the socks at the same time.

In the morning Raymin has wet the bed. The brother has him bent over his wet bed and is swinging a big stick over his head and saying he's going to beat him. He beats him on the backside.

Raymin is screaming and telling the brother that he's sorry and promising not to do it again. Now I'm screaming with Raymin at the brother.

"Please don't hit my Raymin!"

The brother walks away, telling him to tie a sock on his bed every night. If his bed is wet tomorrow morning, he'll get the beating of his life and be sent back to the smelly pissy bed room. Now I'm thinking again that maybe the haunted room wasn't that bad compared to these big brothers and their sticks and straps. If Mammy was here she could get the cruelty man for them.

*

There's a small yard and a big yard in the school, where we play most times during the day, sometimes even when it's raining. In the big yard I can look through the gaps in the wall where the rusty wire fence is. I see the cows from the farm and the River Shannon. Sometimes I see the big cart horses, Sean and Sheila. They're as big and as strong as elephants. I wish I could ride them around the farm all day long. I look up in the sky and I can see the planes flying into Shannon Airport from across the other side of the river, and they make me think of Daddy. The boys say that the planes that look so small in the sky are as big as the playground. But I tell them – 'cos I know more about planes and airport things – that the planes are as big as ten playgrounds. And you can tell different planes from each other without even seeing then, 'cos of the engine noises. I tell them all about the airport and Daddy on the radio making the planes land safely.

There's a fight going on at the other side of the yard. We all go running over. It's Raymin. He's fighting one of the big boys. They're rolling on the wet ground. All the boys crowd round them shouting. I'm shouting at Raymin too, telling him how to win the fight.

"Kill him, Raymin, kill him! Wallop the liten bastard! Choke the feckin shit out of him!"

I know what to say to him. I heard it all when Daddy was fighting with Mammy, when he was drunk and being a liten bastard himself.

"Wallop the feckin big bollix!"

Now the boys go all quiet and the fight stops. I get the biggest wallop I've ever had, on the side of my head. It knocks me over onto the wet ground. It's one of the brothers, a big man, I don't know his name, but I know he's ugly, and that makes me feel more frightened of him. He's telling Raymin and the other boy he'll see to them later. Then he lifts me off the ground by the back of my pants. My toes are barely touching the ground as he drags me across the yard. My trousers are crushing my fork. I look up at him and I can see his big red face and sticking out eyes. He shouts at me.

"Filthy language from the Limerick estates won't be tolerated, boy!"

I see a flash of Raymin's face watching as I'm dragged past the boys in the yard. Now Raymin is running along beside us. He's telling the brother that I didn't mean to be cursing. He says that Grandad said we didn't have a very good start in life, and he says it's not my fault that I'm a little feck. And now he's on the ground after getting walloped for saying feck. I'm thinking about what's going to happen to me now for using the cursing words and I'm trying to figure out what tolerated means. The boys move out of the way quickly as the brother rushes me past them.

Now Raymin is running alongside again holding his ear. But there's nothing he can do to help me 'cos he knows the brothers are to be more feared than God. The door of the chapel is pushed open and I'm thrown in onto the floor between the long seats. The brother, with his face still red, tells me to get to my knees and pray to God for forgiveness for bringing disgrace on the school by cursing. He says he's going to see the principal and I've to be prepared for a good beating when he comes back. The door slams behind me and I look up to see the Saint Joseph's statue looking down at me. There's all the chapel to look around, but he's looking straight at me. My head is sore from the wallop and my privates are hurting from being squashed. I start crying and praying.

*Please God and Saint Joseph and Saint Anthony, please find my Mammy so she can come and take us all back to my Grandad in Dublin where there's no ghosts, no bad teachers, no cruel brothers, and more than porridge for breakfast, and please make my ear and privates better 'cos they hurt.*

I've said my prayers but I stay on my knees. The brother will be coming back soon and I'm frightened. He might give me the strap or the stick, 'cos of the cursing words.

In about 5 minutes he is back. He calls me out, takes me back to the big yard and says nothing. He just walks off. Raymin comes running over to see if I'm alright. He says he thought I'd fallen at first when he saw me with the brother. He's telling me not to use the cursing words again. He says I'm lucky the brother didn't beat me more. He says the other boys said I was lucky that I didn't use the 'c' word on the brother. It's one of the worst things you can do in here. He says no matter how bad things get you must never call a brother from the country a culchie (a bad name for a country person). But I'm not listening to him much. I'm busy trying to pull out the skin on my knees that has gone flat with kneeling on the floorboards in the chapel, and then I remember to ask him what tolerated means. He says he thinks that it means you won't put up with things. Like the brother didn't tolerate me being a stupid cursing little feck. I'm thinking I'm not a little feck, so I tell him to feck off, after I make sure there's no brothers around.

It's a freezing cold morning when the brothers get us up earlier than usual. It's still dark and I'm tired and sleepy. Out the window I can see bright stars in between the fast clouds. The brother in charge tells us that the Russians have sent a satellite called the Sputnik up into space. He says we might see it if we hurry down to the yard. I'm thinking it'll be like Dan Dare in the comics, with flames shooting out the back as it dashes across the sky, all lit up against the pitch black.

It's nearly seven o'clock and all the boys are in the yard looking up at the sky. The wind is whistling down our necks, up our sleeves and up the short pants. Someone shouts "Look out, there it is!" I duck my head in case it hits me. Then I look up and after a while I can see a tiny white dot that takes about five minutes to cross the sky. That's it, no flames, no rocket, no nothing. The brothers are all excited.

"Isn't it wonderful," one one of them says, and then adds, "someday there might be as many as ten more up there."

"I don't think so, it's not natural, the communists putting things in God's sky," another one says.

Now I'm wondering why they didn't leave us in bed and keep all the excitement to themselves.

After all the fuss we go to Mass, like we have to do every morning and then to breakfast in the big dining hall shed. Breakfast is usually tea from a great big teapot that I can't taste any sugar in, porridge that's sometimes watery and alway lumpy, and a thin slice of bread with a thin scrape of marge. There's never a smell of fried bread, black pudding or sausages, never ever.

*

The next time I'm in a parade line in the yard is for a different reason altogether, nothing to do with dots in the sky. It's a Saturday morning and I hear there's a pants inspection. The brothers want to see if there's any scutter marks on the insides of our short trousers. There's a line of boys standing in the yard with their pants in their hands. They are waiting for a bucket of cold water and a scrubbing brush to clean the inside lining. None of the boys in the school have underpants, so it's easy to get marks on the trousers. I run into the toilet block. I need to check the bit of white cloth that covers the rough stitching in the privates area of my pants. It makes me bad with my nerves when I see the marks on my pants. This could be as bad as cursing in here. I pick up some bits of newspaper and wipe the marks but it only makes things worse. The print of the *Limerick Leader* marks the white cloth bit even more. I cut out the cloth with a piece of broken glass and throw it down the toilet. Then I get in the queue to have my trousers checked and I miss out on the scrubbing.

Soon I'm back playing in the big yard and the rough stitching is rubbing against my privates and making me sore. It's making me wish I'd joined the scrubbing brush queue like the other boys, instead of being frightened and ashamed. After the boys have scrubbed their pants they go into the long dining hall shed beside the classroom, where they dry their pants by the big turf fire stove. It is in this hall that one of the old brothers gathers all the boys together on the very wet days to play games or to tell stories. The way he tells the ghost stories he can keep us frightened right to the very end. Some are horror stories, some are old Irish legends, some are fairy tales, some go on for so long that it takes two wet days to finish them. This is one of the few things at the school that I like, and the old brother is liked very much by the boys.

Three days after I cut the nearly white patch out of my pants the inside of my legs are all red and sore. The brother in charge sends me to see the infirmary nurse. She puts a lot of cream on me and says to come back to see her every day for three more days. Then she sends me straight to the tailor's workshop at the top of the big playground to have a new patch put on. Now I'm sitting in the tailor shop with my long vest covering my privates, thinking about if Mammy will ever come back, or has the Devil got her. I want to be back home with Raymin, huffy Helen, Louise and Baby Deirdre. I want to have jam samiches in bed at night and all of us to sleep in the nice warm bed with overcoats on top and breadcrumbs on the sheets to make me feel like I'm at home.

At night in the dormitory the watchman comes around to check that none of the boys are missing. He wakes up the pissy beds three times a night to make them go to the toilet. He carries his big stick with him, and if anyone is acting the goat he beats them with it. I'm thinking he's practising to be a Christian Brother. Some of the boys are so frightened of wetting their bed that they sleep on the floor.

There's another hall at the other side of the big yard where they sometimes show films. Me and Raymin and the rest of the boys are watching 'Reach For The Sky.' It's my first time here. The film is about a pilot with tin legs who limps across an airfield. During the picture Raymin shouts "Give him the *Leader* so he can wipe his arse!" making everybody laugh except the brother in charge, who turns on the lights to look around as a threat to whoever did the shouting out. Now I'm thinking that this is the place where the infirmary nurse was the night I was in the haunted room. This must've been the place where the laughing noises came from. And I'm thinking that Raymin still owes me two squares of Cleeves toffee from the bet when Daddy fell on the floor.

I'm asking Raymin how the man in the film can joke about having his tin legs made longer, 'cos he's always wanted to be taller. He whispers back to me.

"Look, stupid, it's OK to joke 'cos it's only a film."

Then I'm asking him how Douglas in the film can take a fancy to Nurse Brace in the hospital and fancy Thelma the waitress in the café at the same time.

"He's just trying to be like Daddy. Now shurrup an' let me watch the film."

Now I'm being quiet and houlding my whisht. I'm sure I've just seen a mouse running across the floor under the screen.

After the pictures we're all taken up to the farmyard where the turf for the fires is tipped under an open-sided barn. Our job is to throw the turf pieces to the top of the pile against the wall, out of the rain. We always get bits in our eyes doing this job and some of us suffer for days after. While I'm there, in a dark corner of the farmyard, I can see something on an old bit of tree trunk. It is a glowing piece of bark. I peel it off and hold it between my hands. I can peep in and see it glowing. I put it in my pocket. When I go to bed I put it under the covers and it still glows in the dark. Raymin says it's probably something like a Jack-O'-Lantern or a living thing. I don't care what it is as long as it doesn't stop glowing and as long as it's mine. It glows for two days and then, just as I am going to swap it for a square of Cleeves toffee, it stops. I should have taken the square of toffee I was offered for it on the first day.

There's lots of mice and rats in the school. So many that if you catch a mouse you get a penny reward for it. If you catch a rat you get thruppence. Some of the big boys set their traps around the farmyard and they make lots of pocket money. They buy lots of Cleeves toffee at a halfpenny for two squares and then they swap them for other things. Lots of deals and swaps are made in the boot room, between the small yard and the big yard, where every morning your boots have to be well polished, before the compulsory morning parade.

On Sundays we're most times taken for walks around the countryside and down to the River Shannon. In the fields we collect vinegary salix leaves to eat (some boys call them sorrel), and sweet-tasting pink honeysuckle flowers and little yellow leaves from the May bush. At the river, we pick up seaweed. The brother says that some of the seaweed is called dillisk, and it tastes like ginger biscuits. While the big boys are swimming, me and the other small boys move a rock and find an ugly little crawly thing that looks like a snake. One of the boys wants to throw it into the water, but after some serious talking and remembering the old brother's stories about sea monsters, we decide not to put it into the river. We think it might grow into a monster fifty-foot long snake and then someday come back and kill everybody. Baldy Spot Face has a great time standing on it and killing it.

The uniform for walking out is a dark blue, double-breasted, knee-length gabardine coat. Our short pants are grey and have draughty leg holes. The knee-length grey socks never stay up unless you are lucky enough to have swapped some toffee for a hard-to-find piece of elastic. The hobnailed boots clatter on the ground with every step. I think people in Glin village must be afraid of us, 'cos they give us funny looks and some close their doors every time they hear an army of us coming. Raymin says that it's probably because most of the kids at the school are here because they've been bad. It's true. Some of the boys here have stolen apples, and not just one or two, maybe ten or more. On the way from and back to the school, one brother leads the way and another follows behind, just in case any of the boys try to run away. I keep looking up at the planes overhead on their way in and out of the airport. It makes me wonder if Daddy is back there, and if Saint Anthony has found my mammy yet.

Soon it's springtime and the nights come dark later. We haven't had any news from Mammy or Daddy and there's no more news from Grandad in Dublin. The last we heard from him was when he wrote to us at

Christmas, and sent five shillings for me and Raymin to share. Santa Claus brought no presents either, not even an orange or two balloons or some sweets like we got when we lived at Crosbie Row.

*

I'm in the dormitory one day on my own. One of the brothers comes over to me. He lifts me onto my bed and puts his hand on my chest, pressing me down on the mattress. He pulls down my short pants with his other hand, and puts his mouth over my privates, four times. He then pulls my pants up and leaves the dormitory. He doesn't say a word.

My privates are wet from his mouth and they feel cold from the draughts in the room. I don't understand why he did that to me. I stay in the room a while thinking about what the brother did. It might be something that grownups do. I wouldn't want to do that. Even if I was a grownup, I wouldn't want to do that. I hope it's not going to be compulsory, like prayers and things.

I'm thinking I'm going to be sick. When I go back down to the yard the brother doesn't say anything. He's just playing around with the other boys, acting as if there's nothing wrong.

But I'm sure something's wrong.

*

There's more time to play now that the cuckoos are back in the fields and the buds are on the May bush, and the days are a lot longer. At the bottom of the big yard there's a low concrete wall that we play on. We stand on it, pulling our coats up behind our heads to catch the wind. We want to see who can lean forward the most without falling. Bets are made using toffee, mousetraps and pieces of elastic and pennies and halfpennies, if anyone is lucky enough to have any. One of the big boys is really good at it and wins lots of times – until the day he doesn't. He leans forward too much with one hand stuck in his pocket and falls flat on his face. That cost him four squares of toffee, one mouse trap and two of his front teeth.

For toys we make bangers from a hollow key and a nail tied at each end of a bootlace. Sulphur from a match head is put inside the key and then the nail pushed in. A couple of swings around on the lace, a wallop against a wall and there's an almighty bang. You need to dart off quick and hide in case the brothers come to see what the bang is. For this game you have to be friends with the 'fire lighter boy', 'cos he's the only one allowed to have matches.

*

In the summer, the brother in charge of the farm has us going across the fields in a line with hurling sticks chopping down thistles and other weeds. This takes a long time. After a while we get fed up and start lifting cow pats with the hurling sticks and throwing them at each other, or we take a swing at them on the ground and slap them all over. Back at the yard, stinking of cow muck, the brothers make us wash our clothes in the stone baths and showers at the top of the big yard and dry them by the fire in the middle of the big dining hall.

The summer passes quickly and soon we're back to the winter storytelling in the hall. Christmas passes with no presents and no letters, except for Grandad who sends another five shillings for me and Raymin. After Christmas we spend a lot of time digging and levelling the field at the front of the school to make a pitch for Gaelic football and hurling. We dig the ground with picks and shovels, lifting out the stones and levelling off with rakes. One day a boy has his head split open walking behind someone swinging a pick. He's OK after a couple of weeks in the infirmary.

*

At Easter time, I have to learn about the catechism book and how to confess my sins so I can make my first holy communion. I'm thinking of what sins I have to confess. I don't know if running outside in the rain from the haunted room is a sin, or if cutting the stained cloth from inside my pants and flushing it down the toilet is. Then I remember about Baldy Spot Face tying a sock to my bed, and when I found out it was him, I swapped two squares of toffee for a dead mouse and put it in his bed. I'm sure that must be a sin. I suppose calling him Baldy Spot Face is another sin, and also cursing in the yard when Raymin was fighting. That must be another sin there. Now I'm happy 'cos I have a good list of sins to tell the priest when I go to my first confession before my first holy communion. Now I better learn how to say the rosary prayer all the way through, 'cos with a list of sins like that, I'm sure I'll have to say more than three hail Marys for my penance.

Just before my first communion we get a letter from Mammy. She is still in England, she is asking how we're doing and says she will be writing again shortly, and hopes to come and see us soon. Raymin writes back and tells her I'm getting ready for my first holy communion. He has to say the right things in his letter as the brothers read them before they're posted.

After my first communion the storyteller brother says he wants to take a photo of me and Raymin to send to our Mammy who has asked for one. We are given some better clothes to wear for the photo. We're out on the small lawn behind the main entrance. Raymin standing and me sitting. Raymin is wearing his double-breasted jacket, short trousers and long socks and boots. I've got my communion medal on my chest and I'm wearing a double-breasted jacket, short trousers and wellies. The story brother says he couldn't find any boots to fit me.

*

In June 1958 the brothers get a letter from Mammy saying she has come back from England and is staying in Belfast with Daddy who has got a job at Belfast Airport. She says the name of the airport is Nutts Corner, and this will suit Daddy very well. They are living in a flat in Fitzroy Avenue, and they are making plans to take us 'home' in late June. Now me and Raymin are happy 'cos soon we'll be back with Mammy and Daddy. Everything will be fine again, and in the winter when it's cold, we can sleep two in a bed again and if it's really cold Mammy will warm up the iron on the gas stove, wrap it in a towel or jumper and put it in our bed. I'm wondering if God is in Belfast, but I think he will be there 'cos it's not England, where he isn't.

*

It's early July and me and Raymin are at the main entrance hall in our going away clothes, waiting for Mammy who is coming to take us to Belfast to live with Daddy. It's breakfast time and I can smell some cooking, like at Grandad 's house. I think the brothers must be having sausages and black pudding for breakfast and this thinking about it makes me feel hungry now 'cos I didn't eat my porridge this morning. I was too excited thinking about going home with Mammy.

We're dressed in the clothes we wore for the communion photo, except for the wellies. We wait all day long, but Mammy doesn't come for us. The brother in charge says she has been delayed and she won't be here until tomorrow. At night time we stay in the infirmary room with our good clothes, ready for the next day. The nurse in charge tells us that everything will be fine tomorrow when our Mammy comes for us, but I'm not so sure. She told me lies when I was in the haunted room, and no one should tell lies 'specially grownups and more 'specially nurses.

Next morning we go back to the main entrance to wait again. I can hear a radio playing in one of the rooms. In between the songs the radio man is talking about Americans and celebrations and then Mrs Sera Sera is playing on the radio and it makes me happy, reminding me of when Mammy used to sing when we lived in Crosbie Row and reminding me that Raymin still owes me two squares of Cleeves toffee.

Soon Mammy comes and we are happy as happy can be to see her. She looks different, she is looking fatter than she used to be, but I don't tell her she's got fatter 'cos that would be bad manners like staring at ugly people is. Her hair is all nice and she's wearing posh clothes and lipstick. She looks more like a posh than a trollop. The brothers are being nice to her and give her tea with extra sugar in a fancy cup and saucer. They don't tell her about me and the cursing words. Mammy asks how we are and Raymin says fine and I say fine. Then I ask her if she had to go to England for the milk of magnesia for Baby Dierdre and Raymin gives me a dig in the side and says "Shurrup stupid."

We walk down through Glin village to the main road, for the bus into Limerick. On the bus Mammy tells us about Daddy getting a new job at Belfast Airport. Then I'm telling her about the haunted room and the grownup nurse telling me lies, but she's not listening. She's looking out of the window, into the distance. Raymin looks at me and says shush.

Mammy takes us to Mount Convent in Limerick to see Helen, Louise and Baby Deirdre, who isn't a baby anymore, she's three and a quarter now. Mammy is telling them and the nuns that she'll be back soon from Belfast to take them 'home', when her and Daddy find a bigger place to live. Mammy leaves a ten-shilling note and says goodbye to Helen and Louise. Baby Deirdre won't say goodbye 'cos she doesn't know who we are. She stays hanging on to Helen.

In Limerick we walk around the People's Park, waiting to get the train to Dublin. On the platform of Limerick Station I'm looking at the engine man again like I did a long time ago when we first went to Dublin to live with Daddy and Grandad when they didn't know we were coming. I'm wondering if it's the same engine man as before. I don't think so, 'cos the man before had a tooth in the middle of his smile, this one has none. That doesn't stop him smiling at me though. On the train, the wheels are saying 'clickety-click' to me again. This time I don't run around trying to be a train and making noises like I did before. I'm more than two years older now and growing up a lot and being sensible I think.

When we get off the train at Dublin, I'm pulling Mammy's hand to show her a black man from the equator. The brothers in Glin say that's where they come from. I'm telling her he's the first black man I've ever seen. The pennies collected for the black babies in Dublin schools must have brought him from the equator. Now I'm thinking that Limerick will soon have its own black man from the equator brought over with the money collected for the black babies in Saint Mary's School and Glin School. I'm telling this to Mammy as we walk along the platform and she belts my ear and says it's not a nice thing to say. I tell her it's not as bad as when Uncle Colm said shit in Grandad's house. Then I get another clatter on the head for saying shit. Raymin is now doing a bad stare at me. Before he opens his mouth, I say, "OK, I'll shurrup, but you still owe me some Cleeves toffee."

Now I'm thinking about things back in Glin. I'm wondering why the brother in the dormitory wanted to wet my privates, four times. And I'm thinking if Mammy had married McInnery the farmer from Hospital village when he asked her, would we have had a lot more chickens in Crosbie Row?

Mammy leans over and gives Raymin a hard slap across his face. Raymin says "What was that for?" "It's for dropping the front door key in the River Shannon," she says.

# Chapter 7

## We move to Belfast in the North

We get the bus up to the South Circular Road. We are off before we reach the W.D. & H.O. Wills cigarette factory 'cos Mammy says we're calling to see Auntie Nan, who's Grandma's sister and lives down on Maxwell Street. "A nice street with lovely tiny houses," Mammy says. Auntie Josie and Uncle Denis also live on the same street. We see Marie and her friend Chrissy on their way home from school. She says hello and then waves to a man at the other side of the road. He looks like has had a drink or two, or more. He smiles and shouts "Hello ladies!" loudly. His shirt is open down to his belt, showing his vest and his big belly that Marie says is made from beer. Mammy says that Marie shouldn't say hello to drunks. Marie says its OK, he's harmless. Loud but harmless. She says she sees him most days, on his way home from the pub. His name is Brendan Behan, and he lives just up the road.

Mammy tells Marie that we're on our way to Belfast to stay with Daddy, and we'll see her up at Grandad's after we visit aunties Nan and Josie. Auntie Nan and Auntie Josie make us tea and give me and Raymin buns and money 'cos they like us. Auntie Josie has a glass dome ornament with a house and snow in it on the side dresser, and I spend all the visiting time playing with it and shaking the snow up.

Soon we're on our way back up past the cigarette factory and the Boys' Brigade ground entrance next to Grandad's house. This time when the door opens Grandad looks like he's expecting us, and he's glad to see us. In the house the smell makes me remember all about the long summer we stayed here, a couple of years ago. I run out into the back garden to see Bunty the dog and check on the growing apples and pears.

We stay the night at Grandad's and in the morning Donnelly's sausages and Grandad are at it again, calling me down for my breakfast – "Is there no one getting up at all this marning?" Grandad is still in charge of the breakfast.

*

We're leaving for the train to Belfast. I show Grandad that I still have his rosary beads, and I promise to look after them safe and sound forever. When we leave, me and Raymin kiss Nan and Marie goodbye. I don't think Grandad wants any kisses. Mammy kisses no one. There's no crying or tears this time, and I'm happy now 'cos we're going to Belfast to live with Mammy and Daddy. Mammy says Helen, Louise and Baby Deirdre will soon be going there too. Then we will all be back together, she says, with Daddy working at Nutts Corner that suits him. And she can cook us the Donnelly's sausages every morning, if she can get them in Belfast, and Raymin can tell me to shurrup every day, and we will all be happy. Oh, and Mammy told me that 'tolerate' is what we have to do sometimes with Daddy. And I'm still not sure what it means. I'm asking her when we have to tolerate him. "When he's being a bit of a feck," she says. Now I'm thinking it's beginning to make sense to me. It's just another word for wallop.

We're on our way to Belfast. When the train stops at Dundalk some men get on, and as it moves off again they are asking people questions about where they come from and where they are going. Mammy says they are plain clothes policemen, probably looking for IRA men and spies and things like that. Mammy is telling them about us going to Belfast to live with Daddy and I ask them if they have guns, but they don't answer me, and Raymin says I'm stupid. When we get to Belfast Station it looks bigger than Limerick and Dublin stations. Outside at the top it says GNR. Mammy says that stands for Great Northern Railways.

Me and Raymin are carrying two small suitcases. There's not much in them. Mammy just has her handbag and a shop bag made from brown paper, with pieces of string for handles. We get on a bus with no door on the back, like the ones in Dublin with just a pole to hold onto going from the roof down to the floor, where you jump on and off. I'm looking out the window as we pass the shops and the houses. Some of them have big paintings on the end walls. There's a painting of a man on a big white horse. Mammy says his name is Billy – the man, not the horse. Underneath it says, 'No Pope here.' I'm wondering if there's writing that says there's no God on the walls in the Devil's Country where Mammy was. I ask Mammy why people paint on their houses in Belfast and she says she doesn't know.

Soon we get off the bus and there's a signpost for Queen's University and Botanic Gardens Park. We walk the other way, following the sign for Ormeau Bridge. We stop at 78 Fitzroy Avenue and go up to a back room on the second floor, past the bathroom on the first floor. In the room there's two single beds, a wardrobe, two wood chairs, and lino on the floor with squares in it. In the corner there's two gas rings on a shelf and a gas bottle underneath. There's boxes of clothes stacked in one of the other corners and a po pot under one of the beds. There's no taps in the room and Mammy says if we want a cup of tea we will have to fill up the kettle in the bathroom downstairs.

A man called Billy and his wife Mary come up from downstairs to see Mammy and us. Mary says hello and Billy says "How's about yous?" and I don't know what he means. Then he's laughing and saying to Mammy that me and Raymin will make two fine Orangemen. I'm thinking I've seen whitemen, a Chinaman, and a black man from the equator, but I've never heard of an orange man, so I just stay quiet and say nothing.

Mammy sends me down to the bathroom to fill the kettle so she can make some tea for all of us, including Billy who talks funny. Billy gives me and Raymin some pennies with a picture of the Queen's head on them, and he says if we go down towards the Ormeau Road we'll find Dorothy's shop on the corner of Dudley street, where we can buy sweets.

"You can go, as long as you don't talk to strangers or foreigners or anyone who looks like a kidnapper, 'cos there's lots of them in Belfast, especially at this time of the year, in the summer when there's lots of kids on the streets to choose from," Mammy says.

Later, Mammy is cooking some pork chops in the frying pan for Daddy's tea, ready for when he comes home from the airport. There's real butter for him as well. He doesn't like marge. When he comes in he looks like he's happy to see us, not like when he was in bed in Dublin when he let the cruelty man take us away. He picks me up and takes me and Raymin down to see Billy and Mary on the first floor. Mammy doesn't tell him we've seen them already and I don't say anything 'cos I've been told to shurrup a lot lately when I say the wrong thing, so I think it's best to keep quiet like we did a lot in Glin with the Christian Brothers, who Mammy says weren't very Christian but I know they were 'cos it said so on the main gate.

Billy says that I look just like Daddy and that Raymin has more the look of Mammy and now I'm thinking that Daddy is going to like us all again and it looks like he won't be wanting to fight with Mammy like before. Billy asks if Daddy needs a call in the morning for work as he will be out early doing his job turning off the street gas lamps and turning them on again in the evening. "Billy the gas lamp lighter, that's me," he says to me and Raymin, and off we go back upstairs to Mammy.

Me and Raymin sleep in one bed and Mammy and Daddy sleep in the other. Billy knocks at the door early in the morning and Daddy shouts 'OK' and 'thanks'. Mammy is up first to make some tea for Daddy. Then he asks me if I want to go to the airport with him but when I hear it's nearly twelve miles away I say no 'cos I haven't got over the long journey from Limerick to Belfast yet.

When Daddy's gone to work I tell Mammy that I think his clothes are very posh like hers and not like when we left Crosbie Row. She says she's taking me and Raymin into the city to buy us some nice summer clothes and soon we will be posh too. At the shops we get khaki shorts, white ankle socks, slip-on shoes that Mammy says are in fashion and a new shirt and tie each. We wear them at teatime when Daddy is home and he says we look very posh and he calls us toffs.

The next week Daddy is on the night shift when I go to the airport with him. We are on the bus for nearly an hour before we get there. Then a van takes us out to a small brick building near the middle of the airfield next to the runway, and then Daddy's friend who has just finished the day shift is taken back to the main entrance.

Daddy shows me the direction-finder wheel at his desk that turns an aerial on the roof while he listens in his headphones to the voice of the pilot on an incoming plane counting down from ten to nothing so Daddy can read the markings on the wheel and tell the pilot the compass bearing to follow to lead him right to the runway. At the same time the other radio and radar operators at the main building are watching the planes on the big green radar screens.

I spend a lot of the time looking out on the airfield watching all the rabbits running around just as its getting dark. I tell Daddy that there's one rabbit that's bigger than the others and he says that one is a hare, but it still looks like a rabbit to me. Then I make my bed for the night with blankets laid on the lino floor. In the morning when the shift is finished, we call into the radar building to see some more of Daddy's friends. They show me the big round radar screens and point to the little green dots that light up to show where the planes are. Then the airport van with the front sliding doors takes us back to where the bus is so we can go home, where Daddy and me go straight to bed, after the hard night's work.

Next day it's the 12th of July when Billy asks Daddy if it's alright to take me and Raymin up to Sandy Row to see the bands playing and the Orangemen marching. Billy says to Daddy, "Och, it's only a band, Brendan," so he says it's alright for us to go. Billy's wife Mary is saying she wants to come with us, but Billy says she has to stay and wait for his brother John who is bringing something over for him. Now Mary is not looking happy and Billy says "Mary – go talk to the sheep!" I'm thinking he wants her to hould her whisht.

We go up near Queen's University and then down towards the city where there's crowds of people all along the streets shouting and waving at the bands. I'm sat on Billy's shoulders waving at the band and eating one of the ice creams he bought for me and Raymin, and wondering how many sheep Mary and Billy have got. The men marching are wearing orange scarfs over their shoulders and now I can see why they call them orange men. I'm thinking when I grow up I might get a job like the man at the front of the march, turning a stick around and throwing it up in the air and catching it before it hits someone on the head. Billy tells the people around that he's training us to be orange men and they're all laughing and having a great time and I can't wait to get home and tell Mammy and Daddy what a good time we've had down at Sandy Row.

When we're nearly home Billy says "Hello Harry" to a man fixing his car, with lots of banging, outside number 82. He tells Harry about us going to see the marching bands down Sandy Row but he's not interested. Billy tells him, "Fine Orangeman you are." And we carry on to number 78. Before we get inside at home I ask Billy how many sheep him and Mary have. He says they have none but his friend out in the country has some. I ask if I can see them sometime and he says I surely can. He says there's one really special baby sheep called Mary after King Billy's wife, Queen Mary, who's deaf – the sheep, that is, not the queen. On the way up the stairs to the back room where I live I'm thinking about Billy taking me to see the sheep some time. He knocks on the door and calls to Mammy.

"Does Mary the sheep know she's deaf?" I ask him.

*

Mammy and Mary McDonald are talking about babies and drinking tea when we go into the room. There's bacon and cabbage boiling in a pan for the tea. I ask Mammy where babies come from, 'cos I can see she's getting fat, like a cow does when it's having a calf. She says she'll be having a baby alright but the baby will be left under a cabbage leaf and in order to know where they are left, if you want one, you have to say your prayers and then go to the hospital to see if you want a boy or a girl. She says she's been getting fat 'cos she's been eating more to calm her nerves 'cos the 'fenobarritone' tablets from the doctor haven't been working properly to calm her down.

I say that I think she laid me, like a cow lays a calf and a cat lays a kitten. Then Mammy says babies are surely found under cabbage leaves, and I've to stop saying stupid things like 'Mammy's laying babies' and I've to go out the back lane to play 'cos she wants to talk to Mary now, in peace. Mary is sitting on the bed with her hand covering her mouth, trying to make a cough noise. I think she's laughing. I look into the boiling pan to see the bacon and cabbage and I'm thinking the bacon looks all pink and wrinkled like a new baby, and now I'm not so sure if I want any dinner.

"For the love of God, will you ever get out so I can talk to Mary!"

Now Mary is laughing again under her hand.

"And don't talk to strangers, and watch out for Marie 'cos she's due from Dublin any time now to visit us."

I'm out on the landing listening at the door. Mammy is telling Mary about Daddy shouting at her. He said there's no need to go to the hospital to have a baby. Mammy told him she wants to be safe with this baby. Daddy said what about all the women down the centuries who had their babies in the fields, and then went back to working the land, and Mammy shouted back at him, "And what about all the babies and mothers that died in the fields!" She says he had no answer for that. Mary says that was a terrible thing for him to say. Now Mammy is calling him a liten bastard again.

I'm out on the back lane trying to figure out about the baby thing when Raymin comes through the yard with Marie. They are talking and I'm wondering if I have to ask her about the baby question. I'm nearly eight now and I need to know these things. I'm trying to make up my mind when to ask. I'm leaning forward with my hands on a window sill on the back lane pushing myself back up and onto my feet. I let myself fall forward and stop myself with my hands on the window sill. I push myself back up and I decide that after the next push up I'm going to ask Marie all about the baby question.

I lean forward and my shoes slip on the dust and the pebbles on the lane, my hands miss the window sill and as I gather speed, heading for the ground, the window sill comes up to meet me on the forehead. Marie comes running over and as I get up onto my knees I can feel the wet running down my face. I put my hand to my head and it's covered in blood. I grab Marie's dress and push it to my head to stop the blood. She takes me into the house and Raymin calls for Billy, telling him not to tell Mammy what happened 'cos she's bad with the nerves and will panic if she sees my head and all the blood on Marie's dress.

Billy carries me down to the doctor's house on the Ormeau Road and the doctor stitches my head and asks me what happened. So I tell him, and then I ask him if he knows where babies come from and he just says, "You'll have to ask your Mammy that one."

Now Billy is carrying me back up to the house and I'm still thinking about the baby question and I can't understand why even the doctor doesn't know where they come from and maybe I should get Mammy to tell him. Then I think no. No I won't ask her. I'm never ever going to ask anybody ever about babies ever again. Marie has washed the blood off her dress in the bathroom. When Mammy sees my head and the stitches she has to take a tablet for her bad nerves. Mary is trying to keep Mammy calm, to stop her worrying about my cut head and where Marie is going to sleep. Mary says that Marie can sleep in her room if she wants. She has a spare bed with a screen in front of it. Marie stays for a while and then goes back to Dublin when my head is better.

*

Marie is back in Dublin and Mammy is waiting for an ambulance to take her to hospital to pick a new baby. Mary says she will look after me and Raymin while Mammy's deciding which baby to pick for us. I'm shouting after Mammy to make sure that the doctor has a bigger bag this time, so the new baby won't be squashed and wrinkled.

Two days later she's back without a new baby. I don't think the hospital looked after her much as she doesn't look as well as she was when she went in. Later I hear her talking to Mary again, and it sounds like the baby was a little boy, but when she went to collect him he had died. Now I'm feeling sad 'cos I could have had a little brother and it's making me wonder if a big cabbage fell over on top of him and killed him, God bless him, but I can't ask Mammy about it yet 'cos I'm not supposed to know what she has been saying, and she would say that I've been bad with my manners for listening to her and Mary talking about private things. And now I won't have a little brother for when we get older, to tell him he's too small to come around with me, like Raymin says to me when he wants to go around with Michael Kennedy from across the road. And in winter the bed won't be any warmer without an extra boy in it.

Later I say to Mammy that I think she was codding me when she said she was going to hospital to collect a new baby, but she doesn't answer me. She's sat on the edge of the bed, looking out the window, far into the clouds, like she sometimes does when her nerves are bad or when she thinks Daddy might be late home. I think she's sad that she didn't bring a baby home, so I sit down beside her and hold her hand, and hould my whisht.

*

After about two more fortnights at number 78, Mammy tells Daddy there's a room at number 82. It's on the first floor at the front and it's bigger, and nearer the bathroom, and owned by the same landlord as number 78. After lots of cups of tea and cigarettes – Senior Service for Daddy and Gallagher's Blues for Mammy – and her calling him Bren and love, Daddy says it's OK for her to see if she can get the room at 82, even though it is an extra five shillings a week for the rent.

Soon we move into number 82, the house where Harry Waddle with the broken down car lives with his wife Sybil, who always buys him soft tissue paper to wipe his tender arse, Mammy says.

She also says that Harry has lots of pictures of Doris Day on the wall in his room, and Sybil has lots of pictures of the Lone Ranger on her side of the wall, 'cos Harry loves Doris Day and Sybil loves the Lone Ranger. But Mammy says they also still love each other, God bless them.

The new room has a tall folding screen inside the door, a double bed, a single bed, a square table with big round legs, two chairs and an old two-seater settee in front of a coal fire grate. In the corner there's a two-burner gas ring with the gas bottle under it.

Mammy says that this room is posher than the other 'cos it's bigger and the gas bottle is hidden behind a nice curtain hanging on a piece of string. The floor has a big square of brown carpet and some lino around the outside edge of the room. And there's a space between the wardrobe and the bed for the po pot. Mammy says this will do fine 'til we can get a bigger place or a house when Helen, Louise and Deirdre can come to live with us in Belfast from the nuns in Limerick.

*

After about two more fortnights in the big room, some men come to the door and ask for Daddy. They look like snobs. Behind them is a policeman with a gun on his belt. The snobs say they are from the antitourist police. They ask Mammy to take me and Raymin out of the room onto the landing where the policeman with the gun on his belt is. When Mammy goes back inside we can hear them all talking. The snob men say they have been watching Daddy since he moved up from Dublin with his homemade radio on the train. One man says that the other is a radio specialist. They want to examine the radio and search everything in the room. Daddy asks them what they're looking for and one says that they'll know when they find it. Mammy starts shouting when they search her handbag. One of them is searching up the chimney and Mammy asks him what the feckin hell does he think is up there. Then the specialist asks Mammy if the radio can transmit as well as receive and she turns round and says, "You're the feckin expert, you tell me!"

Things go a bit quiet, but they're still talking. Then I ask the policeman if he can fix cars and he says yes 'cos he's got one himself. Then I ask him if he is an Orangeman and he says why do I want to know, and I tell him that Harry Waddle the Orangeman who has the room next to the bathroom and a tender arse is always having trouble with his car and maybe he could help him to fix it so he can take me for a drive in it like he promised. And now the policeman is laughing.

"Now that we're friends, can I have a look at your gun and bullets?" I ask him.

But that has stopped him laughing and now I'm thinking we weren't friends for long.

The door opens and Mammy is still being grumpy with the two snobs. They are leaving and taking the radio with them, telling Daddy that they will be checking on his details and will be back to see him later. When they're gone Mammy is smoking a lot and cursing them and Daddy says it would serve them right if they had found a toy gun up the chimney, and Mammy agrees and says they were two clever feckers anyway. Daddy says no, just one of them.

For weeks afterwards Daddy says he is followed everywhere he goes. He borrows Billy's lamp lighting bike and cycles all around Belfast, sometimes around in circles and back home to see who is following him. One day when he is followed home by some men in a car that parks near the house, he takes the bicycle through the house to the back lane and round the block and past the men in the car and into the house again through the front door just to give them something more for their note books. After about a month and a fortnight they bring his radio back and apologise to him and Mammy for searching the room. They say they were only doing their jobs. Daddy says it's OK and Mammy tells them they can feck off.

And I'm thinking Billy hasn't taken me to see Mary the deaf sheep yet.

# *Chapter 8*

## Dumped again

Raymin is friends with Michael Kennedy across the road. His mother runs the nursing home at the corner of Magdala Street and Sandhurst Road. One of the old ladies there is blind and if I see her on her daily walk around the block I sometimes walk around with her, thinking I'm helping her but she's probably used to finding her own way around, always the same way round, but even so, she always thanks me.

When Michael Kennedy gets a new bicycle he gives Raymin his old one. It's one of them black bikes that has square handlebars and strong wire levers for pulling on the brakes that are nearly working. I keep asking Raymin to teach me to ride the bicycle, so he lets me have a go on the back lane between the houses. He holds onto the saddle to keep me straight 'til we cross Dudley Street by Dorothy's shop, then he lets me go on my own and I'm going from side to side trying to keep straight. If I use the brakes they just pull me to one side so I let go. Further down, the lane bends to the left and there's a wood fence that slows me down with very little help from the brakes. It's just as well the fence is rotten, or I could be hurting a lot more. I look back up the lane and Raymin is jumping up and down laughing and shouting down to me that I've passed my first test. Now the handlebars are twisted and my knee is all grazed and my jumper is ripped. When I'm bigger I'm going to give him a good clatter and get him back for this.

In the evenings we listen to the radio that Daddy built. He tunes it in to the Light Programme station so we can listen to the Lone Ranger, and Michael Miles on 'Take Your Pick,' but we have to imagine the pictures for ourselves. Daddy says that in a couple of years there should be another TV station coming out. Sometimes when the Lone Ranger is on me and Raymin go down the street outside number 49, across from Dorothy's shop. We stand on the garden wall where we can see the rich woman's television through her front window. We watch Clayton Moore, who is the Lone Ranger, in his white hat shooting the bad cowboys, who always wear black hats. Soon other kids join us, looking through the window at the television. So we either watch the Lone Ranger through the window without hearing it or hear it at home on the radio without watching it. Sometimes the woman in the house tells us to go away. I don't really know why, 'cos there's usually only about six or seven of us watching her television, and most of the time we're quiet. Well, except when the baddy gets shot.

Grandad in Dublin sent me a crystal set radio with headphones and I can listen to the BBC radio station Home Service and the Light Programme by myself. I spend a lot of time hanging wires out the window for aerials and others tied to drainpipes for earths to make it work better. John upstairs, Billy's brother, lets me lower wires from his window down to mine to make the aerial higher and longer. After tea the table is cleared so that Daddy can work on his radio building, and soldering things together. Sometimes, when we have our samiches in school the next day we find bits of wire and solder in them.

*

We've been going to school at Rosario, up at the top of Ravenhill Road, since September, and now it's nearly Christmas. Helen, Louise and Deirdre are in Nazareth House at the top of the Ormeau Road with the nuns, and we can go up to see them on Sundays. Sometimes the nuns let me go in and watch the films at the school with all the girls. Helen and Louise have a friend called Helen Sweeney, so I go to see her too.

When I go to school I get the bus up to Rosario on the Ormeau Road near the convent and if there is plenty of time I try to get the Sunnyside bus 'cos it goes the long way round along the banks of the River Lagan and up Sunnyside to Rosario.

During one of the lessons at school the teacher asks everyone to write down the name for a small pig. The answer she wants is piglet, but I put down Irish word 'banbh.' It takes a while to convince her but in the end I get a tick for getting it right. One day on the way home from school I remember about my bus money being lost in the morning as the Sunnyside bus was moving off and I dropped my tuppence and watched them roll along the rubber mat and out onto the fast-moving road. Gone. Running around the corner from school onto the main road I see a man and ask if he can lend me tuppence to get home 'cos my money rolled off the bus. The man gives me tuppence and I tell him I will pay him back when I see him again. Then I run all the way home, as it's a nice day, and spend the money on sweets. I'm hoping it's not a sin that I've done.

At teatime Mammy, Daddy, Raymin and me are sat at the square table with bits of solder on it. We're having mashed potato with chopped onions in it, fried egg, sausages and peas. Daddy is having mashed potato with chopped onions in it, fried egg, sausages and peas and a pork chop on top of his, and plenty of brown sauce for his peas. I'm telling them all about the lost tuppence and a man lending me the money for the bus. I don't tell them about spending the money on sweets. Daddy asks me how I'm going to pay the man back if I don't know him and I have no answer for that. Raymin is asking Mammy for the last sausage off her plate and I tell him to leave her alone. He keeps asking her until she gives it to him and says, "My God, you'd take a penny from a beggar, you would!" I'm telling Raymin it's bad to take Mammy's last sausage and he's just grinning to himself like he does if he wins a row sometimes.

After tea Raymin asks me if I want to go out and around with him. I'm thinking there's something wrong 'cos usually it's just him and Michael Kennedy and he doesn't want me with him. So now I'm wondering if he wants to fight with me over the sausage thing. He says he just wants to go for a walk down the Ormeau Road as far as Donegall Pass, to do some window shopping. I say OK, but I'm wondering what he wants a window for.

By the time we get down near the gasworks, where they suck gas out of coal and the air smells bad, it's getting dark. Raymin tells me he wants me to do the borrowing bus money thing. Now I know why he wants me with him.

There's two women together across the road and he tells me to go across and do the borrowing thing. I go across the road to ask them. Raymin stays and pretends he's not with me while I ask one woman.

"Please missus, I've lost my bus money and I've got to get home to Rosario and my Mammy will be getting bad with her nerves if I'm not home soon, can you lend me tuppence please?"

"Oh you poor wee child," says the other, as she looks in her purse and says "I'm sorry I haven't got tuppence."

I'm thinking I knew it wouldn't work twice.

"I'll have to give you half a crown, now take this and get the bus straight away and don't talk to any strangers."

"Thank you, missus, thank you very much," says I.

I'm waiting at the bus stop and I'm thinking how I've done very well 'cos half a crown is worth about fifteen tuppences. The kind women look back and wave as they make their way towards the city centre. Raymin is across the road waving for me to go over to him, but I can't 'cos the women keep looking back at me and waving. Now the bus is coming and the women are looking back to see if I'm safely on the bus. I don't know what to do. Raymin is shouting across the road for me but the women can still see me. Now the bus is stopped, the women are *still* waving at me. I'm waving at them, Raymin is waving at me and shouting and I pretend I don't know him. I get on the bus and ask for the next stop, and the conductor takes a penny from the half crown and gives me the change. Raymin is running up the other side of the road shouting at me to get off the bus, but the bus stop isn't far enough away from the two kind ladies and I can still see them so they must be able to see me. So I say to the conductor again, "Next stop, please," and offer him another penny, but he doesn't take it. He says something about 'bloody rebels,' scratches his head and presses the button for the bus to move off just as Raymin is catching up at the other side of the road. Now Raymin is trying to shout but he's getting out of breath with chasing the bus again. Then I say to the bus conductor, "This stop, please," and he asks if I'm sure and I say I am and when the bus stops I jump off and run across the road to Raymin and explain what happened. He's trying to shout at me but he can't 'cos he's out of breath. When he sees the change from the two shillings and sixpence the kind women gave me, he's my best friend again, and he takes the money and buys himself cigarettes and matches and lets me keep sixpence. Then he tells me not to tell anyone about the borrowing thing. Now I'm feeling guilty and thinking that I've committed a mortal sin. When I tell Raymin he says that it's not a sin 'cos it was him who made me do it. And he just keeps on puffing on the Gallagher Blues and grinning to himself.

*

It's Christmas 1958 and this year we get some presents. Helen, Louise and Deirdre have come from the convent in Limerick to stay with us. I get a carpenter's set with a saw, a hammer, pincers and some nails. The saw bends if I press too hard on it, but I can straighten it again with the hammer. Helen, Louise and Deirdre come to stay with us for a week. Louise gets a cowboy outfit with a gun and holster. Helen gets some girls annual books and Deirdre gets books and crayons. We all get some sweets. Raymin asked for some money to fix the brakes on his bike and asked Daddy to buy him a secondhand violin. Daddy just gave him enough money to fix his brakes, so he spent it on cigarettes.

The man at the grocer's shop on Dudley Street lets me have some wooden orange boxes so I can make a small ladder with my new tools. The steps look good when I've finished them, but you can't use them, they're not strong enough to stand on, they're just good to look at. After making the steps I'm playing cowboys and Indians with Louise, then we go down to number 49 to stand on the wall and watch the Lone Ranger. There's some other kids on the wall so we swap some sweets with them to get a better watching place to see the television through the window.

After the Lone Ranger, we go back up to the room for teatime. On the way back, me and Louise are talking like cowboys. Raymin is in the backyard smoking and grinning. He says he used the steps I made to try and get something from the top of the wardrobe but they broke. Now he's grinning more than before. Louise says let's arrest him and put him in jail. No, I tell her, let's arrest him and beat the shit out of him.

We're all sitting around the table, on the two chairs, the end of the bed and on the arm of the settee. Helen is dishing out the grub. We're all having cowboy food, bread and beans 'cos we wanted cowboy food. Mammy asks Helen if she has given me some beans and I answer her in my best cowboy accent.

"She sure did, ma'am."

Everyone bursts out laughing at the cowboy answer, and for the rest of the evening we are all talking in our best cowboy accents, except Raymin who is still sad because he didn't get the secondhand violin he asked Daddy for at Christmas, after his teacher told him that he is very good at music. Now I'm thinking that Raymin needed the cigarettes for his sadness.

That night after we all had a really good wash in the bathroom, me and Raymin are at the top of the bed and Louise and Deirdre are at the bottom and Helen is on the settee, being huffy and not wanting anyone near her. Raymin is crying. He's trying to cry quietly so Daddy doesn't hear him. He whispers to me that Daddy is earning twenty pounds a week and can easily afford a secondhand fiddle. Now I'm feeling sorry for him. I wish I had enough money to buy it for him. I wish I could do something to make him feel better. I know what I can do. I might let him off the two squares of Cleeves toffee he still owes me.

Next day we're all sitting round the table having fried turnip in bacon fat and spuds boiled in their skins and bisto gravy for dinner. I tell Mammy I don't like the turnips, and I'm not happy 'cos Mammy says I can't go down to number 49's wall to see what's on the TV unless I eat my turnips. That's not fair. She says I'm just a sulking little white bull, like Tommy Steel sings about on the radio. Now they're all laughing at me. Now I'm really not happy, enough not happy to tell them all that I'm going to kill myself after dinner. Raymin asks if he can have my turnips when I'm dead. Mammy asks how I'm going to do it. I tell her I'm going to wring my own neck, like she did with the little chicks in Limerick. Now they're all laughing at me again. I'm really mad at them. So I tell them that I'm not going to bother killing myself. Not if it makes them this happy. I'll just hang around and annoy them. Mammy says you can't wring your own neck anyway. Raymin says he'll help if I want. Mammy says, "If I send for the Bisto Kids badges for you, from the Bisto gravy adverts on the radio, will you promise not to wring your own neck?"

Now I'm thinking, sounds a good enough deal to me.

"OK, Mammy, but don't forget now, you've promised!"

The dinner is finished and Mammy is clearing the plates and washing them in the tin washing up bowl on the table. The man on the radio is saying the news. He says that the police are on the lookout for a confidence trickster who robbed two elderly women in the Ormeau Road area. Mammy tunes the radio to another station before I can hear anymore of the news. Now I'm thinking the old ladies who gave me the two and sixpence for my bus fare must have seen me get off the bus at the second stop. They must have decided to tell the police about me. They'll have gone straight down to the police station at Donegall Pass. Now the police are looking for me, not Raymin 'cos the women won't have seen him. Louise is asking me if I'm going for a run around the block like we sometimes do, after the dinner, so we don't get fat. I tell her I'm not bothered about getting fat today. I'm a wanted man. I have to hand myself in to the sheriff's office, tomorrow, or the day after. When I tell her why, she says if they lock me up she'll get an outlaw posse together to break me out. Louise asks Helen if she'll join the posse and she just says "Huh." Louise looks at me and says don't worry, that's Red Indian for yes. I'm thinking Louise is a really kind cowboy.

Next day I ask Raymin if he'll play cowboys and Indians with me and Louise. We need help arresting Deirdre, who is going to be a bank robber, and tying her to the gate on the back lane 'til the Sheriff comes for her. Raymin says he's too big to play cowboys with us, and anyway, he's going out on his bike with Michael Kennedy. Now I don't feel sorry for Raymin not getting the fiddle anymore.

At dinner time me and Louise are going down the avenue to the shops. I've got some money for Joe at the bakery across from Dorothy's shop and Louise has some money for a bottle of milk from Dorothy's. Louise comes to the bakery for yesterday's bread with me because she loves the smell of the bread and buns, and I've told her that Joe, who is taller than the Lone Ranger, always gives me extra buns. When we leave the corner shop the milk bottle slips from her hand and smashes on the ground. She says Daddy will go mad. We both do a really good job of picking up all the pieces of glass and throwing them into someone's garden. We've no money for another bottle, so Louise goes home and gets some out of her red money box, that looks like a post box, 'cos she's too frightened to tell Daddy.

Early in the evening Daddy tells Louise it's time for her to go to bed. She tells him that Deirdre should go to bed first 'cos she's the youngest. Louise says she always goes to bed later than Deirdre. Daddy starts shouting and says you can both go to bed now. She complains to Mammy saying that Deirdre goes to bed usually at about seven and she goes to bed about eight and it's only seven o'clock now and she doesn't want to go to bed. Daddy grabs hold of Louise and one of Mammy's slippers with its tough leather sole. He wallops Louise hard on her backside and legs. She's screaming with the pain. He's shouting, asking who does she think she is, to be answering back like that to him, at her age, as he carries on walloping her. We're all shouting at him to stop. Louise is crying out in agony. Mammy grabs his arm and pulls the slipper from his hand. He goes to the other side of the room and sits on his bed. Alice and John from upstairs are at the door shouting to Mammy, checking if she's alright.

Louise is on the other bed being comforted by Mammy, who is looking at the bruising on her bottom and legs. Twenty minutes later there's another knock at the door. It's a policeman. One of the neighbours has rung the station down on Donegall Pass about all the screaming going on. He says the neighbour was worried that someone was being kilt so he came as fast as he could, on his bicycle. Daddy says that it was just the children playing loud games and the policeman goes away. In another couple of days the girls are with the nuns in Nazereth House. Mammy says we can't all live in this room and they can come home again soon when her and Daddy get a bigger place.

*

I'm sitting on the cold pavement in the morning sun making sparks by banging a big spanner that I got from Harry Waddle the car fixer on the stone kerb step. I've no one to play cowboys and Indians with now that the girls are not here. Daddy comes around the corner from the night shift and I stand up to run to him. He asks me what all the banging is and kicks me on the top of my leg, knocking me over, then he shouts for me to get upstairs and wash my hands and face. My leg hurts and I'm crying now as I run up the stairs. Daddy goes in the room and doesn't say hello to Mammy. He tells her I should have a wash before going out to play on the street. I'm thinking I haven't been up long enough to get dirty. Mammy is looking sad and puts the kettle on the gas ring. Outside, Harry is making a banging noise trying to fix his car again. Daddy opens the window and shouts.

"Harry, is that engine you're trying to fix a precisely engineered machine?"

"Of course it is, Brendan," Harry says.

"Well tell me, how the feck can you fix a precisely engineered machine by banging it every day with a feckin hammer!"

Harry says nothing, Daddy bangs the window shut. Mammy bangs his cup of tea on the table and I'm rubbing my sore leg thinking, there goes my chance of a ride in Harry's car even if his hammer does ever fix it. Mammy tells Daddy that I didn't need a wash 'cos I wasn't going to school and there's no need to give me a kick in the leg anyway. Then she gets the wet rag that she uses as a dishcloth and wipes my hands and face and says now I can go back out to play but don't do anymore banging and don't talk to strangers.

Out on the street I can hear Daddy shouting at Mammy like he does when he's not happy. It seems a long time since Mammy and Daddy had a proper fight. Soon Raymin comes back from Michael Kennedy's but he stays down the stairs with me 'cos Mammy and Daddy haven't finished shouting yet. Things go quiet when Daddy goes to bed for the rest of the day and then we have to be quiet too. In the evening Daddy gets all dressed up and goes out to the bars drinking. Me and Mammy go upstairs to see Alice, who is John's wife and has a little boy called Danny who is sick with leukaemia and they don't think he'll get better. Mammy is drinking tea and telling Alice and John her worries, like she told Mary before, when she said, "We got married on Boxing Day and we've been feckin fighting ever since!" I go back downstairs to Raymin. Mammy comes down at about nine o'clock and says she's going out somewhere and won't be long so we have to go to bed and be good and don't let any strangers into the room.

We're in bed when Daddy comes in with Mammy. He's shouting at her about when she left us in Dublin to run off to the Devil's Country. I think he's due for a proper fight with her, but she is calming him down, asking if he wants a cup of tea and saying "Do you want a cigarette Bren love?" and "Don't shout in front of the kids," and things like that. And when she talks like that I know she's getting bad with her nerves again and getting frightened. Then Daddy sees me and Raymin looking out over the blankets and things go quiet.

The next morning is Sunday. Mammy cooks bacon for all of us for breakfast, but she just has a cigarette and a cup of tea. There's no more talking about the milk of magnesia or the Devil's Country now. Mammy says I have to finish my breakfast 'cos we're going for a walk down to the City Hall to take some photos with Daddy and his new Box Brownie camera. He tells me to eat my bacon but I don't like fried bacon, we didn't get bacon in Glin School ever. Then Daddy grabs me by the hair and starts shoving the bacon in my mouth with a fork, and he shoves it so hard that it cuts my gums, and he's shouting that it cost a lot of money for food and I should be grateful to have food on the table. Now my mouth is full of bacon and I think I'm choking and I spit the lot back on the plate and tell him I'll have it later. He says if I was going out to the Congo in Africa like the Irish soldiers might be soon, I'd be glad to have food like that on my plate. I don't see what the Congo has to do with not liking bacon. Maybe he's just being domineering like Mammy sometime calls him – a domineering bastard.

We're nearly ready to go out now. Mammy is just combing Raymin's hair, but there's a bit of hair that won't lie flat. Now Mammy is testing the iron to see if it's still warm from ironing Daddy's shirt. She wets Raymin's hair with the dishcloth and then irons it flat to his head with the warm iron. That's better she says – not quite right, but better than it was.

We spend most of the morning looking around the closed shops and then sitting on the grass in front of the City Hall building in the cold sunshine. When I get the chance I ask Mammy what a domineering bastard is and she says I mustn't say that word. And I don't know why 'cos she says domineering all the time. So I don't ask again 'cos this is the kind of day that if I do ask anything, someone is sure to tell me to shurrup anyway.

Me and Raymin are sitting on a cold stone seat at the front of the City Hall when Daddy wants to take a photo with his box camera. He tells us to smile and it's hard to smile when you're cold. Then me and Raymin start laughing and he says that's good, but he hasn't seen Mammy behind him, pretending to hit him with the pointed heel of her shoe.

After tea, at home in the room, Daddy is shaving and looking in the mirror and blowing his cheeks out to get a better shave. Then when he dries his face his cheeks are all shiny so he puts talcum powder on so they don't shine so much. He's putting on his best clothes with his white starched shirt, and he gives me sixpence to polish his shoes. He's off out to the bars again on his own. He says he won't be late and Mammy says nothing, she just smokes her cigarette. Daddy goes out and leaves the white tin basin on the table with the dirty water and shaving bits in it for Mammy to take down to the bathroom and wash it out before boiling some water on the gas ring so she can wash up the dirty dishes from the tea.

Mammy is washing the dishes in the basin and tapping her fingers on the edge of the tin and chomping her teeth in time with the tapping and looking through the wall into the distance again, like I've seen her do lots of times before when she doesn't want to answer my questions, and wants me to hould my whisht. So

I do. Then she says out loud to herself, "That lazy vain bastard! He never cleans anything away after himself. Never cleans up. When he was on his own, the only thing in the place that was clean when I came back was the feckin mirror."

Later Mammy gets her coat and handbag. She says she's going out somewhere and she won't be long and don't open the door to anyone. I say what about Daddy and she says nothing.

Raymin finds two squashed cigarettes in Daddy's pocket. We are listening to the radio. I tell him I've thought of a better way of making some money than being a criminal. If all the singers are at the radio station, they'll be needing cups of tea and samiches. And we could sell them some and make lots of money. Raymin lights one of Daddy's cigarettes and says, "There's nobody there stupid, they're playing records." I'm thinking yeah, I never thought of that.

Daddy comes back early, shouting about Mammy not being in. He's asking where she is but we can't tell him 'cos we don't know. He goes back out again, cursing and banging the door. Soon Mammy comes back and we tell her about Daddy shouting and cursing and going out again. Then Mammy says stay there, and now she goes out again but she doesn't bang the door. Then Daddy is back again asking has she come back yet and we say she did and he asks where she is. We say she went out again, then he pushes me and Raymin over to the old settee in front of the fireplace and says watch this. And with sweat running down his forehead and his eyes staring and his mouth cursing, he takes clothes from the wardrobe drawer, his own shirts, some of them still in new bags, and puts them in the fireplace and lights matches and sets them on fire and says "There!" He goes out again and slams the door shut. I'm standing there crying, watching the bags the shirts are in, burning, and then the shirts catch fire. Raymin is just standing beside me saying nothing. He looks at me and says "Do you want a cig?"

Not much later Mammy is back, she asks if Daddy came back and we say yes and show her and tell her about him setting the clothes on fire and she says oh Jesus. Then she tells us to go to bed, "Don't be frightened, 'cos Daddy won't hurt you, he's only mad at me" she says, and then she goes out again.

It's very late when Daddy comes in again, staggering and shouting "Where is your mother!" and calling names at her, even when she's not here to hear him. Then he falls on his bed and starts snoring. Mammy doesn't come home.

In the morning me and Raymin get up and make some tea and bread and butter with jam on. I'm telling Raymin we shouldn't be eating Daddy's Kerrygold butter, but he says it'll be alright, he'll never know. Then Raymin searches Daddy's coat pockets, taking some change and more cigarettes. Daddy doesn't get up 'til nearly dinner time. He asks what the shirts are doing being burnt and I tell him he did it last night. He asks where Mammy is and we tell him we don't know, and she didn't come home last night. He has a cup of tea and I offer him some buttered bread and jam but he doesn't want any. After about an hour of being quiet, Daddy says he's taking us to the park with it being a nice day and the sun shining.

On the way to the Botanic Gardens he buys us a white plastic ball so we can spend the afternoon in the park playing football. Later, after football and some ice cream, we go back to the room. It's not long after that when Mammy comes in, but there's a policeman with her, standing with his arms folded and a gun on his belt. She says she's just come back to take me and Raymin to stay with the nuns at Nazareth Lodge on Ravenhill road, near Nazereth House where the girls are. Daddy asks the policeman what he's doing here and he says he's just here at Mammy's request and to see that there's no trouble. Daddy says he doesn't want us to go and we say we don't want to go either. We want to stay at home. Mammy says she's not leaving us here with 'Him.' So we have to go with her, as it looks like it's compulsory. On the way out she points to the fireplace and says to the policeman, "That's what that mad bastard did last night, I'm sure it's them feckin headphones at work that put a kink in his head. It's like a comical farce," she says, "or it would be, if it wasn't so serious, the mad bastard."

Mammy takes us on the bus up to Nazareth Lodge home for young boys where she tells us that the Belfast cruelty man says we can stay for a while 'til things get sorted out and it'll be alright 'cos God is good and things will get better. And now Mammy is going again and I'm shouting after her not to forget about the Bisto badges that she promised.

The nun is asking us what happened at home. So I tell her all about the fighting and shirt burning, and Daddy drinking and wanting to fight Mammy again, and about Mammy telling the policeman that it was all just like a comical fart. Now Raymin is looking at me and calling me stupid, and the nice nun is smiling.

*

We've been here two weeks now waiting for Mammy to come back and take us home again. But it looks like she's not coming. I hope she hasn't gone back to the Devil's Country again. In Nazareth Lodge all the boys are smaller than me and Raymin, except for a boy called Kevin Halfpenny who's bigger than us but he can't talk, he just makes noises. I try to make friends with him but he just tries to scratch me. There's a nun who is with him all the time and she tells me to leave him alone. One of the other boys tells us that Kevin is a new boy there like us. Some boys found him living in a shed with chickens with no clothes on – Kevin that is, not the chickens with no clothes. The boys had heard noises coming from the shed and when they looked in they saw a dirty naked child. They asked his name and he didn't answer them. Later they could hear him crying and when they saw him there again on another day they told their parents, who told the police, who told the cruelty man from the NSPCC who told the nuns. The police took Mrs Halfpenny to the courthouse but she wasn't sent to jail or anything like that, for not letting Kevin in the house. The Court said she will suffer enough just knowing what she's done. The cruelty man took Kevin to Nazareth Lodge where the nuns dressed him and washed him. Now the nuns are praying that soon, on his 12th birthday, God will teach him to speak, like we do, instead of making noises like a chicken.

The nuns are having me and Raymin learning the Irish dancing. Dancing to the side and counting 1-2-3-4-5-6-7, then a-1-2-3 and a-1-2-3. They say if we practice the Irish dancing they will take us on holiday soon with the other boys, to the seaside at Portrush, where we will be staying in a boarding house for two weeks. The dancing nun tells us a story about a man who entered a competition, and after he danced all the steps he knew, the band kept on playing, so he just made up his own steps and carried on 'til the band stopped, and he won the competition. I'm thinking I've been making up my own steps for the past two weeks and I've impressed no one.

I've never heard of a boarding house before, and I'm thinking it must be a house on the sands made of boards like on a beach that I've seen pictures of. A week later when we get off the bus with the other boys at Portrush the house we go to is made of bricks and it's nowhere near the sands, so I'm a little bit sad, but I don't let it confuse me more by thinking about it a lot.

On the holidays Kevin Halfpenny has his birthday, but the nuns prayers don't work to make him talk. I'm thinking the holiday is a good one, but I don't really know 'cos I've never had one before. The nuns say it is great, so I take their word for it.

I've been practising the dancing on holiday, but it isn't very good 'cos the sand keeps filling my shoes and the sea keeps wetting them so I keep falling over in the sand.

*

Back at Nazareth Lodge it's dancing time again, but I'm still no good, and two weeks later I don't have to dance anymore when the nuns tell us that Mammy is coming to take us home again.

Mammy comes to collect us from the nuns who tell Mammy lies, like we are great dancers. I ask Mammy if Daddy still has the football and Raymin says I'm stupid and tells me to shurrup. I'm thinking Raymin's cranky 'cos he hasn't had any cigs. Mammy says everything is alright back at the room at number 82 and Daddy is sorry for burning his shirts. I ask her if the policeman will be there and Raymin calls me stupid again and Mammy says no he won't. She says her and Daddy will be looking for a bigger place so that, please God, soon Helen, Louise and Deirdre (who is now 4 and not a baby anymore) can come to live with us again.

We're back at the room. Daddy is at work and Mammy says he doesn't drink so much these days. On the next Saturday we all go into Belfast city centre and Daddy buys me and Raymin some more new clothes. Grey short trousers and jackets to match. I'm thinking we're lucky to have some new clothes 'cos it's only about nine months since we got some new shorts.

That night, Mammy says she is praying to God to make Daddy go to Mass on Sundays again, like we used to, most of the time, when we first lived in Crosbie Row. In the morning when we're all getting ready to go to Mass at St Malachy's, she tells us her prayers have been answered. After Mass, we're walking through the city centre and when we're looking into the shop windows I get a wallop from Daddy for leaning on the dirty shop window ledges and getting the front of my clothes all dusty. I don't like all this being clean and tidy and having to be careful where I lean or sit on things.

Soon we are back at the room where I can change into my other short pants and go out on the street to play and I don't have to worry too much about getting dirty. Then I go down to the house wall across from Dorothy's shop, to watch the television through the posh woman's window and make my own mind up about what the cowboys are saying to each other.

When there's other kids are on the wall with us we take it in turns to speak what we think the cowboys are saying. It hardly ever makes sense with the pictures, but it's good fun. The woman in the house tells us to be quiet or get off her wall. I still don't know why she tells us off, there's never more than seven of us. I can't see the harm in it myself.

At dinner time Mammy is giving Daddy his chops and peas and potatoes and butter and brown sauce and telling him that there's a place to rent down the street at one of Mr Madowl's houses, and it's got two bedrooms and a kitchen and it would be big enough for all of us and the girls too. It's at the lower end of the avenue down past Dorothy's shop. Daddy doesn't seem to be interested in the moving but when Mammy asks him again and calls him Bren he says if she sees it tomorrow and she thinks it's alright then we can move.

In the morning as soon as Daddy is off to work, Mammy takes me and Raymin down the road to see the two rooms and the kitchen, and she says it'll do grand. She says it's big enough for the girls to come home and that makes me feel happy. I'll have someone to play cowboys with. On the way back up to number 82 we call at Dorothy's shop to get some cardboard boxes for moving things from her and wooden orange boxes from the grocer man round the corner. We borrow a pram from Mammy's friend that I didn't know she had to move Daddy's radio and other things that don't want to be broken (it's the friend I didn't know she had, not that I didn't know her friend had a pram. You know what I mean!). We're up and down the street for hours carrying everything from the room at number 82 to the bigger place down the road and we're all tired out, Mammy, Raymin and me.

Now Mammy is making Daddy's tea. Fried steak, potatos, peas with brown sauce and butter and bread for him. She says she got him steak to celebrate the move. Me and Raymin are going to have mashed potato, sausages and Bisto gravy. Daddy comes home from work and says he doesn't like the place, 'cos he says the walls smell of the damp. He eats his dinner while Mammy is looking out the window and smoking. Me and Raymin are having our dinner and I'm trying to fight him 'cos he wants one of my sausages, but he's not getting one and Mammy tells us to whisht and be quiet. Then Daddy changes his clothes and goes out to the bars to give us time to get all the bedclothes bundles, and all the boxes and everything back up to number 82 and I think it's a good job we still have the pram to make the moving back easier.

By ten o'clock we're back in the room and Mammy is drinking tea and smoking her cigarettes with Alice from upstairs, telling her it must have been one of the fastest moves since the war times, and she's laughing now. Then Daddy comes in from the bars and Mammy asks him if he wants a cup of tea and if he's brought any cigarettes home, but he doesn't answer 'cos he's too busy talking to Alice from upstairs. Now I'm thinking the girls are going to have to wait a bit longer before they come home to stay.

Alice visits Mammy a lot these days and I can see Mammy's face turning sad if Daddy and Alice are talking for a long time. Some days I think he likes Alice more than Mammy. Sometimes he goes upstairs to talk to Alice and her husband John. When I go up to their room, I go to see little Danny who is always in his cot and smells of pee.

When Mammy is on her own and Alice comes down, I hear them talking about Daddy going up the Ormeau Road to see a woman who's husband is nearly always away in the south. Mammy says he is away doing his bit for his country and she says Daddy goes up there doing something for the woman, so I think he must be fixing her radio or something and I don't understand why they're talking quietly about Daddy 'cos everyone knows that he's good at fixing radios. Then Mammy realises that I've been in the room listening to them talking, so she tells me that I better shurrup about what I heard, and I haven't even said anything but I shurrup anyway.

# Chapter 9

## The De la Salle Brothers who are not very Christian

Mammy and Daddy take me, Raymin and the girls to Dublin for two weeks. Me and Raymin stay at Grandad's, and Helen, Louise and Deirdre stay at Dun Laoghaire with Uncle Declan and Auntie Peggy. Me and Raymin are at Grandad's with our cousins from a place called Ballyfermot at the other side of the city. Connor is 12 and Donal is 13. They are both mad, crazy mad. Grandad catches them smoking in the bedroom at night and gives them a good walloping, but they just don't care about anything.

One day they take me up to the shop at Dolphin's Barn where Nana has a slate. They call it a slate but Nana calls it an account. They tell me to go in and ask for 20 Sweet Afton cigarettes for them, on Nana's slate, and half a pound of butter, to make it look genuine. I tell them that I don't want to do it but they are calling me a 'softee' and 'souper' and bad names like that. I don't know what a souper is but it sounds like it's a bad thing to be. So I do it. They took the cigarettes and I got the job of sneaking the butter into the cupboard in Nana's kitchen. Now I'm a criminal again. Just before teatime Nana asks me if I would like to go to the shop with her and make sure that I'm wearing the same clothes I had on earlier in the day. She knows. She knows about the cigarettes thing. Connor says she's taking me to the shop to be picked out of a line and be arrested by the Guards and put into Mountjoy Gaol down by the canal where the criminals sing rebel songs out the windows. Now I'm thinking that the Lone Ranger was right when he said crime doesn't pay, with Nana catching me straight away and me still being a wanted trickster by the Belfast police.

I'm standing at the front door with my coat on, crying. Connor says don't worry, if it's a first offence you won't be locked up for long, maybe only ten years. Raymin is grinning and pretending to be smoking. Nana comes up from the kitchen and tells me to take my coat off and go down for my tea, saying to the others, "Leave the poor child alone." Connor and Donal are sent home to Ballyfermot that night. I guess Nana knows I don't smoke. Before they go I ask them what a souper is. They say they don't know. They heard it being used on the Ballyfermot estate when people were calling each other names.

For the rest of the time in Dublin we have days out with Willy and Margaret McDonnagh, who are Auntie Josie's sister and her husband, in their van, with visits to Dun Laoghaire and into the country hills to light campfires and sing songs, like we did before.

On the last day in Dublin the girls are back from Uncle Declan's and Auntie Peggy's house. Daddy asks Louise if she prefers to stay at Grandad's or with Declan and Peggy. Louise says she likes it at Uncle Declan's house better. Daddy doesn't like her answer so he throws his dinner plate at her. It misses her and smashes against the kitchen wall into lots of small pieces.

We all go back to Belfast together. Louise, Helen and Deirdre go back to the nuns at Nazareth Lodge. The next time we see them Louise tells us how, when she was getting changed for bed the night they went back, bits of broken plate fell out of her clothes. She also tells us that while she was playing on the climbing frame one day she saw Daddy walking down the Ormeau Road outside the convent. She says he didn't even call in to see them. I'm thinking he'll have been up to fix the woman's radio again.

The next Sunday we go to Mass without Daddy. Mammy's prayers haven't been answered this time 'cos he's still in bed and won't get up. When we get back home, he's gone out. Mammy says he's probably gone down to Charlie's Bar on the Ormeau Road. Later Mammy sends me down to tell him that Marie has come to see us again from Dublin and the dinner is ready. He sends me home, saying he won't be long. When I get home and tell Mammy she sits on the bed, smoking, looking out the window saying things to herself. She's tapping her fingers on the window sill to help her think. Marie tells me to go and find Raymin for his dinner and when we come back Mammy is washing clothes in the bowl on the table. In between she's tapping her knuckles on the side of the bowl while me and Raymin sit on the bed eating the dinner and listening to Mammy telling Marie what we have to put up with. And saying that

Marie would be better off staying in Dublin. The radio is on. There's a man called Vic Damone singing 'On the Street Where You Live', but Mammy doesn't join in today like she usually does. I can tell she's sad again and getting more bad with her nerves.

Most of Daddy's dinner is in the fireplace now, there's only a bit of it on the wall at the side. He threw it there after he came in shouting about me going down to Charlie's bar and asking him to come home in front of his friends. Mammy says that she only sent me to tell him that Marie has come to see us, all the way from Dublin, and Daddy says he doesn't give a shite if she brought President de Valera himself from Dublin to see him. Then he looks at me and tells me never, never to come to the bars for him again. Now he's sweating and his face is going red and he's shouting louder. Mammy calls him a rotten bastard for frightening us kids. Alice and John come running down the stairs to see what all the noise is and Mammy pushes them and Marie, Raymin and me out onto the landing and closes the door so that she can talk to Daddy on her own. She's trying to calm Daddy down, so she's calling him Bren now instead of rotten bastard. Marie has her arms around me and Raymin when the shouting gets louder. I can hear things breaking, and now the shouting is getting louder again and turning into screaming. I hear Mammy screaming and now I'm getting frightened. I pull away from Marie as the screaming gets louder still. I push the door in. Mammy and Daddy are fighting. Daddy has hold of Mammy's wrists, holding her away from him. She's trying to pull a pair of sissors away from Daddy and she has a cut on her arm. Now I'm screaming at Daddy. I drop onto my knees and put my hands together like a prayer and scream.

"Please Daddy, please Daddy, please don't kill my Mammy!"

They both look down at me. My face is frightened and wet with tears. The room is full of people. They stop fighting, Daddy sits on the bed and puts his head in his hands, and Mammy gets a towel and wraps it round her cut arm. Marie puts her arms around me and Raymin. Mammy tells Alice and John to go back up to their own room.

Alice and John have gone back upstairs and nobody speaks. Raymin takes the scissors from Mammy's hand and wraps the towel tighter on to her arm. She sits down and lights a cigarette and says in a low voice, "The liten bastard." I'm thinkin why does Mammy say liten instead of dirty, but I know now is not the time to ask, 'cos I'm getting bigger and trying to have more sense. Mammy turns to me and whispers, "It was me trying to stab him, not the other way round!"

Me and Mammy walk down to see the doctor on the Ormeau Road to get her arm stitched. I don't think he believes her when she says she tripped and fell on the scissors. It takes three stitches and a nerve tablet and a bandage to fix her arm. The doctor asks her how she was holding the scissors when she fell and was Daddy there when it happened . Then he asks me to wait outside while he talks to Mammy about her tablets. He must think I'm stupid. I know it's not the tablets he wants to ask her about. He wants to ask her about where babies come from.

*

It's Monday morning and Marie is on her way back to Dublin. Daddy is back down at Charlie's Bar with his friends and Mammy is leaving me and Raymin back at Nazareth Lodge with the nuns. After the nuns have put a clean bandage on her arm, she tells us not to worry 'cos God is good and things won't always be like this and then she leaves. She doesn't say where she is going or for how long. I'm thinking she's off back to the Devil's Country, Daddy won't know what's happening until he gets back from Charlie's Bar, and the girls up in Nazareth House won't know anything at all about what's happening. I ask the nuns if Kevin Halfpenny can talk like us yet. She looks at me as if she's thinking about what to say to me, then she says nothing and Raymin looks at me and this time even he doesn't say anything like he usually does. I'm thinking he's looking sad and he probably needs a cigarette.

In the evening, the nun in charge tells us that we will be going to stay with the De La Salle brothers in Rubane House, Kircubbin, down past Newtonards. That's where the bigger boys have to go. It's another home for bad boys. I'm thinking it looks like it'll be a long time again before Mammy will be back. There's a

Brother Ignatius coming soon to collect us. We're too big to stay at Nazareth Lodge and in Kircubbin we'll be with boys of our own age. But I'm thinking the nuns want to get rid of us 'cos they're thinking that maybe we just came back for another free holiday. The next day in the afternoon Brother Ignatius comes to collect us in a black square-looking car. The number on the front of the car is VWW 522. The seats are red and they smell of leather, like the cruelty man's car did in Limerick.

We're leaving Belfast on the Newtonards road and soon we pass a hill in the distance with a tower on the top and then the road goes alongside a loch that looks like the seaside. The brother is asking us questions about Mammy and Daddy and what sorts of things we have been learning at school. Raymin does most of the answering. I'm busy looking at the back of the brother's nearly bald head and wondering where all the dandruff on his shoulders is coming from 'cos only people with lots of hair get dandruff and nits and things like that. Then Brother Ignatius asks why we have no bags or a case with us and Raymin says we left the room in a hurry. And I say to the brother, "Will you be taking us on holidays like the nuns did?" And Raymin tells the brother to take no notice of me, so he does take no notice of me, at first, then he says, "Sometimes the brothers take the boys out for the day in the school minibus, if they behave themselves." And I say, "That'll be good." I'm thinking a holiday would be better, but a day out is a good start. And I'm not sure what a minibus is exactly, but I've asked enough questions for now.

We drive through a place called Grey Abbey, with a bad bend in the road where the cars have to slow right down to be safe. I see a church and it reminds me that I have left the rosary beads that Grandad gave me in the room at Fitzroy Avenue. It's getting late and a bit dark as we drive through a village called Kircubbin, and then a smaller village called Rubane with a post office shop, and then we turn right and soon right again onto a farm lane and left under a brick arch and stop in a big yard at the back of a great big old house. We go up some steps and along some railings and into a hall with big pillars that hold up the top of the house above, in front of a great big staircase. The brother takes us up the stairs and says in future we must use the side stairs 'cos the main stairs are only for the brothers to use. Then he shows us into a big room that is over the front entrance and the hall. There's about 12 beds in the room and me and Raymin will have a bed next to each other by the windows. The brother asks us if we're hungry and we say yes, so he takes us down to the kitchen for a plastic cup of tea and some bread and jam. The brother then shows us where the other boys are in the cellar dining hall watching the square television that has a twelve-inch screen. The boys are staring at us in our new clothes that Daddy bought us. Their clothes look all worn and patched up and some of the boys have shaved heads. When we go to bed some boys are asking what we've done wrong to be sent here. Raymin tells them about Mammy going away and leaving us but I don't think they believe him. I kneel down and say my prayers and ask God to look after my sisters, Marie, Helen, Louise and Deirdre who isn't a baby anymore, and look after me and Raymin in this strange place, and please look after Daddy and stop him being a liten bastard and a hopeless case. God bless everybody and even Mammy who has left us again and has a cut arm after trying to kill Daddy, amen.

Next day after breakfast of porridge, bread and tea in the cellar dining hall me and Raymin are given numbers that will be put on all our clothes and things. He is number 23 and I am number 10. Our good clothes are taken away from us and we are given old clothes like the other boys are wearing. There's a locker room next to the dining hall with open boxes under the bench seats. They call them lockers and that's where I have to keep my shoes and polish and brushes and personal things that I haven't got. Then there's a parade out in the yard before we go to the school building next to the lower yard. Brother Ignatius tells us that the boys go back to school early here at the end of summer to make up for three weeks off in September when all the boys go picking spuds for the local farmers, to get some money for the school. But that's a long way off.

Down along the other side and the back of the school building is the garden area where the vegetables and fruits are grown. Below the lower playground is the concrete outdoor swimming pool, that's used only in the middle of the summer. Beside the pool is a big 'eccaliptus' tree from Australia, the only one in Northern Ireland, says the brother.

Brother Ignatius is in charge of the school, then there's Brother Jarleth O'Donoghue who runs the farm; Raymin says he is a big horse of a man. Brother Selba has white hair and is old and quiet. Brother Stephen has hair going grey and he is old and grumpy and moody and not nice. The big boys say he is ruled by the moon but I don't know what that means. Brother Felim and Brother Gerrard are young and happy, and there's another brother from Malta, where he got a bald head and glasses, and he seems kind but I don't know his name yet.

Every morning each boy has his own job of housework to do. Then on Saturday mornings you have more time, so the jobs have to be done properly. My job is to sweep and dust the main wide stairs and on Saturday I wax and polish them better. Sometimes there's a competition to see who does the best job, and if you win and you have done a really good job, you get a bag of sweets. I once got a sweet.

At Eastertime there's lots of masses and benedictions and rosaries and hymn singing. After that it's back to school where Brother Ignatius is giving me different school books to the other boys. He says he wants me to take the eleven plus exam at the end of the summer.

Sometimes after tea the boys help clean up after the building works on the the old barn beside the top yard that's being made into a sports hall. There's going to be a snooker room, table tennis room, and a badminton hall that's nearly finished. Over another two days me and Raymin and a boy called Andy McLoughlin help

Brother Ignatius clean out the concrete swimming pool with a hose pipe ready for the summer. The only water supply is from a small tap at the other side of the big boundary wall beside the farm. The brother says it takes three days to fill the pool, usually at the beginning of June.

One Saturday after the morning cleaning duties, Raymin is up in the chapel loft space with Brother Ignatius looking for a roof leak when he puts his foot through the ceiling. Raymin that is, not the Brother. After this, we are not allowed to help as much with fixing things around the school. There's still no news from Mammy or Daddy.

The days are getting longer and we can play in the top yard later in the evenings. Some of the boys take up running and do circles of the yard to see who can do the most. The brothers let them stay out late if a competition is going on. One evening two boys start running together, but they start late. The brothers let them stay out when all the other boys are called in. It was a Saturday, shower night. The showers are down the cellar behind the dining room and the locker room. The change of clothes and socks and towels are all laid out. We all rush into shower in case the water goes cold like it sometimes does. When we've done it's a rush too for the front seats in the dining room to watch Rawhide on the TV.

Just before Rawhide ends Brother Stephen comes in and turns the TV off. He's asking if the two 'runner boys' have come in because he can't find them. He turns the TV back on and rushes out. All the boys give a big cheer. 'Stevie' (that's what Brother Stephen is called behind his back) comes running back in shouting, "What's all the cheering for?" The room is quiet. One of the big boys says "'Cos Rowdy Yates is back on, brother."

In the morning after Mass, Brother Ignatius is in the locker room where we are queuing for breakfast. He's shaving the heads of the two boys who ran away last night. One of the boys has a black eye. The brothers are all very serious, even Brother Gerrard and Brother Felim. After a breakfast that never smells like Grandad's, we are all told to go over to the school. The big partition between classrooms one and two has been pulled across to make one big room to fit all the boys in. The two runaway boys are standing at the front dressed in only swimming trunks. Brother Ignatius is standing beside them. He tells us that the two boys ran away last night and were caught by the police in Grey Abbey while trying to get to Belfast. Due to a brief struggle one of them now has a black eye. The boy with the black eye looks at Ignatius, then at the floor shaking his head. He says running away will never be tolerated, and this is what happens to boys who run away. He holds the stick in the air for everyone to see. He tells the first boy to bend over and lean on the front desk. He lifts the cane high in the air and with all his strength brings it down on the boy's backside. The boy jumps up in the air screaming with pain. By the third wallop Ignatius has sweat running down his face. The boy is crying out for the beating to stop but the brother beats him three more times. Now it's the turn of the boy with the black eye. He leans on the front desk. Ignatius wallops him as hard as he can. Even with the swimming trunks not protecting him from the cane he doesn't cry out. I can see by his face that he's in pain. I'm thinking the pain would be as bad someone having their arse nailed to a floor. Ignatius is getting mad. His face is getting red and he's sweating more, but the boy won't give in. The brother carries on to the sixth wallop, with a deep breath before the last one. The boy won't give in. Ignatius looks around at all of us and shouts – out of breath – "That's what you get if you run away!"

Later, out in the top yard, I see the boy with the black eye. He's limping. I wait 'til there's no brothers about before I can ask him if he's OK. He says no. He says he has a headache with the beating and the black eye. Then he says it wasn't the police who gave him the black eye.

# Chapter 10

## If I don't say my prayers at night I will go to Hell

The weather warms up and we spend lots of time on the football field. Some of the boys have small plots of garden near the fence behind the goal posts where they grow lots of flowers and veg and things. On the really hot days we can go swimming in the pool and sunbathe under the Australian eccaliptus tree. On the way back up to the house for tea we sometimes risk going round the back of the school to help ourselves to the tomatoes in the greenhouses. Wednesday evenings is the chanter practice for the bagpipe band

It's a sunny afternoon and all the boys are coming up to the top yard from the football field. I haven't seen Raymin for a while. He's leaning against the sports hall wall, grinning at everyone. He's says he's been at the altar wine. Brother Stephen is at the other side of the yard getting ready to get the boys into the cellar for tea. I call Gilly Gilmore over to help get Raymin out of the way and stop him grinning and telling us to feck off. I go over to Brother Stephen and tell him that Raymin has tripped and fallen while he was running around the yard and that he is feeling sick and dizzy 'cos of the hot sun. The brother tells us to take him inside out of the sun for a while, and if that doesn't help then we've to get him up to his bed, out of the way. Me and Gilly take him straight up to bed. Later, at tea time, Brother Stephen says I can take Raymin's beans and two slices of bread up to him. I'm sat on my own bed eating the bread and beans, telling him that Brother Stephen says he shouldn't really be eating if he's still dizzy. I ask him if he agrees and he says "Huh, yuh". And then he starts crying.

"Daddy wouldn't buy me a secondhand fiddle, even when the teacher said I was good at music, even when Daddy could afford it!"

I'm feeling sad for my brother Raymin and I'm thinking that I'm missing Belfast, and Louise being a good cowboy and Helen agreeing to help me get out of jail, and Raymin giving me sixpence out of the money I made from the two nice ladies, and I miss Deirdre being Deirdre, and Mammy. Now I'm feeling sad and getting a lump in my throat. I don't like feeling like this. It's making it hard for me to swallow the bread and beans.

I'm thinking about all my worries. I think my nerves are getting bad and I need a cigarette. I find some matches and a cigarette butt in Raymin's pocket. I light it up and lean out the window. It's making me cough and it tastes awful. I throw it out the window when I hear footsteps coming across the hall. Brother Felim comes in. He says I have to go to chanter class for the bagpipe band. He's asking how Raymin is and I tell the brother he's fine now that he's sleeping after eating most of his beans.

"Has someone been smoking in here?" he says.

I can feel my face going red. He leans down to smell my breath. I'm holding my breath in but he stays there 'til I feel myself changing from red to blue and breathe out. He puts his hand out and asks for cigs and matches. I tell him they went out the window when I heard him coming. He puts his hand in his pocket and pulls out his leather beating strap.

"Bend over your bed, I'm going to give you six of the best."

"I'm sorry, I'll never do it again, and it's the first time, and I only dit it because my nerves are bad and I don't even like it, and I'll never do it again!"

"Where did you get them?"

I tell him I found them on the locker room floor. Now I'm bending over my bed crying, waiting for the beating to start. I hear his footsteps walking away from me. He looks back and says if he ever catches me smoking again he'll give me twelve of the best. As he crosses the hall he shouts back to me, "Why can't you behave yourself, like your brother?" I'm up off the bed, drying my eyes. I look at Raymin. He's got one eye open and he's grinning at me.

*

It's a Sunday afternoon and we're getting ready for spud-picking time. There's a big pile of secondhand clothes on the classroom floor to pick from, to keep us warm. There's long trousers, coats and jumpers, boots and wellies to pick from. We use old socks as gloves, and cut up the sleeves of old woolly jumpers to make hats. Some of the lucky boys find hats to wear or knit them themselves using a cotton reel with four nails in the top and wool stripped from the old jumpers ready for the Monday morning start.

The farmers pick us up in their tractors and trailers at about 7.30 a.m. on the frosty mornings and we work 'til about 4.00 p.m. We take samiches with us and the farmers give us cocoa to drink at dinner time. Sometimes we catch the field mice that run out after the tractor and plough have passed, and we take them back to the school in our pockets to keep as pets.

One of the farmers uses horses instead of a tractor, like the big horses called Sean and Sheila on the farm in Glin where me and Raymin stayed for our own good when we were small.

In the evening at the school I get into trouble when one of the brothers finds me with a mouse in my pocket. He says if any boy is caught bringing a mouse back to the school he will lose his shilling a week pay. But he didn't call it a mouse, he called it a vermin. I'm thinking I was unlucky to be caught with a vermin in my pocket, but on the second week I got lucky 'cos I got tonsillitis and had to stay in bed 'cos I was sick and didn't have to go out spud-picking in the cold frost. My friend Kevin Brady comes in to see me in the mornings to see if I am alright, before he goes picking the spuds. He walks round and round my bed sucking in the air, trying to get sick too, but he was unlucky 'cos he didn't get sick.

He asks me if I need anything, and I say I don't, but he can bring me back a mouse if he catches one, but he's to check to make sure it's not a vermin first.

In the wintertime we play in the yard or go into the school building in the bad weather. In the evenings we can watch the TV in the dining hall. We watch Rawhide and Bonanza and the Lone Ranger and things like that. It's a lot better when we watch the Lone Ranger here and can hear what they are saying, not like when we were on the wall looking through the posh woman's window on Fitzroy Avenue.

Sometimes, when Brother Stephen is in charge of the television watching and he's in bad form, he makes us wait outside in the locker room until there's complete silence before letting us in to watch it, and sometimes he does the same at food time.

On a Wednesday evening we get beans for tea, beans and bread and marge. One of the other boys doesn't like beans so I swap some of my bread for his beans. We call the end slice of the loaf 'the healer' and during Hail Mary prayers in the chapel, when the brothers can't hear us, we say things like "Hail Mary full of grace, put a healer in my place." On the next Wednesday the boy who gives me his beans says he doesn't want any of my bread, he whispers to me that he wants a kiss instead. He's a year younger than me. He says his Mammy and Daddy used to kiss him and his Mammy died and his Daddy couldn't look after him and now he never gets any kisses. I feel sorry for the boy, but not that sorry, I'm thinking about the beans. I give him a hug instead.

There's lots of morning masses, evening benediction and rosaries to say and there's no dodging it 'cos it's all compulsory. Me and Raymin are learning to be alterboys and singing in the choir. We can read all the hymns and Mass prayers in Latin; we don't always know what it means but we can still read it. We have to say the 'Credo' (I believe) in the Mass service, and in the middle of it we say *Mea culpa, mea culpa, mea maxima culpa,* that means 'Through my fault, through my fault, through my most grievous fault.' It's about our sins, but when the priest can't hear we change it to 'me a cowboy, me a cowboy, me a Mexican cowboy'.

One morning Raymin stays in the sacristy after Mass. He's been at the red altar wine again. He's been missing for an hour. Me and Kevin Brady find him staggering down the side stairs and laughing to himself. He tells us he's been drinking wine and asks us for a cigarette. We help him up the stairs and on the way to put him to bed Brother Gerrard sees us and asks us what's wrong with him, so we say he's sick and Brother Ignatius has told us to help him to bed. Brother Gerrard asks if he's banged his head again.

We put Raymin to bed with all his clothes on and Brother Gerrard comes in to see if he's alright. Then he asks Raymin about the red jumper he's wearing. He asks him what shade of red it is and Raymin says "It's red, brother, yes just red." Then Brother Gerrard says he thinks it might be a wine red, a deep wine red, then he looks at me and Kevin and says, "Do you think it could be wine red?" And I say "Yes brother, it could be a wine red I suppose." Then he leaves the room, and we all know that he knows what we know, and he never says anything about it again. He's just letting us know that he knows, and he's not stupid. Then Raymin says, "Have you got me a cig yet?"

*

Most days when we're not at school, we are at Mass or in the choir or saying the rosary or at evening benediction. Then fitted into the time that's left we're practising reading music for the bagpipe band that Brother Ignatius wants to start up at the school.

Christmas 1959 passes without any presents or news from Mammy or Daddy. In the spring we help the other boys painting the games rooms in the old barn by the top yard, in between all the other learning and practising. As the longer days come along we play Gaelic football or sometimes hurling.

During a hurling game one evening, Gilly Gilmore is knocked unconscious by Paddy Ryan from a wallop with a hurling stick. As Gilly is being carried into the main house to be put in his bed, Paddy is ordered by Brother Stephen to go to the chapel, get down on his knees and pray to God that Gilmore doesn't die. Half an hour later Gilly is back down the field to finish off the game, and Paddy is left in the chapel by Brother Stephen praying for him, 'til bedtime.

In the early summer, when the sports rooms are finally finished, some priests come down from Belfast for a few days. We practise a high Mass with plenty of singing by the choir, so that Brother Ignatius can show off to them before he has to rush off to Belfast himself. While he's away the priests are playing football with us down on the field. After a while they get fed up with the Gaelic football and want to play soccer. We tell them that we're not allowed to play soccer 'cos it's a Protestant game and Brother Ignatius never lets us play it. He says that after what the English did to the Catholics and Ireland, even going back to the times of Cromwell, we should never play their national game. The priests from Belfast don't agree, so we have a great game of soccer.

The next day when Brother Ignatius finds out, he calls all the boys into the school building and gives us a lecture for an hour on the English, Cromwell, the siege of Drogheda, Protestants, the Black and Tans, the Irish Potato Famine, and anything else he can think of as reasons for us not to play soccer. Not only must we not play soccer with the priests, it's compulsory that we never ever play the game again. The priests from Belfast weren't invited to the lecture.

Later, before the priests leave for Belfast and while we are all still in the school, one of them comes in to give us another lecture. This time it's all about why it's compulsory to say our prayers at night.

"Now boys, you must always say your prayers. You must always get down on your knees at night before you go to sleep and say your prayers. You must ask the almighty God to forgive you for any sins you may have committed during the day. Because at night when you're asleep there is only one thing between you and Hell, and that is your breathing. And if you stop breathing when you are asleep you will die, and if you have not said your prayers and asked God for forgiveness for your sins, you will go to the burning fires of Hell. And on judgement day at the end of the world, you will know when it's time to face God with your sins, 'cos the bible tells us that there will be three days of darkness and three days of light and the world will end. That is the time when God will send you to Hell if you haven't said your prayers. So saying your prayers is not only necessary, it is compulsory. Good night now boys and don't forget God loves you all, as long as you say your prayers."

So now we've got more compulsory things to do and compulsory things not to do as well as all the other praying and singing the Latin and serving the Mass as alter boys. And I've something else to worry about if I stop breathing at night. Now I'm getting frightened of dying in my sleep and being sent to Hell.

I've been in bed a while and I'm thinking about what the priest said. I've said my prayers but I'm still checking my breathing. I know if I stop breathing now I'll go to heaven 'cos of my prayers, but that means I will have to die first and I don't want to die while my mammy is in the Devil's Country across the water, and really I don't want to be dead for any reason, and now

I'm crying 'cos I'm frightened of dying. Raymin shouts over to me from the next bed.

"What's wrong with you?"

"I'm thinking about the breathing and dying thing that the priest said, and that I might die in my sleep."

"Don't worry, I'll listen to see if you stop breathing, and if you do, I'll wake you up and you'll be alright."

"Are you sure?"

"I am. The priest from Belfast was only trying to frighten us into saying our prayers."

Now I'm thinking he's done a good job of it.

I feel a bit better after saying the compulsory prayers and listening to Raymin and soon I'm trying to go to sleep, still listening to my breathing even though I've never noticed it much before tonight. A few minutes later I'm crying again. Raymin is leaning out the window smoking.

"What's wrong now?"

"It's dark outside."

"Of course it is, it's night time."

"What happens if it doesn't get light in the morning?"

"It gets light every morning, doesn't it?"

"Not if it's the end of the world, it won't."

Now Raymin says he'd love to choke the shit out of the priest from Belfast who frightened the shit out of me from Limerick, and then he shouts at me to shurrup and go to sleep or it'll be him that stops me breathing. I think I'll stay awake tonight.

In the morning it's nice to see the daylight, but I'm not happy and I don't want to get out of bed. I tell everyone that I've got a toothache and I stay in bed. Brother Ignatius says I can stay in bed for a while to see if I get better and Kevin Brady says he will bring me up some tea from the dining hall. By dinner time I'm getting fed up and hungry, so I get up and say the toothache is gone and I'm alright now. A couple of weeks later I'm feeling tired again, so I say I've got toothache again and stay in bed. After the boys' breakfast is over Brother Ignatius comes into the room and asks which tooth is hurting. I tell him it's the same one as last time.

"Right, get up and get dressed, we'll have to sort this one out. We can't have you in pain all the time." He takes me to the dentist on the road by the Lough, Strangford Lough. It's like a trailer cabin in a layby. I can't figure out whether admitting that there's nothing wrong with me will be harder to stand than having a good tooth pulled. I'm soon back at the school, with one tooth less than I went out with and a sore jaw that wasn't sore before. In future, if I want to stay in bed I'll have to think of a better excuse, or stop being tired.

In the longer evenings, when we go down to the field to play football or hurling, me and Kevin Brady are together most of the time and Brother Gerrard calls us the terrible twins. Kevin has some sisters, and they are with the nuns in Belfast with my sisters. Sometimes we climb the wire fence and go over the little bridge to the tower building that is hundreds of years old. We think it must have been used as a lookout tower in the olden days. Then we go around the back of the field and up to the hay barn by the old school house that's now used as dormitories. We climb up to the top of the barn and dive down into last year's soft hay and have great fun, but we have to keep a watch out for Brother Jarleth from the farm, who would give you a wallop as quick as look at you.

After football one evening I'm going up to the house early because I've got a bad headache. I leave my boots in the locker room and I'm sweating, but I don't bother having a wash. I'm lying on my bed when Brother Ignatius comes in and asks me what's wrong. I tell him I have a headache and I feel sick. He says he'll soon make me better and brings me a glass of water with two fizzy Alka-Seltzers in it. I'm drinking the Alka-Seltzer and when I'm finished the brother does something. He puts his hand up my shorts and touches my privates. I start getting up off the bed but he holds my elbow to slow me down, still touching me with his other hand. When he hears footsteps coming across the landing he stops and walks out of the room. Now I'm thinking about the brother in Glin and what he did. I'm thinking it must be something that grownups do. It must be. I know it's a bad thing to do, and I still have the headache, so it can't be a headache cure. Then I'm thinking it can't be anything about religion or a Latin thing 'cos I'd have known by now, being an alter boy and choirboy. I'm thinking maybe it's something grownups have to do. Then I say a little prayer while I'm still on my own.

> "Dear God, I don't understand what it is that
> the brothers do or why they do it. And if it is

> something that grownups do, I don't think I'd like to do it when I grow up. So please, is it alright if I don't have to do it? And please please don't make it compulsory like the night prayers and begging forgiveness for my sins is compulsory, so I don't have to worry about that as well as stopping breathing in my sleep, and it not getting light in the morning, and going to Hell, and God bless everyone."

But I can't stop thinking about what the brothers did. What will I do if it's compulsory for grownups?

What age will it become compulsory? Now my stomach is feeling funny. I think I'm going to be sick.

In the morning Brother Ignatius comes in to wake all the boys up. I'm thinking he's going to say something about the touching the privates thing, but he's just the same as any other morning, as if nothing happened. So now I'm wondering if it's not an important thing after all. I don't tell Raymin about it or my best friend Kevin Brady, I just tell God about it when no one is around. But I'm still confused.

# *Chapter 11*

## A holiday at 'home'

It's June and nearly Raymin's birthday. Brother Ignatius has bought him a bicycle. The bike has been left with Daddy in Belfast so nobody at the home will find out. Raymin says we'll be going to see Daddy soon to stay for a couple of weeks. Then he can have the bike to use at home.

Mammy is still in England and we haven't heard from her since she left us with the nuns up the Ravenhill road. I think about when we were all together in Belfast when we were all happy. When she would sing along with Doris Day and Victor Damone, on the days that Daddy wasn't being a hopeless fecker. At night I still say my prayers to Holy God to bring Mammy back safe, but he might have to sneak into England to get her. It's been a while now since I told God about the privates-touching thing by the brother and nothing like that has happened since. Now I'm thinking that if it's compulsory, it might only have to be compulsory once, for each brother.

Soon it's school holiday time and Brother Ignatius says me and Raymin can go to see Daddy in the room in Belfast for a two-week holiday at home. Most people go to boarding houses made of bricks by the seaside for holidays and it seems funny to be going home for one. So we're on our way now with Brother Ignatius to the room in Belfast for our holidays. We have some extra clothes with us and there's a big television with a small screen on the back seat of the car that I have to hold onto so it doesn't wobble about. The car we're in is a new one. It's a green Morris 1000 and there's a picture of a bull on the horn button in the middle of the steering wheel that the brother won't let me press. He says I'm not allowed to press the horn because I haven't got a driving licence. He says the broken secondhand television in the back seat came from some other brothers at a school in Belfast, so me and Raymin and Daddy can have it. He says that the yanks in America have televisions with coloured pictures but we're not as lucky or as rich as them. I tell him that Daddy might make it into coloured 'cos he's good at fixing things like he did for the woman up the Ormeau Road who's husband was always in the south, doing his best for his country, while Daddy was doing his best for her, and I'm not supposed to know about it, 'cos Mammy told me to shurrup, when I was being quiet anyway. Brother Ignatius says "Oh is that so," and I'm thinking he's good at keeping secrets too, isn't he. Raymin looks back at me and tells me to shurrup.

When we get to Fitzroy Avenue Daddy is sitting on the front step. Raymin dashes past him and up to the room to see the new bike.

"It looks brand new!" he shouts.

"It is," the brother says.

I've never seen Raymin as happy as this, even when he was drunk. He grabs hold of the bike. On his way out he says hello to Daddy and tells me that I can have the old black bike that's out in the backyard. Daddy clears away the pots and dishes from the day before so we can put the television on the table for him. Then him and the brother go downstairs to the front door to have a talk. Raymin is soon back, still all excited, and runs up to the room. I'm waiting for the kettle to boil on the gas ring so I can wash the dishes. Raymin tells me to listen at the door while he searches Daddy's pockets.

On the first night Daddy is on the night shift so me and Raymin stay up late. We try to stay up all night like grownups do sometimes. By midnight we have to splash water on our faces to keep awake and by one o'clock we're dipping our hands in a basin of cold water on the table and still wetting our faces, and trying not to get the television wet. The next thing I remember is waking up in the morning when Daddy comes in from work and goes straight to bed. In the evening, when he gets up, he fries some chops and peas for himself. He gives me and Raymin a key for the room door and some money to go to the picture house down by the Ormeau Bridge and buy some chips for our dinner.

"That's a nice surprise," I'm saying to Raymin.

"He's trying to get rid of us. Usually we have to ask him if we want some money."

We go off down Ormeau Road but we don't go to the pictures. We spend the money on sweets and Raymin's cigarettes. We go home early but the brass key that says

Yale on it won't open the room door. Raymin says in a whisper that there must be someone inside with Daddy and they don't want to be disturbed. I say they must be watching the television and Raymin says they must be, but I'm wondering why the TV sound is not on and everything's quiet. We sneak back down the stairs and out again across the road for Raymin to see his friend Michael Kennedy and then he tells me to get lost 'cos they're talking big boys' stuff.

Later when we go back to the room there's nobody in. There's plates on the table from when he had his chops and peas, and a bowl of water and a razor. There's no bits of wires or solder on the table, so he hasn't been fixing his radios or the television. He must have been asleep after all. Raymin is going around the room sniffing the air and he says he can smell perfume, a bit like Mammy used to wear, and then he finds a cigarette butt in the fireplace with lipstick on it. I ask him if he thinks maybe Mammy sneaked in and had a cigarette 'cos she was afraid to wake him up in case he wanted a fight, and Raymin says shurrup. We put the kettle on for water to wash the bowl on the table. I have a look around to see what food is in, while Raymin searches Daddy's pockets again. He finds some Senior Service cigarettes in one of the pockets and in the top pocket of Daddy's jacket there's a one-pound note. Raymin takes half the cigarettes for himself and leaves the pound note where it is. I make some tea and we have some triangle cheese spread on burnt toast. And it's good being home 'cos I can have more if I want.

Daddy is going out a lot more now 'cos he has time off work after doing all his shifts. The next night Raymin waits for him to go out again before he takes the rest of the cigarettes. The pound note is still in the top pocket and Raymin wants to take it. He says Daddy will have forgotten that it's there. I'm not so sure that we should take it. First because it'll be a serious sin and second because we might get found out. And there's a lot of difference between taking some cigarettes and a whole pound. So we decide to take the pound down to Dorothy's shop and change it for two ten shilling notes and put one of them back in the pocket. So now it's only half a sin.

Two days later after Daddy has been to the bars again, the ten shilling note is still there. Raymin wants to take it. I'm telling him I'm having nothing to do with it. I'm sticking at half a sin. He can do the full one if he wants. I'm thinking the gates of Hell will be only half open and the gates of Heaven will only be half closed and I'm sitting on the gate or the fence or whatever I'm supposed to sit on to play safe.

Some of the sinful money is used to fix a puncture on the new bicycle. I now have the old black bike with wire brakes and metal levers that Michael Kennedy gave to Raymin before. We go for rides during the day when Daddy is in bed or when he is at work. Raymin has fixed his puncture again and the brakes on my bike nearly work now.

Daddy says he wants me to take a letter to Alice up the Falls Road. Alice and her husband John and little

Danny have moved from the room above us. Raymin waits 'til Daddy is busy writing and whispers to me that he'll wait at the top of Magdala Street to meet me when I set off on my secret mission. This job must be more important than cleaning his shoes, 'cos when he seals the letter he gives me a shilling for the letter delivery and says there won't be a reply to bring back, just deliver this one.

Raymin has already gone out when I set off on my bike with the nearly working brakes, leaving Daddy getting ready to blow out his soapy cheeks with his razor at the ready and the bowl of hot water on the table and a clean mirror propped up against the teapot. Raymin is waiting for me at the top of Magdala Street where it meets Rugby Road. He takes the letter from me and rips it open. I'm telling him he's mad for opening the letter. And I'm mad 'cos I'll get into trouble for it, not him! My bike is lying on the road and I'm dancing around in a panic. Now I'm going to be in deep trouble. Raymin reads the letter out loud.

"Dear Alice, meet me at the same time, same place, Brendan."

Raymin lights up a cigarette, takes a new envelope from his pocket for the letter and stands there grinning. "Shurrup and stop dancing will yer!" I'm thinking that that's just saved me from getting into serious trouble for double-crossing Daddy. But I'm also thinking that Raymin's a bit of a feck.

I'm on my way up to the Falls Road, past the signs to the road works to the new motorway that's being built, and up past the Donegal Road to Alice's house to deliver the secret letter. After stopping a while to make it look like a normal visit, I leave and go back by the Grosvenor Road and down through Sandy Row, where all the houses are flying the English flag out of their windows and the end of the houses have pictures of King Billy and his big white horse, ready for a fight. King Billy that is, not the horse. Others have writings saying that there's no Pope there. Everybody knows that the Pope, who's name is John the 23rd, lives in Rome near Italy 'cos he's been in the Sunday papers for sneaking out of the Vatican house and riding around Rome on his motorbike when the Vatican guards weren't looking. And he got into trouble for it. And now I'm wondering who he confesses his sins to, if he's the boss of the Vatican and there's no priests above him. He'll probably have to tell them straight to God.

I'm pedaling like mad through Sandy Row where there's a boy shouting at me asking what I'm doing around here. He's riding his bike beside me and when I tell him I'm going home to Fitzroy Avenue and he hears my accent he calls me a rebel and a Fenian and I say I'm not. Well I don't know what he means anyway. Then a woman shouts at him to "Leave the wee boy alone," as she calls him back to her house that says there's no Pope, and my pedaling gets faster and faster 'til I'm up near Queen's University and out of breath and Sandy Row is well behind me.

I'm back at the room now and Daddy is happy that I've delivered his letter, and I'm happier still that he doesn't know that we've read it. I tell him about the boy calling me a rebel and a Fenian and he says I shouldn't have gone down Sandy Row anyway. I ask him what a Fenian is and he tells me to polish his shoes and I can have another sixpence. He's getting ready to go out. His pants are ironed and neatly creased, his shirt is ironed with a starched collar and cuffs, ready for his dicky bow and fawn Crombie coat with leather buttons. Now he's just waiting for his shoes to be polished. He goes out looking like a professor in a film at the pictures.

The plates from his quick dinner are on the table along with the bowl of water from his wash and shave. I fill the kettle in the bathroom and while I'm waiting for it to boil on the gas ring in the corner, I rinse out the bowl in the sink in the bathroom, then me and Raymin wash the dishes and make some tea for ourselves, beans on one-sided toast. It's toasted on one side only because that's how Mammy always did it. Then it's time for the pocket searching again, but this time there's no money or cigarettes for Raymin. So it's back to finding cigarette butts from the ashtray and fireplace for him.

Later in the evening Daddy comes in drunk. He's telling me and Raymin that he's been seeing Alice. Me and Raymin pretend to be surprised by the news but Daddy's so drunk that he's only interested in himself. He's telling us that Alice is a lady, a real lady, and that's why he likes her. He says Mammy is not like Alice, Mammy is different, she's not a lady like Alice is. He asks if we understand what he's saying and I say yes, 'cos that's what I think he wants to hear. But I don't really understand 'cos he's my Daddy and a man, and Mammy is my Mammy and a lady too, and now while he's talking to me and explaining things to me that I'm not interested in, Raymin is behind him taking cigarettes from his coat pocket.

Daddy's gone to work in the morning when a letter comes from England for him. Raymin says it looks like Mammy's writing. He can't open this letter 'cos he hasn't got an envelope with stamps of the queen's head on it to fool Daddy. Now I'm telling Raymin that the queen might have given Mammy some of her stamps for Mammy reading her tea leaves and giving her advice on how to run the Devil's Country. Raymin says not to be so stupid with my ideas 'cos the queen would be paying in English money and not in stamps, but now I'm thinking that Raymin isn't being serious and he's just mocking me.

When Daddy comes home from work he opens the letter and says it's from Mammy. When we ask if she's coming home he says he doesn't know. Then he starts getting ready to go out with his clean shirt that's been hanging on the wardrobe door with his dicky bow and Crombie coat, and now he has some new lemon-coloured woollen gloves to finish off his posh outfit. I get another sixpence for polishing his shoes. Raymin is watching where he puts Mammy's letter, but when he goes out he takes the letter with him. When he's gone me and Raymin are cooking sausages from Dorothy's shop for our dinner, with money that Daddy gave us. He didn't bother having any dinner today.

We're watching the television now that Daddy has fixed a fuse inside it. He fixed it when his drinking money ran out the week before his monthly payday. We're using two lengths of copper wire hanging out the window to get a better picture that's not too fuzzy. The television programmes have just finished for the day and the little white dot in the middle of the screen has just faded away when Daddy comes in. He's drunk again. His dicky bow is in his pocket, his face is red and he's sweating. He takes Mammy's letter from his pocket and says he's going to bring her home. He says he knows Alice is still a lady, but he wants to bring Mammy home. Now he's crying and he says that Mammy is his Mammy as well as ours. Now I'm crying and Raymin isn't. Daddy says he's going to the post office in the morning to send her some money to bring her back from England. When I go to bed I'm still crying but I'm not sad anymore. Mammy's coming home, and if she comes home straight away, we won't have to go back to the home in Kircubbin.

In the middle of the night there's a noise that wakes us up. It's Daddy chasing around the room in his baggy underpants trying to wallop a moth with a newspaper in one hand and the other hand holding his baggy underpants close to his privates while he's jumping on and off the bed chasing the moth around the room. He asks what we are laughing at but we don't answer. It's hard to get back to sleep now ’cos I’m all excited about Mammy coming home.

*

When I get up in the morning Raymin and Daddy are still in bed. It’s Daddy’s day off so I try to be quiet. Raymin gets up and goes out on his new bike to find Michael Kennedy and Daddy finally gets up at dinnertime. I make him a cup of tea, but he doesn’t want any one-sided toast. I’m dressed in my summer khaki shorts and my sandals. Daddy puts on a clean shirt and his ‘going to the bars’ clothes. He asks why I’m not out with Raymin like I usually am in the mornings and I say it’s ’cos we’re going to the post office. He’s going to the door and when I follow him, he asks me where I’m going.

“I thought we were going to the post office.”

“What for?”

So I just stand there and say nothing as he walks off saying he’ll be back at teatime.

When Raymin comes in I tell him about us not going to the post office and he says he’s not surprised. He lights a cigarette and says it was the drink talking. I’m sitting on the bed now looking out the window like Mammy sometimes did, and I’m thinking about the drink talking and grownups telling lies and I’m getting fed up of getting confused, and I’m wondering why Raymin doesn’t seem to get confused like me, but it's probably 'cos he's too busy going through Daddy's pockets again looking for cigarettes and money. I ask Raymin why he doesn't worry about things like me and Mammy do, and he says, "I have my worries but I don't worry about them." I think I'll go and help him look through Daddy's pockets. I might take up smoking again too.

A couple of days pass and there's no more talk of Mammy's letter. Daddy will soon be back at work and it's nearly time for us to go back to Kircubbin. Now I have another letter to take to Alice up the Falls. I meet Raymin at the top of Magdala Street, where he reads the letter – 'same place same time' again – and with the letter in a new envelope, I'm off to the Falls Road again. So it looks like Alice is still a lady, and Mammy isn't. On the way back I don't go through Sandy Row in case the people there might still think I'm a Fenian rebel (Raymin found out what a Fenian is from Michael Kennedy).

When Daddy comes in there's a parcel for him that's been delivered from a place called Practical Wireless. He's all excited when he sees it. He opens it up and shows us a transistor radio. He says it has tiny transistors instead of valves, and that means you can run it off a battery. He says you can use it anywhere and the battery is only the size of a big tin of Heinz beans. He doesn't mention Mammy.

After tea with Daddy's chops, and sausages for me and Raymin, Daddy gives us some money to go to the pictures again, but this time we don't come home early. In the morning Daddy is at work at the airport when

Brother Ignatius comes to take us back to Kircubbin. After a few weeks of being back, Marie sends us a letter asking how we are and says that Alice's little Danny has died, just after his fifth birthday.

# *Chapter 12*

## Cruel Brothers and Raymin turns to the drink again

There's some summertime left and Brother Stephen is in charge of the boys down at the swimming pool. He's in one of his 'full moon' moods. He's throwing little Billy Lafferty, who is just a bit younger than me, into the pool. The brother thinks it's great fun. Billy doesn't, he can't swim. He's screaming for help and clawing at the water trying to get to the side before he goes under again. Some big boys are going to jump in to help him but Stevie won't let them. Billy clings to the side of the pool scared and crying. The brother pulls him out saying, "See I told you, you CAN swim." Now Billy is clinging on tightly to the blue railings around the outside of the pool area. Stevie is pulling at him, trying to throw him in again. Billy is shaking and screaming.

"Please brother no, don't throw me in again, I can't swim! I'll be drowned. Please brother, I'll give you my shilling pocket money, I'll give you my extra spud-picking money when I get it."

Stevie can't pull him off the railing on his own. He tells two of the big boys to help him. The three of them throw billy into the middle of the pool, kicking and screaming 'til he goes under the water. When he comes up he's gasping for air and clawing at the water like a wild cat, trying to get to the edge of the pool, he is still promising all his pocket money to Brother Stephen. Stevie now realises that all the other boys are watching what is going on and he's the only one who thinks it's funny. He pulls him out and says "See, I told you it's easy to swim." Billy's shaking, his nose is running, and he's trying to smile through his crying: "Yes I can swim now brother, can't I?" Stevie walks off up the path towards the house but Billy won't let go of the railing 'til he's out of sight. Now the boys gather around Billy and ask if he's all right. "No I'm not, is he gone?"

During September and early October, we're out in the fields again picking spuds for the local farmers and collecting field mice vermin in our pockets. Back at school after the break for spud picking, Raymin tells me that Brother Ignatius says the nit nurse is coming to check our heads. All the boys have to line up in the main entrance hall of the big house to have their heads examined by the nurse. Raymin goes out to play in the yard with the boys who get the all clear, and I join the queue down in the basement locker room where Brother Ignatius himself is doing the hair cutting to get rid of the nits and head lice. My curly hair is falling onto the pile of hair building up around the chair from the dining hall that I'm sitting on. I feel sad, like I'm being punished for doing something wrong, like the criminals in jails, when the baddies in the pictures have their heads shaved and have to wear prison suits with arrows on them. I feel like crying but I can't, not in front of all the other boys in the queue watching.

Soon it's all over and now I'm a baldy. In the queue we were all blaming each other for spreading the nits. But now it doesn't matter who got the nits first 'cos we're all baldies together. I'm running my hand over my head and it feels like Daddy's chin when he needs a shave. I go out to the yard where the other hairy, nit-free boys are waiting to see who the next baldy is to appear, so they can tease us and make fun of the prickly bonces. They call us baldies and we call them hairies. My friend Kevin Brady is a baldy too, and this makes me happy 'cos he is on my side when we have mock fights with the hairies. There's no more cowboy and indian fights in the playground now. It's just straightforward baldies against hairies and it's cold being a baldy in late October.

There's a shortage of hats in the school, and with the sudden need for bald heads to be covered the demand for knitting reels is increased. The reels have four nails in the top with wool wrapped around the outside of the nails and then each piece of wool is lifted over every nail in turn and the knitted 'tube' is pushed down the middle of the reel and eventually pulled through as the knitted piece gets longer. The wool tube is then sewn together to make things (the knitting is done with another nail to lift each new line over the old one). The boys are knitting hats and scarves and some of them are even making socks. There's some balls of new wool around, but most is unwound from old jumpers. Gilly Gilmore has knitted himself a scarf nine inches wide by eight foot long and won't swap it for anything. The wool hat I have made for myself has earflaps on it and the stubble on my head grips the hat and stops it falling off when we are fighting the hairy boys out in the yard. It takes about a month for my hair to grow into what looks like a crew cut, like the soldiers in the American films. Raymin says I look like Tony Curtis, but I think he's only mocking me.

In November Brother Ignatius takes me and Raymin down to Dundalk to meet his relatives. We all stay with his sister and her husband and kids for a few days. Another of his relations has a pub in the town. On the way back to the school at Kircubbin the brother buys some tobacco and puts it under the seat of the car to smuggle it past the border checkpoint. The policeman calls Brother Ignatius 'Father' 'cos with his collar on everyone thinks he is a priest. Later, in the car, he asks us if we would like to move to Dundalk and stay with his sister and her husband. If we did, he says, we could go to the same school as his nephews, so at least we would know someone there. We say that we would prefer Dundalk to Kircubbin. I ask him if we can go straight back now, and Raymin tells me not to be so stupid. I'd forgotten that the brother would have to get rid of the smuggled tobacco first.

It's a few weeks now since we went to Dundalk to see the brother's relatives and do the smuggling. I've written a letter to them and thanked them for being nice to us while we were there. I've also thanked their relatives in the pub, where the floorboards smelt of beer. Brother Ignatius checks my letter and says it's OK, then as I'm going down to Rubane post office I remember that I have forgotten one of the husbands, so I put an extra note in the letter saying, "Tell your man I was asking about him," and later when they're all joking about my letter, they tell Brother Ignatius the sooner I get to Dundalk the better 'cos I'm beginning to sound like an Orangeman to them

It's nearly December and Brother Ignatius says me and Raymin can soon go to Dundalk to live with his relatives. He has agreed it with Daddy in Belfast and has written to Mammy in England and they can both write to us when we go, but he says we mustn't tell the boys or the other brothers about it. We have to tell them we're going back to Belfast to stay with Mammy and Daddy. We think it's because Brother Ignatius might get into trouble for helping us so much.

On the first of December we're off to Dundalk. I'm saying goodbye to Kevin Brady and telling him I'll write to him when we get home to Belfast. Soon we're going through the border point in Armagh, where one of the policemen seems to know Brother Ignatius, 'cos he says "Hello again, Father" to him. We settle in at Dundalk and then we join the local school with the brother's nephews, where the teachers are just teachers and not Christian Brothers or De La Salle Brothers. After school we have fun with the brother's nephews and the rest of the family, sometimes at the pub, and I'm wondering when we'll get a letter from Mammy and Daddy like Brother Ignatius promised. The school is alright and I'm meeting lots of new friends, and some of them have promised to take me and Raymin fishing by the sea. I think I'm going to like living in Dundalk by the sea where Brother Ignatius's relations are nice and kind and where we all go to Mass on Sunday mornings, and in the middle of the Latin Mass I don't say "Me a cowboy, me a cowboy, me a Mexican cowboy" anymore 'cos that's not a nice thing to say in front of people who don't know us too well. I'll probably say it when I get to know them a bit better.

We've been in Dundalk for two-and-a-half weeks now and Brother Ignatius has come down from Kircubbin to see us. Well, we think he's come to see us. He's in the front room talking to the grownups. He's telling them about some trouble at the border where there's a car covered with a wagon sheet, and he has seen bullet holes in the door of the car. Then they close the front room door and they're talking more. It sounds like there's something wrong; there's no one shouting or anything like that, but they're talking serious. I can just make out someone talking about babies and a shadow on the lung. I'm thinking it must be the cabbages at it again. I don't understand what they are talking about. Then out comes Brother Ignatius and his sister and her husband, who I called 'your man' in my letter. They're smiling at us but it's not their normal smile. It's a smile that tells me something is wrong, or they're going to tell us a lie, or Brother Ignatius has been caught smuggling tobacco or impersonating a priest even or something like that. They're looking a bit like Nana and Grandad in Dublin did, when the cruelty man came to take us away.

There's very little explanation and there's very little time for us to get our clothes together for the brother to take us back with him to the home in Kircubbin. I manage to find my school jotter where I have changed the school name on the front cover and now I'll have to cross it out and change it back again, and the kids at Dundalk school will have to learn to pronounce their 'th's without my help. Like when they say things like 'tunder' instead of 'thunder'.

We're in the car with the brother. His sister and 'your man' have come out to wave goodbye to us, saying they hope to see us again sometime, and God bless us, and God love us, and then she says "Ah God is good" just like Mammy says when things are going wrong and she's sad.

On the way back, Brother Ignatius says that there's something wrong and he can't tell us, and his sister can't look after us anymore. He says it's nothing to do with me and Raymin, that we've done nothing wrong. It just can't be helped and we have to go back to Kircubbin where we must tell everyone that things didn't work out with Mammy and Daddy in Belfast.

When we stop at the border I can see the car with a cover over it, and the bullet holes in the door. The policeman looks in our car window at me in the back seat. I ask him if the covered car was shot for smuggling. Raymin turns round and gives me one of his looks and tells me not to be so stupid. He's being grumpy with me, probably because he's run out of cigarettes. Brother Ignatius tells the policeman that I'd talk the leg off a donkey and gives me a dirty look in his mirror. The policeman says "Carry on, Father," and I'm thinking I was only asking.

It's dark by the time we get back to the school, two weeks after leaving for good. I'm confused again as to why we couldn't stay in Dundalk. I'm wondering if it's really worth trying to figure things out, and why grownups tell lies and why they ask us to tell lies too. So I think for now I'll just stay confused and not bother trying to figure things out. I think I really will start smoking again. It seems to stop Raymin from getting confused about things.

In the morning I go and find Kevin Brady and give him the letter for him that I wrote in Dundalk that was supposed to be from Belfast. I tell him the truth about us going to Dundalk and being told not to tell anyone where we were and not being told the reason why we couldn't stay there. Now I feel a bit better 'cos I've someone to share my confusion with.

*

Christmas comes and it's just normal, with plenty of choir practice and no presents and lots of singing the hymns in Latin, and now I'm singing 'me a Mexican cowboy' again in the middle of the Credo and there's no news or letters from Mammy and Daddy or the Brother Ignatius's Sister and 'your man' from Dundalk or anyone else at all.

After Christmas we still haven't heard from Mammy or Daddy. Brother Ignatius gets me Mammy's address from Daddy. So I write to her to find out when she is coming to see us at the school. Then just before the end of January a letter comes from Mammy who is back in Belfast with Daddy and a new baby called Amanda. She says she hopes to be bringing us home soon. I write to Mammy.

"Dear Mammy, I hope you are keeping well, as I am. Raymin got your letter Friday morning. Tell Helen to write if she may, and tell her I was asking for her. Did you hear from Marie yet? Raymin was asking for you. In your letter you said that Daddy was going to write to me and I did not get a letter yet. How is Daddy keeping? How is Amanda too? Did she fit into the English doctor's bag OK, or was she squashed to ugliness for a week like Deirdre was? I have not much else to say for now, so goodbye and God bless you. Has Daddy stopped being a hopeless case yet? I've said a few prayers to St Jude for him. Have they worked? Raymin says will you write soon to let us know when we will be coming home to Belfast. From you loving son, Brian Óg."

Two weeks later there's another letter from Mammy. Brother Ignatius gives the letter to me 'cos he can't find Raymin who usually gets the letters first. I'm reading the letter jumping up and down with joy. I'm so excited, running all around looking for Raymin in the yard, in the school and in the sports hall. I find him in the school storeroom office opening one of the new boxes of Tato crisps and stuffing some of the packets up his jumper.

"It's a letter from Mammy!"

"OK calm down, calm down. Is it good news?"

"It's brilliant!"

He turns to Gilly Gilmore and shouts "YES! WE'RE GOING HOME."

"Ah, no we're not."

"So what's the good news then?"

"Mammy has sent the Bisto Kids badges!"

He stops stuffing crisps and calls me a stupid fecker and chases me out of the school and up the steps to the top yard. Lucky for me he has to stop to pick up the crisps falling out of his jumper before any of the brothers see them. I go back and see him when he has had enough time to calm down but he won't give me any crisps. He says him and Gilly have to go to the sacristy now to get some things ready for tonight's benediction.

"It's a bit early for that isn't it?"

"No," he says, "We've got to do it now."

"In the sacristy?"

"Yep."

"Where the wine cupboard is?"

"Yep."

"With your bags of crisps?"

"Yep."

"And your cigarettes?"

"Yep."
"Can I come with you?"
"NO!"

# *Chapter 13*

## Cursing Brothers and going home to Mammy

I'm in Belfast with Brother Ignatius, who is going to see the man from the secondhand shop on the Shankill Road where he buys new and secondhand clothes and shoes for the boys at the home. He leaves me sitting in the car outside the shop for ages. After a long time a woman comes to the car and asks me if I'm alright. I tell her I'm fine but I haven't to talk to strangers, especially in this area. Soon the woman is back to give me some warm cakes in greaseproof paper. I thank her and put them on the shelf in front of me. They smell lovely, and I'm starving with the hunger, but I can't eat the cakes 'cos this is a Protestant area and if the woman thinks I'm a Catholic, she might be trying to poison me. It takes ages more for the brother to come back. When he does come back he asks me about the lovely smelling cakes. I tell him about me being starving but not wanting to be poisoned. He ask why I think she was a Protestant so I tell him that I couldn't see any crosses or medals of the Virgin Mary around her neck, so I wasn't taking any chances. He says that he'll eat one of the cakes and if he's alright in five minutes and he's not poisoned then it'll be safe for me to have the others.

We're going to see Mammy in Fitzroy Avenue while we're in Belfast. When we get there Mammy is there with Amanda the new baby girl, my new sister, that I didn't know I had until we got the letter a few months ago. Mammy tells us Daddy is out in the bars. He's not needed at the airport at Nutts Corner anymore due to the new machines they have to guide the planes in without him. Mammy says Daddy got extra money for him losing his job and she says he's spending more time out drinking again and when he's drunk he says things like, "I don't want that new baby 'cos she's not mine, and you're a hoor!" and bad things like that, and soon he'll have to sign on the brew when there's no money. "Hasn't the baby even got the look of him?" Mammy says, and I can see that her nerves are still not better. Brother Ignatius gives me some money to get myself some sweets from Dorothy's corner shop. I'm thinking he wants me out of the way so him and Mammy can talk about me and Raymin coming home. Mammy won't let me take Amanda to the shop on the crossbar of Raymin's bike. She says the baby might fall off

On the way back to the school home, I ask the brother what a 'hoor' is. He says the Bishop told him it's an awful bad word to say, it's the worst word in the world, and it's as bad as the word f-u-c-k that he told all the boys at the school that they must never say 'cos a bad word is a mortal sin if you say it and 'hoor' is another mortal sin word. Now I'm thinking these words are so bad that children must never know what they mean, and if I ever say these words I'll have to run straight to confession in case I die in my sleep and go straight to Hell with a mortal sin on my conscience. I'm looking at the water in Strangford Lough at the side of the road. But I'm still thinking about the two worst words in the world. I'm wondering, maybe even Brother Ignatius doesn't know what they mean. I'm going to ask him if he knows. Or if it's only bishops and cardinals and the Pope that know. I'm going to take a chance on being told to keep quiet and stop asking questions about words that grownups can use and children can't. I'm going to say "Excuse me brother, but do you know what the two words mean, and if you use them together is it one sin or two, and if I'm too young to be told, then what age will I need to be before I can find out what they mean?" I'm going to ask him now, just before the bad bend in the road at Grey Abbey. We're near the bad bend now.

"Excuse me brother ..."

The car swerves and just misses one coming round the corner in the middle of the road and he shouts.

"What the feck!"

Then he looks straight at me and says "What?"

"Excuse me brother, would you like another piece of the lovely smelling cakes?"

*

We're practicing with the choir for the Masses all Easter week. A lot of the words in Latin are the same as before, but the music is all different, it's more fast. The brother says it's modern. In the evenings there's choir practice and now once a week there's also practising for the pipe band again with the chanters in the classrooms. The choir practice is doing alright but we're not very good with the chanters and reading the music sheets.

After Easter the choirboys go on a day trip down past the border to Skerries on the coast near Dundalk. Brother Ignatius and Brother Selba take us in the school minibus as a treat. It's a cold and windy day. The brothers leave us on our own for a while and they drive off south; I think Brother Ignatius is off down to Dundalk to visit his family. We've each been given some money and buy sweets and ice cream that collects the sand blowing around in the air. The brothers come back in the middle of the afternoon and take us to a little gift shop on the seafront. Each boy is allowed to pick a small gift and Brother Ignatius pays. I see a brass cross with black wood in the middle. I'm wanting it. But it's five shillings so I think it will be too much. Brother Ignatius tells us to hurry up so I point to the cross and to my surprise he says OK. It's a really good cross. Now that I've got such a really good present I'll have to look after it and never swap it for anything, not even more Bisto Kid badges.

After Easter the choir practice has eased off. So we have two evenings a week practising for the bagpipe band. Brother Ignatius has brought in a man to teach us how to read music and play the chanter. Raymin is losing interest in the band 'cos in June he will be fifteen and have to leave the school and get a job. The brother is keeping in touch with Mammy so that Raymin can stay with her and Amanda and Daddy when he leaves.

They are also arranging for me to go with him; they don't want me left here 'on my own'. I'm keeping up the practice with the pipe band, just in case.

About a month later it's the middle of May when Brother Ignatius tells me and Raymin that Mammy has left Daddy again. With the brother's help she has rented the bottom floor of a three-floor house in Kinnaird Street on the Antrim road, up past Carlisle Circus, but she doesn't want Daddy to find out where she lives. Helen is out of Nazereth House and is living at Kinnaird Street helping to look after Baby Amanda with Mammy and Marie. Now they're all hiding from Daddy again. Brother Ignatius says there will be enough room for me and Raymin when we leave the home. He says Daddy is living back in Dublin.

At the end of June school finishes for the summer holidays and me and Raymin are soon to be going to Belfast to live with Mammy, Marie, Helen and Baby Amanda, who is now trying to walk. In early July the brother takes me and Raymin to the clothes store on the Crumlin Road to pick out some clothes for us to take with us. I root through the pile and I find a three-quarter length overcoat and some brown slip-on shoes and knee-length socks. Then we pick out a second set of clothes so we have something to change into at home. Ignatius takes us into the city centre to get something to eat. He takes us to a place that has a waitress. On the way in we walk past a beggar man with a dog. They both look hungry.

The brother tells us to pick anything we want to eat. The waitress says that a mixed grill might be too big for me and Raymin but that's what we all have. When it comes the waitress says be careful, the plates are red hot. It smells lovely. I'm thinking about the hungry man and his dog out on the street. I start to eat the lovely juicy meats that we're not used to having. When Ignatius isn't looking I grab my two sausages and stuff them in my short pants pocket. As soon as I start eating I have to stand up. The sausages are burning the tops of my legs. I'm pulling the pocket away from my skin. Brother Ignatius jumps up and pulls the sausages out of my pocket and onto the table and asks me why I put the sausages in my pocket. I tell him I was taking them for the poor beggar man outside. The waitress sees what's going on and brings a wet cloth over to cool down the skin under my pocket. Raymin calls me stupid. The waitress tells me I'm not and smiles at me. I finish the mixed grill, standing up to let the cool air up my shorts to ease my pain. When we've finished I take the sausages out for the beggar man and his dog. They've gone. I'm thinking now that I might as well keep them for myself and put them back into my other pocket.

*

It's the 2nd of July 1962. We are ready to go 'home'. It's about 11am, the sun is shining. I find Kevin Brady to say goodbye. He's looking sad. I'm feeling sad for leaving him but I'm also feeling happy about going home, or maybe I'm just getting used to saying goodbyes and that's why I'm not so sad. Then again I might be back in three weeks like when we went to stay in Dundalk for good, and I wrote him a letter from Belfast, that was really from Dundalk.

I'm waving to Kevin as we drive out of the yard onto the farm lane and past the big wall behind the swimming pool where Brother Stephen had his fun by nearly drowning ten-year-old Billy Lafferty. I look back at the big old house for the last time.

The house in Belfast is near the top of Kinnaird Street on the left, by the gates of the Territorial Army barracks. Mammy is sitting on the doorstep smoking and stands up when she sees the brother's car. The front room is a bedroom, the back room is the dining room with a coal fire grate and there's a door leading out to the kitchen, and another leading up some steps to another bedroom above the kitchen where the two floors stick out from the three floors of the main part of the house. In the kitchen there's another door leading out to a small backyard, and in the middle of the back wall there's a wooden gate leading out to a lane. There's no one living on the second and third floors. Helen and Baby Amanda are in the dining room talking to Raymin. It sounds like Marie is at work doing a waitress job.

Mammy, Marie, Helen and Baby Amanda have been living in this house for a few months now, since they had to run away from Daddy, who started drinking heavy again after losing his job at Nutts Corner Airport, where a new machine, called a computer, was brought in to do his job. Louise and Deirdre are still with the nuns in Nazareth House. Now me and Raymin will be living here with them and a cat called Tommy. Mammy says the cat's a stray and he just came to visit and decided to stay. Tommy the cat can play hide and seek. If I run and hide upstairs Tommy will come and find me and then run away and hide until I find him, probably under one of the beds.

After Brother Ignatius leaves, Mammy tells us that he found the flat for her 'cos he knows the landlord. She says that shortly after moving in, the brother called one evening to see how they were getting on. They were all sitting at the table by the back window having a cup of tea, when suddenly bricks came through the window showering glass all over the table and the pram with Baby Amanda in it. Then they heard Daddy outside shouting and kicking at the back door.

Mammy and Marie were screaming with the fright. Mammy was struggling to get Baby from the straps in her pram, while the back-kitchen door was bending in from being kicked. Brother Ignatius ran out the front to get his car started and they all piled into it. By this time, he had pulled off the collar that made him look like a priest. On the way down Kinnaird Street he had to swerve the car to avoid hitting Daddy, who was now running up the street trying to get to the front door of the house. The brother drove straight down to the police station near Carlisle Circus roundabout. Mammy says Daddy was arrested and sent back to Dublin for being drunk and breaking the windows. The next day Brother Ignatius got some money from the school funds to pay for the windows being fixed, so that Mammy and Marie could drink their tea and read the tea leaves in peace again, with no draughts coming in through holes in the windows. Mammy says that the brother has an awful time trying to balance the books at the school after taking money out to help us, and she says he puts some of it down to 'charity work.'

Brother Ignatius has gone back to Rubane house and I'm thinking we won't be seeing him anymore. Mammy is happy getting her National Assistance money every week to help pay the rent and feed us. Raymin has applied for a job as a waiter at the sportsman's club, and at McGlades bar down in the city, and is hoping to get one of them. Things seem to be going alright for a few weeks, then the National Assistance money stops and we have no money for food. During the next week there's a man from the Salvation Army called Captain Carrol who comes to the door collecting for his church. Mammy says she has no money to give him since Daddy rang up the National Assistance Board out of badness and had her money stopped by telling them she had a job when she didn't. She tells the captain he can have a cup of tea if he wants, "That's all we have, we haven't even any milk for the baby, not since that liten ba— not since my husband got my money stopped."

Captain Carrol stays for about half an hour talking to Mammy and Marie. Mammy is telling him all about Daddy and the drinking and the fighting and not having any money for food and how she's dying for a cigarette. The captain is standing by the fireplace. He's telling Mammy that cigarettes are very bad for her. He's banging his hand on the mantelpiece and saying that cigarettes are no good, and that food is more important, and then he says he's going back to his office to see if the can get some food to bring to us, and he'll try and get in touch with the National Assistance office and explain about Daddy's badness in case it happens again. Mammy says she's been to see them and she can't have any money 'til they've checked out Daddy's lies about her having 'other income'. Then with one more bang on the mantelpiece before he goes, the captain tells Mammy again that cigarettes are not good for her. After he's gone, Mammy is standing by the fireplace, and just where he was banging his hand down, she sees a ten-shilling note! "God bless you, Captain Carrol," she says.

It's not long before the captain is back to see us with a cardboard box full of food. There's loaves of bread, potatoes and other vegetables, and lots of tins of different things, and tea, sugar and milk. Mammy is thanking him for his kindness, she's nearly crying, and thanks him more when he tells her he's rung up the National Assistance office, but it was no good, 'cos they wouldn't tell him anything over the 'phone.

Raymin is out again looking for a job. Mammy has rung Brother Ignatius and told him about the money being stopped and that we're all starving with the hunger. She has told him about Captain Carrol feeding us after he saw her trying to stew the tea leaves to make him a drink of tea. She says the brother is on his way to see her now. Raymin comes in, starving but happy ’cos he’s got the job at the sportsman’s club down in the city. He says he can start the job straight away.

It’s evening time when Brother Ignatius comes. He’s brought a box of food and now Mammy has some more money for cigarettes. There’s a lot of talking and tea drinking and smoking going on. It’s getting late and Mammy says the brother can stay the night if he’s tired. She says he can sleep in the little bedroom over the kitchen. She tells him there’s only one bed and he’ll have to bunk up with me. I don’t really want him to stay. Raymin says I can sleep upstairs in one of the empty rooms with him, but Mammy says no, and that I’ll be fine as I am.

I wake up during the night and Brother Ignatius has turned me to face him. He’s trying to put his privates in my hands. I’m half asleep, I turn away from him and go back to sleep. I wake up again and he’s doing the same thing, but now my underpants are pulled down a bit. I sit up as if I’m getting out of bed but he lays me down and tells me to go back to sleep. In the morning he’s up and dressed. I’m glad he’s up ’cos that means he won’t be trying to touch me anymore. Then he turns the bedcovers down, pulls my underpants down, and holding me on the bed he puts his mouth over my privates and he moves up and down over me about five times, making me feel wet. Then he kisses me on the forehead and goes down the stairs. I pull my underpants up to cover my privates, that feel cold from the breeze coming in through the small bedroom window. I'm thinking it's the same thing that happened to me in Glin. I'm thinking, why would anyone want to go round wetting a boy's privates?

*As I write this, I find it very difficult to stay in the child's memory. At this moment I would like to pull the Brother's head off! I need to go for one of my calm-down walks!*

I get dressed and go downstairs. The brother is laughing and joking with Mammy. I'm thinking I want to tell Mammy what the brother did. But I don't. If I do tell, who will Mammy be able to ask for help when we're all starving with the hunger? Will she believe me? I'm thinking that Raymin doesn't want to talk to the brother much these days. He keeps his distance from him. Yep, I'm thinking a lot. I hope to God that it's not compulsory to do things like that when you grow up. I'm feeling a bit sick again. The brother turns to me.

"I've just been telling your mother that, because it'll soon be your birthday, I'm taking you down to the secondhand market to buy you a bicycle."

"Isn't that good of Brother Ignatius, Brian? Well, don't you think you should thank him?"

I look at him and say a reluctant 'thanks'. Yes, I'm thinking. I'm thinking a lot.

It takes another week 'til Raymin gets his first wage and the Assistance money comes in again. I offered to sell my five-pound secondhand bike to feed us last week but Mammy said no. During last week we lived off the small amount of tips that Raymin gets doing his waiter job and the money Marie gets from her job, and the food from Captain Carrol and Brother Ignatius, who always manage to avoid meeting each other.

On the Tuesday mornings, I go up to the baker's shop on the Antrim Road to get the leftover bread from Saturday when they were last open. I get two big paper bags of bread, soda bread and buns for just two shillings and sixpence. At least we won't be hungry for the rest of the week. Tommy the cat isn't too keen on the one-sided toast dipped in milk that I make for him. The soda bread is going a bit hard, but when it's toasted it tastes good.

# *Chapter 14*

## Daddy is back and I explore the Army Dump

During the summer holidays I get to know some boys and girls that live up past the army gates on Thorndale Avenue. Sometimes we play football in the grounds of the Salvation Army home for young women at the top end of the avenue. Mammy says that the young women stay at the house to have their babies born. After all this time she has finally admitted that babies don't grow under cabbage leaves. It's taken her a long time to tell me that babies are really born in the hospitals, when the woman lays a baby, like a cow lays a calf.

It's good being at home. When we play football now, we can play soccer, and there's no Brother Ignatius there to stop us playing the English game. It's better still when the girls are around and we play kiss catch, especially when I let Bridie Gallagher from down Dawson Street catch me, and she lets me catch her sometimes. Then we have to have a proper kiss, on the lips. Bridie is lovely. She has long brown hair and she's a good kisser and I might marry her when I get older, 'cos she doesn't make fun of my short trousers, like some of the others, and she has her own bicycle.

On Saturdays Raymin has his wages and pays Mammy some money for his board and lodgings, and if she has some money left from the National Assistance she sometimes gives me a shilling and says I can go down to the Plaza dance hall in the city, where kids can go on a Saturday afternoon. I'm going with some of the boys from Thorndale Avenue, who go most weeks. They have long trousers and some of them have new winkle picker shoes with pointed fronts that have just come into fashion. I just have my short trousers, long grey socks and my slip on shoes, but that doesn't stop me going with them when I get the shilling off Mammy and she's forgotten about the kidnappers and criminals that she normally uses as an excuse not to let me go anywhere.

In the dance hall there's a fancy silver ball with lots of small square mirrors on it, hanging from the ceiling, reflecting little dots of lights everywhere. We're all dancing. I'm doing the Twist that Marie's friend Francis, from down Carlisle Circus, has shown us at home. It's great fun at the dance hall, especially when I meet a girl from the Malone Road who's the same age as me. She wears red lipstick and she doesn't mind me dancing the Twist, in my short trousers and my long socks sliding down to my ankles and my ugly shoes. When the dance is over we're outside with the other boys and girls, swapping names and addresses. We're planning to meet again next week. Some bigger boys are talking about one of their school friends who died because of a hole in his heart. Red Lipstick from the Malone Road turns to me and asks me what happened to the boy. I'm telling her that I didn't actually know him, but I explain to her that there was probably a fight and he most likely got kicked by one of them new pointed winkle picker shoes and that probably caused the damage. Some of the boys hear what I say and they start laughing at me. But Red Lipstick from the Malone Road is not laughing. She's smiling, and she leans over to me and kisses me on the lips and says "See yews next week, noi," then she wanders off slowly with her friends and leaves me wondering what the other boys are laughing at. I'm thinking they're laughing at my short trousers.

When I get home I'm telling Mammy about meeting a girl who wears proper lipstick, and how we had good fun doing the Twist, like Francis Boyle showed us, but Mammy's not listening to me. She tells me to hould my whisht while her and Raymin are reading a letter from Daddy in Dublin.

*

I'm inside the fence of the Territorial Army barracks exploring. I've got through a hole in the fence and I'm rooting around their rubbish dump. I find lots of pairs of goggles and some old helmets and an old pram and some planks of wood. I load the helmets and goggles and wood into the pram to take them home, along the low ground by the fence, away from the road that runs through the barracks. I'm thinking the wheels from the pram will make a good bogey cart. I can't get the pram through the hole in the fence, so I push it along to the main gate that's usually open with no one around. Just as I'm going through the gate, there's a soldier coming, running up to me. He's telling me that I'm trespassing. Then he's looking in the pram to see what I've got. Now he's telling me if I trespass again that he'll fetch his gun and have me put into the Crumlin Road Gaol, and he shouts at me to get out of the barracks. But he still lets me take the pram and other things with me. I'm wanting to ask him if they ever throw old guns away. I don't think I'll ask him just now.

Mammy's shouting out the back door for me to stop hammering and banging things while Baby Mandy is trying to sleep. She doesn't know how hard it is to make a bogey cart without making noise. When Mammy's not looking, I'm knocking Mandy's pram, and soon when she is awake I can go back out into the yard and start banging and making the bogey cart again. In between the hammering, I can hear the others inside talking about Daddy's letter. It sounds like he's sorry for saying that Alice was more of a lady than Mammy and he wants to come back to live with us. He tells Mammy he didn't write to the National Assistance and that he's sorry for breaking the back windows, and he only did it 'cos he still loves her. Mammy says she's heard it all before. Raymin says he's not too sure about letting him come back to live with us. He says that when Daddy rang up the home in Kircubbin, before we left, trying to find out where she was living, he gave him an address up the Falls Road and sent him on a wild goose chase, and Daddy won't have liked it when he didn't find her there. Marie says she's wanting to move in with her friend

Una, over by Queen's University, and be well away from Daddy, if he does come back. I'm looking in the door saying that if he promises not to drink too much and not start wanting to fight Mammy then maybe she should give him another chance, and anyway it might be handy having him here, just in case the telly breaks down or we need another aerial so we could get that other TV station as well.

Mammy says there'll be no quick decision made. She'll have to think long and hard about it, and if he does come back and starts being a liten bastard again she'll split him wide open with the poker. Then she lifts up the poker and swings it over her head showing us how she'll do it. Now we're all having a good laugh at her, so she threatens us all with it, saying that it's not that funny, but we think it is. "Somebody put the kettle on," she says, "we'll have a cup of tea and read the tea leaves."

By the next Saturday I've managed to do something important. I've finished building the bogey cart. Mammy says I can have another shilling like she gave me last week to go to the Plaza dance hall again. But some of my friends are going to see a film called Ben Hur so I make my mind up to go with them instead. This means that I won't be seeing Red Lipstick from the Malone Road. I've been thinking about her this week when I haven't been making the bogey cart, and I've been thinking that Bridie Gallagher doesn't need lipstick to look pretty and Bridie likes riding bikes, so she'll probably like the bogey cart I've made too. I won't be missing seeing Red Lips too much even if she is a good kisser, and she never mentioned anything about having a bike.

At teatime I'm telling Mammy all about the film and how Mr Hur gets hurt in the chariot race when his horses jump over a broken down chariot and he nearly falls off. Mammy says "Oh is that so" and then says she's busy making the tea and can I keep out of her way and go and tell the others all about 'Mr Hur' and the chariot race.

Soon I'm out in the backyard, thinking that if I cut the front of the bogey cart off, and nail two wood handles to the sides sticking out the back, I'll soon have my own chariot. I'm thinking I'll risk going to root around the army dump again. Maybe Sunday morning, when all the soldiers will be at church, would be a good time.

Summer has been good, playing football, playing kiss catch, pulling my Ben Hur chariot behind my bike, going for bike rides, and all of us going for long walks up Cave Hill with picnics. It's nearly September now and it seems a long time since me and Raymin left the children's home in Kircubbin. Marie was finished at her other job down by the docks with no explanation after she told her boss about her friend Captain Carrol who liked to play detective sometimes. When she told the captain about being finished, he admitted that he had been watching the café at night and that there had been some suspicious comings and goings. Marie said that now she knows why he told her about the job in the first place. She was a spy and she didn't even know it.

Now she has a new waitress job and is living with her friend Una.

Raymin has his waiter job. Helen is at home looking after Mandy most of the time and soon I'll be starting at a new school called St Joseph's, out the Antrim Road, and Mammy says that Daddy might be coming back. I'm thinking that there's no need for Daddy to rush back soon 'cos at the moment the telly and the radio are working fine. Louise and Deirdre come from the convent to stay some weekends, to play on the bogey cart that's now a chariot. Me and Louise still watch the Lone Ranger and play cowboys and Indians when Bridie Gallagher isn't around. We're trying to pick cowboy names for ourselves. Louise is being called Calamity Jane and I'm being called Roy Rogers. Helen says Trigger would suit me better.

# Chapter 15

## A rat in the kitchen and another one in the dining room

I've been at the new school about two months now. Daddy has been back a month and the National Assistance money has gone up a little bit. There's two women moved into the flat upstairs. One's called Harriet and the other's called Dorothy. They both have daughters, about 5 years old, with them. There was a policeman staying in the top flat with his wife for a time, but they left after a short while. Mammy says she's glad they've gone. Not because they weren't nice, but because every morning at half past six we would be woken up by the clatter of him running down the stairs, and if he didn't drop his handcuffs it would be his gun falling down the stairs in front of him and bouncing along the hallway to waken the whole house. He was always late for things.

There's a man in the top flat now called Tommy. He's about the same age as Daddy, with a daughter called Jean who's about nineteen, and a wife who we don't see much of. Mammy says we'll have to change Tommy the cat's name so as we don't offend Tommy from upstairs.

Top Flat Tommy moved in before Daddy came back. He doesn't have a regular job, but he goes out sometimes with an empty suitcase and brings it back full of cigarettes. If we see him on his way out he says he's off to 'see a man about a dog'. Then he comes back in a taxi and he gives Mammy some cigarettes for nothing. Mammy says that he's a smuggler, a kind smuggler. I'm thinking he's a better smuggler than Brother Ignatius, who only smuggled a couple of packets of tobacco under the car seat. His daughter Jean comes down sometimes to have a cup of tea and fancy Raymin. She doesn't know that Raymin fancies Harriet from upstairs, who fancies him back. I know he fancies her 'cos they have cups of tea late at night and go for long walks together. Mammy reads everyone's tea leaves for them, but not as much now since Daddy came back. She say's she's been reading Raymin's cup and she hopes she's wrong but she can see lots of trouble in it. Marie's friend Paddy Kane calls to the house with his sheepdog to see her. He doesn't know she's not here. Mammy brings him in for a cup of tea and tells him that Marie has moved in with her friend Una over by Queen's University. I'm in the backyard with Paddy's dog. Tommy the cat, whose name we haven't changed yet, ran away down the lane when he saw the dog. I'm measuring the dog up to the chariot, but it's no good, the dog would never be able to pull it with me in it. We'll have to find a bigger dog somewhere. Paddy is asking lots of questions about Marie and where exactly she lives now and does Mammy think it'll be all right if he went to see her. Mammy says it'd probably be alright, she'll ask her next time she sees her.

"You still want to take my dog for a walk then?" Paddy asks me.

"Ah, no thanks, I need a bigger dog to take for walks."

"Oh. I see."

But I'm thinking that he doesn't really see 'cos he's probably thinking too much about Marie.

The trouble in Raymin's tea leaves is coming true. It's a Saturday night, about twelve o'clock. Mammy is in the kitchen making tea. Daddy has been back from the pub about an hour. He's shouting at all of us 'cos we've all done something wrong.

Mammy is in trouble again now and he's calling her an 'effin hoor'. Mammy's telling him to calm down and have a nice cup of tea. She's calling him Bren and being bad with her nerves again. Now he's leaning on the table with his fists closed across from Raymin who is sitting down counting the tips he has made doing his waiter job. He's shouting at Raymin.

"You feckin bastard, you sent me on a wild goose chase up the Falls Road!"

Then without any warning he punches Raymin in the face, knocking him back and off the chair and his tips money all over the place. Mammy and Helen are screaming. We all grab Daddy and pull him away from Raymin who is looking dazed with his nose bleeding and his left eye is swelling up like a balloon. Daddy is shouting and bawling, with sweat running down his face, trying to convince us that Raymin deserved the wallop that he got. Raymin is back in the chair with his hands up to his face. There's blood dripping through his fingers and onto the plastic table cloth. Mammy gets a dishcloth and is wiping Raymin's face and then the table. She turns to Daddy and calls him a liten bastard.

Mammy goes into the kitchen to wash out the dishcloth. She screams out loud and I rush in to see her with one hand on the sink and the other on the cooker, with her legs kicking in the air and a big rat running around under her feet. I grab the sweeping brush and try to wallop the rat. Mammy's shouting to open the back door to "Let the feckin thing out!" but before I can open the door the rat has got out by squeezing under the door where the stone step is worn down in the middle. Mammy puts her feet down onto the floor.

"Oh my God," she says, "I'm gone all weak at the knees, somebody give me a cigarette before I faint." Mammy's hands are shaking, so are mine. Helen and Mandy are crying. Raymin is trying to pick up his money off the floor, holding a handkerchief to his nose and his closed eye. Mammy brings Raymin in a cup of tea and she looks at Daddy.

"If you want one, you can get it your feckin self!"

Just then the door from the hall opens and in runs Top Flat Tommy, in just his underpants with his hands covering where his privates are. He's looking around.

"Jesus Christ," he says, "I thought someone was getting kilt!"

Now he's looking at Daddy, who's telling him there was a rat in the kitchen and Mammy says yes there was.

"Well if everything's alright I'll get back to bed then."

As he's leaving the room Tommy sees Raymin at the table with a bloody handkerchief to his face.

"I think there's more than one rat here," says Tommy as he closes the door behind him.

Mammy tells Helen to take Mandy and the cat upstairs to Harriet and Dorothy 'til the morning. Now Daddy is up again and shouting about Top Flat Tommy.

"Who the feck does he think he is coming in here and talking to me like that? He wants his jaw bursting, that Protestant bastard!"

Mammy is standing between Daddy and the door.

"Them Protestants were the ones that gave us food and cigarettes when there was no National Assistance coming into the house, so you can sit down and shurrup, 'cos you've done enough damage for one night."

I'm helping Raymin pick up his money and counting it for him. Then I look at Daddy sat by the fire now, breathing heavy and smoking his cigarette, and I'm thinking, "I'm Twelve years old now, but someday when I get older I'm going to beat the shit out of you, you bullying bastard."

It's late into the night when everyone gets to bed, except Mammy, who says she's happy just to sit by the fire with Tommy the cat who has just come down from upstairs with Helen and Mandy. Sunday morning I get up late. Mammy is in the dining room still in the armchair in front of the fire that's still lit from the night before. She's drinking tea and smoking one of her Gallagher's Blues cigarettes, staring into the coals. I don't think she notices the red marks on her legs from the heat of the fire, with her varicose veins showing through like a map of the Mourne Mountains that I've seen at school. Raymin is still asleep in the bed we now share in the front room. He's usually with Tommy the cat too but Tommy didn't come to bed last night. Daddy is snoring in the other bed that he shares with Mammy. Helen and Mandy are in the little bedroom above the kitchen. Mammy sees me.

"Go and put the kettle on and do some toast in front of the fire and don't burn yourself."

I'm in the kitchen making some tea and toast. I can see Mammy getting up off the chair and looking at Tommy the cat lying still, not moving, at the back of where she was sitting. She cries out.

"Oh Jesus Christ, the cat's dead, I've smothered the cat, oh God I've kilt the cat!"

Helen comes running down the stairs to see what's going on.

"I've sat on the poor feckin cat and smothered it, I've kilt the poor thing!"

Helen is wiping her sleepy eyes and saying she thought the comotion was Daddy causing his trouble again. I'm standing at the kitchen doorway at the bottom of the bedroom stairs. There's a rumbling noise on the bedroom stairs and I turn around just in time to see Mandy tumbling down. I just have time to catch her, saving her from hitting the dining room floor head first. She isn't even crying 'cos she's still half asleep. I give her to Mammy who starts looking for lumps and bruises on her head. Now I'm rushing over to see Tommy the dead cat. I stroke his head. He opens one eye, looks at me, and goes back to sleep. I'm telling Mammy that the cat's alright.

"Here," she says, "hold the baby. I'm needing my tablets. Jesus, my nerves are getting worse."

Now Raymin is coming into the kitchen. One of his eyes is fully closed and still blown up like a balloon, the other is blue, and his nose is swollen. He says he's got an awful headache. Mammy gives Raymin a cup of tea and some of my one-sided toast. Then she soaks a rag in vinegar and ties it tight against his forehead to make his headache go away. After a while with the vinegar rag taken off his head and his headache still there, Raymin says that he's off out to the phone box to ring his boss at work to tell him he can't go into work 'cos he's sick.

It's Tuesday morning now and I've missed two days' school. Raymin comes out of the bedroom. He's going to see his boss at work to explain what really happened and show him that his eyes are still black and blue, and that's why he can't hold his job for him. When he sees his boss at work, he says he can't wait for Raymin's eyes to get better, even if it isn't his fault, so there's no other way but to finish him and pay him up. Raymin is really upset when he comes home. He says jobs are so hard to get in Belfast, and harder still if you come from the south, and he's nearly in tears when he tells Mammy.

"He's a lousy liten bastard, God blast him!" But I don't think that it's Raymin's boss she's calling names.

Raymin says that the next time Daddy starts his trouble, we should all jump on him and beat the shit out of the bullying gobshite, and now I'm agreeing with them and calling Daddy a bullying bastard, but Mammy tells me I'm too young to be swearing and that I'm not old enough to be saying words like bastard. Mammy looks into the front room where Daddy is still in bed to see if he is still snoring. Then she comes back into the dining room to carry on talking to Raymin and call Daddy names. I go out into the backyard to measure up the chariot I made after seeing Mr Hur at the pictures and sit and wonder how old I will have to be before I'm allowed to say the serious cursing words. Mammy shouts out for me to go up to the baker's with two shillings and sixpence from Raymin, to get the Tuesday stale bread bargains before it's all gone.

On the Wednesday morning I go to school. After the morning assembly the headmaster calls me to one side and asks me why I missed school. I'm telling him all about Daddy getting drunk and wanting to fight all of us, and keeping us late with his shouting, and about him drinking Mammy's money and there being no food at home until Raymin's tips money bought the stale bread, and Mammy being bad with her nerves and weak at the knees. But he's not listening to me properly and he butts in before I finish telling him.

"Shut up, boy! If you're off school again I'll send you back to the De La Salle Brothers' home."

Now he's made me very upset and I'm crying.

"Stop your slavering, child, and get off to your class!"

I'm thinking he'd make a really good De La Salle Brother.

When I get home I tell Mammy what the headmaster said.

"Don't worry you won't be going back to any homes again."

Daddy comes into the room just as I'm telling Mammy about the headmaster wanting to send me back to Kircubbin for missing school. Daddy says the head wants his jaw bursting. I'm thinking he's not the only one.

After school the next day I'm walking home with some of my friends who want to spend the bus money on sweets. I'm walking 'cos I have no money for the bus anyway. They show me how to get home on the 'hop.' When wagons slow down at the traffic lights we are supposed to hop onto the backs of the flat wagons, or hang onto the back doors of the tipper wagons, then jump off when they slow down again nearer home. When me and my friends jump onto the back of an empty flat wagon the driver sees us. He's shouting at us to get off, but by now he's moving fast, too fast for us to get off. He's swinging the wagon from side to side, trying to make us fall off. He's shouting out the back window at us, I can't hear what he's saying but he's definitely swearing. I'm thinking he surely was never an alter boy. We're hanging onto the head board and the sides and when he turns fast right onto Cave Hill Road it takes us all our strength to hold on, and as I'm swinging across the rough wood planks, my knees get grazed and my blazer catches and gets ripped by a sticking up nail. Now he's braking hard with the back wheels of the wagon giving off blue smoke and bouncing up and down on the road at the same time. It's still moving when we jump off and run like hell back down towards the Antrim Road, away from the big mad fat driver who is now running after us, threatening to kill us.

I don't think I'll be doing that again.

When I get home it's Mammy's turn to get mad when she sees my bleeding knees and ripped blazer. She's so mad that she makes me sew it up myself. Now Daddy is shouting at me too. Mammy tells him to be quiet and sit down and eat his tea of beans on one-sided toast, and she's sorry that the toast has marge on it instead of the butter that he usually wants, but beggars can't be choosers. In the evening I walk down to the city with Raymin to see if he can get his job back but he can't. It's about half past nine when we're walking back up the Antrim Road, it's dark and it's been raining. We've past St Malachy's College and we're nearly home. There's two Teddy Boys coming across the road carrying a loud-playing transistor radio, one of them modern ones with a small battery about the size of a jam jar, so it can work outside the house. They're coming over to us.

"Hey, have yous ever had the balls in a sling?" I'm not sure what he means, but it doesn't sound a good idea to me. Raymin looks straight at them.

"No I haven't, have you?"

I'm thinking maybe Raymin should try and be a bit nicer to them, then maybe there'll be less chance of me getting a black eye like him, but I guess it's too late now.

I'll just have to look straight at them and try to look tough, but it's hard to look tough in short pants.

"Are yous looking for trouble?" the other one says.

Raymin looks at me. "Go and fetch Malachy and his brothers."

"OK," I say, walking off up towards Kinnaird street, doing my best tough walk.

"Right, see yous back here in five minutes for a fight!" one of the Teddy Boys says.

"Yeah!" says Raymin, following me up the street.

"Yeah!" says I, loud enough for them to hear. I think.

Off we go up Kinnaird Street to get reinforcements, and off go the Teddy Boys down Dawson Street, to get their gang, with the sound of Telstar playing on their new transistor radio fading away into the distance. Halfway up the street, Raymin looks back across the Antrim Road to make sure the Teddy Boys have gone, then we run like hell up the street and home. I'm asking if he still wants me to get Malachy and his brothers.

"No, we'll sneak out the back lane and see where the other gang is first."

For fifteen minutes we're peeping around the corner, watching across the road to the top of Dawson Street, between Mrs O'Kane's grocery shop at one corner and the fish & chip shop on the other. Then we see them. The two Teddy Boys are peeping around the corner of Mrs O'Kane's shop. They're on their own, looking for our gang.

"Thought so," says Raymin. "They aren't that tough."

"Yeah," says I, in my new tough voice. "Who is this Malachy fella and all his brothers anyway?"

He says they live up Thorndale Avenue. We go back up the lane and into the house, and I feel a lot better now that I've missed out on the chance of getting a black eye from some balls in a sling. Now I'm thinking that the Teddy Boys will be thinking that we're not that tough either. Maybe we should have just got Daddy to burst their jaws.

*

Raymin's eyes are better now, so he's out all the time on his secondhand drop handlebar bicycle he bought with his tips money, looking for another job. After about a month, he gets another waiter job at McGlades Bar in the city. Daddy's started drinking heavy again and being cantankerous. And a liten bastard, says Mammy when she's complaining about him. Most of the time when he's drunk he's shouting and looking for a fight, except when Harriet from upstairs, who still fancies Raymin, and Top Flat Jean who still likes Raymin 'cos she doesn't know yet that Raymin fancies Harriet back, are all in our dining room, then Daddy tries to be nice and tries to get the girls to sit on his knee and give him a kiss, while Mammy is making tea for him and calling him 'love' and 'Bren' to please him so he might stay calm. Three times the police have had to be called to the house since he came back from Dublin.

Lately, he's been to see a doctor, who's given him tablets and told him to stop drinking, and says he'll have to go into Musgrave Park Hospital to help him stop drinking altogether. He stays there in the winter of 1962/63 and we all go to see him in turns. Even Harriet and Dorothy from upstairs and Top Flat Jean go to see him. Raymin won't go to see him, 'cos he says he never came to see us in the children's homes.

It's snowing when me and Mammy go to see him. We get the bus across the city and out the Lisburn Road. We're all walking around the grounds in the snow and the cold wind. Daddy is looking for the visitors' tearoom. There's a man walking up the road, talking away to himself.

"Excuse me," Daddy says, "can you tell us where the visitors' tearoom is?"

The man keeps on walking past us as we stop, waiting for an answer. Then he looks back and says "Cup of tea? Cup of tea? I don't want a cup of tea. You can shove your tea up your feckin arse!" Then he continues with his talking to himself as he's walking faster and faster away from us.

Me and Mammy can't help ourselves from laughing. Daddy isn't laughing though, he's not happy. He looks at Mammy.

"Listen to that, bejesus, if I wasn't nuts when I came in here they'll drive me nuts before I feckin leave. That ignorant bastard wants his jaw bursting."

"No he doesn't," Mammy says, as she pulls Daddy's sleeve and guides him towards what looks like a little café on the corner of one of the big buildings. We sit down and drink our tea listening to Daddy grumbling.

"This place is full of nutty people and madmen and that includes some of the feckin doctors!"

He says that one of the patients in his room is getting drunk every day and no matter how much the doctors and nurses searched the place they couldn't find where he hid his drink, until last night, he says, when a nurse found him drinking his hot water bottle.

Now Daddy's showing me the watch he bought when he was working at Nutts Corner Airport, telling me that it never loses as much as a second from day to day. Then he's asking Mammy to send him some Brylcreem the next time someone comes to see him, so he can comb his hair into neat waves. When he's not listening Mammy whispers to me that his hair looks more like a walnut whip every time she sees him, and I'm trying to stop myself from laughing in case Daddy wants to know what I'm laughing at.

At the hospital, Daddy always wears a brown sports jacket and a collar and tie, and has his hair combed up and to one side, with waves in it. He says he feels better being properly dressed, when some of the others go around looking like tramps, including one of the doctors, who's as mad as a hatter and should be a patient.

When it's time to leave, Mammy gives Daddy some packets of Sweet Afton cigarettes that Tommy the Top Flat Protestant smuggler sent for him. Daddy tells Mammy to tell him thanks, and says that he shouldn't have called him a bastard when the rat was running around the kitchen. Then he says that the hospital is doing him good, except for the odd mad fecker that can't talk civil, and that he won't be drinking anymore when he comes home. Mammy says that's very good.

As we are leaving, walking off down the hospital road, Daddy shouts and asks if Upstairs Harriet and Top Flat Jean might come next week. Mammy shouts back, "Someone will."

It's getting dark now, there's more snow in the air and the cold wind is blowing as we get on the bus to go home. There's no talking on the way home. Mammy is looking out of the window into the snowflakes chomping her teeth together, tapping her knuckles lightly on the seat in front of us. There's words coming out every now and then, quietly, one at a time, a few at a time, long gaps in between.

"Bastard ... liten bastard ... won't always be like this ... God is good ..." all the time looking out the window into the passing snowflakes. "Things will get better ... shit! I think we've missed our stop." Mammy's complaining about the cold and the freezing snow. The buses have stopped running out to the Antrim Road because of the bad weather so we have to walk the rest of the way home. It was even on the radio news last night that Lough Neagh, the biggest lake in England and Ireland, has frozen over and people have been walking on it, and even driving across it.

When we get home Raymin is at work at McGlades Bar, Helen is looking after Mandy, and Marie has come to visit us from the flat she shares with her friend Una, who works with her. She's visiting now 'cos she knows Daddy is still in the hospital, and he doesn't agree with her having a flat with Una and living away from home, even if there's not enough room for her here.

Mammy and Marie are sitting drinking tea by the window in the dining room. They're talking about the night Brother Ignatius was there, when Daddy broke the windows in. Mammy says she wonders what the brother is doing now, since she heard that he had left the school at Kircubbin. Then she says she's wondering how Captain Carrol from the Salvation Army is, 'cos it's a long time since he's called to the house to see us.

Soon Mammy is talking about her sister, Auntie Mary Murphy, and her brother Paddy Reilly who live in Keighley in England. They keep writing and telling her there's plenty of jobs going in Keighley and around Yorkshire. They say that all the mills are busy and there's plenty of building work, and isn't Peter Black's shoe factory always looking for people to fill the vacancies there. She says that when she was in England she never once saw a hungry child, or one with no shoes on their feet, and that England is the place to be for all of us. She's going to write to Uncle Paddy and his wife Edna, to see if we can go and stay with them for a while 'til we can find a place of our own and jobs as well. "And if that liten bastard in the hospital, with his feckin walnut whip haircut doesn't agree with me, he can stay here on his own!"

# Chapter 16

## Making important things

The snow is lasting a long time and there's been no more talk of going to live in Keighley in the Devil's Country. Daddy is still in the hospital. Marie, Harriet and Dorothy are sat around the table drinking tea. Mammy is telling them stories about when she lived in the Devil's Country and especially when she lived for a while in a place called Leeds, that she calls 'sin city.' She tells them that a visit to Leeds city would open their eyes, especially in if they worked in hotels. Then she tells me to go out and play so that she can talk to the others about grownup matters.

"Don't go too far from the house, and watch out for drunks coming home from the bars early because of the snow, and don't talk to strangers."

I am glad she sent me out 'cos Bridie Gallagher was up at the top of Thorndale Avenue with the rest of my friends and soon we were all playing kiss catch in the grounds of the Sally Ann. Bridie lets me catch her and do a kiss on the lips. It's all great fun. Except for the time I have to explain to a boy called Roger that it's the girls that he's supposed to be chasing.

When I'm kissing Bridie I'm dreaming about marrying her. Probably down at St Malachy's Church in the city. But my dreaming is stopped by the sound of Helen's voice shouting for me to go home. I'm telling her that it's only early and it's still light 'cos of the snow, but she says that Mammy said I have to go home 'cos it's Saturday night and the drunks will be coming home from the bars early, due to the snow, and it's not safe to be out on the streets at this time of night. Now I'm sad to have to leave the girl I'm going to marry, just when I was going to ask her if she would be my proper girlfriend. Bridie gives me a ride on the back of her bike, even though it's hard to keep it straight in the soft snow, down home where Mammy is waiting at the door to make sure I get back safe. When I get off the bike I'm whispering to Bridie not to kiss anyone else. Then I'm standing in the middle of the street, in my short trousers, doing the Twist, with my legs all wet and scratched from the snow and the brambles in the Sally Ann. She's off on her bike down the street laughing and singing Bobby Vee's song 'The night has a thousand eyes'. Mammy comes over to me and grabs me by the ear and drags me into the house, threatening to give me such a clatter if I don't get in to the house straight away. But even with sore legs and now a sore ear I'm still feeling happy.

Marie is in the kitchen doing some beans on toast for me. It's better than Mammy does 'cos it's toasted on both sides, and cut into triangles before it's buttered and filled with beans, like they do where she works as a waitress. I'm thinking it looks very posh. I'm telling Mammy that it's better having two-sided toast, but she just tells me "For God's sake hould your whisht and eat it!"

*

The next morning I'm at the army camp dump again. It's easy to get in 'cos there's no soldiers on the gate, probably because of the snow. I'm thinking they might even all be at church. Still, I keep to the low ground by the fence so nobody sees me. Under the snow I'm finding more pairs of goggles in a box, another tin helmet, some six-feet-long planks of wood and a pair of boots. The boots are a bit big for me but I think I have a use for them. When I take them all home, Mammy is complaining about me filling the backyard up with "feckin junk." I'm thinking that that's an awful thing for her to say, calling my stuff junk.

I spend the day cutting the planks with a rusty saw. I'm making a pair of snow skis. I nail the army boots to the planks and look for lots of extra pairs of socks to help me fit the boots. Top Flat Tommy lends me a sweeping brush so I now have two to help me push myself down the street. I'm in front of the army gates on the hard snow facing down the street. This is it. One big push and I'll be sliding down towards the main road. I better not go too fast so I can stop safely at the bottom of the hill. The brushes are dug in. Here we go. One big PUSH!

The wood skis stick to the snow like glue. I go flying forward and slide out of my boots, landing flat on the road and my nose is bleeding. Now I'm at home drying out in front of the fire and Raymin is telling me how stupid I am because skis should be polished and waxed before you use them. Mammy says I need to stick to making bogey carts. "I shouldn't have said stick, should I!" Raymin is grinning.

On Monday I'm taking the goggles to school to sell them for tuppence each. I come home with nearly three shillings. On Tuesday morning, early, before going to school, Mammy sends me up to the baker's shop with my money to get bags of Saturday's bread and buns and soda bread for two shillings and sixpence. She lets me keep the six pence that's left from my money. When I get to school, three boys bring back their goggles and ask for their tuppences back. Now all my money is gone. Something tells me that I have a lot to learn about selling things and keeping the money – which is the way you're supposed to do it.

On Wednesday morning before school the soldier on the gate catches me again trying to sneak along the inside of the fence. He's not happy today. He's telling me that if he catches me again he'll definitely have me locked up in the Crumlin Road Gaol. Then he gets more excited and red in the face when I ask him if they ever throw their old guns away. Now I'm thinking it's time to take Mammy's advice and hould my whisht as I run out the gates.

*

Daddy has been in the hospital for four months now and he'll soon be coming home. When he does come home Raymin will have to stop letting Harriet go up to his bedroom in the evening to say good night. He'll just have to say good night in the dining room. He's still working at McGlades Bar. Helen is mostly looking after Baby Mandy, who is running all over the place now. Louise and Deirdre are still with the nuns at Nazareth house. Marie is still in her flat with her friend Una, and Top Flat Jean has told Mammy that she thinks Harriet is after Raymin. And I'm thinking she shouldn't have told her when Raymin and Harriet were sitting on his bedroom stairs listening. Top Flat Tommy still brings Mammy cigarettes. No one is looking forward to Daddy coming home from the hospital.

I've missed my chance to try skiing again now that the snow has finally melted and gone. Anyway, the snow skis and boots went on the fire and helped to keep the dining room warm. I've found a better way into the army camp, through a hole in the fence near the dump. I've been getting lots of old wood for the fire in the cold weather. The cold lasted a long time this year but it's getting a bit warmer now. Well it is April. Mammy says that Daddy will be coming home soon.

*

It's the middle of May and Daddy's been home about a month. He's only had a couple of bottles of Guinness since coming out of hospital. There was no trouble with the drink but it did make him a bit tipsy. He was telling Mammy that he loved her. Harriet and Dorothy were in the dining room with us. He told them that he loved them too. He asked me if I loved him and I said yes.

"How much do you love me?" he asked.

"Lots," I told him.

"How much is lots?" he asked. So I told him I loved him more than I love Tommy the cat. He gave me a funny look. "Sure we all love you, Brendan," Harriet said, then he looked happy again. And he stopped looking at me funny. Anyway, I love Tommy the cat more than I love him. He starts telling us again how lots of people in America have colour televisions and someday we'll have them over here he says. Mammy joins in and says that someday everyone will have a colour telly and some might have even two. Now we're all laughing 'cos we all know that that'll never happen.

Soon Mammy's telling everyone to go home or get off to bed. Daddy doesn't go until he gets a good night kiss from Harriet and Dorothy. Mammy sleeps on the armchair in front of the fire again with Tommy the cat.

# *Chapter 17*

## More important things to make

I've been very busy in the evenings and weekends doing important things. I've being fixing a leak on an old paraffin heater I got from the army dump. I drilled a hole with a nail in the tank where the leak was and then plugged it with a piece of wood. It'll keep us warm next winter. And I've been experimenting with melting margarine by the fire and mixing it up to make it more like butter. I changed the broken front wheel on my bike with one I got from the dump. It's not the right size. The wheel is a bit small, but I can still ride it. Raymin says it looks stupid, like a penny farthing bike going backwards. Mammy says it looks fine and when I look at Daddy he just shakes his head. I ask Helen if she thinks it's OK and she says "Huh." And as we know, that's Indian for yes. Baby Mandy says, "It's lubbaly."

Now that the bicycle is fixed, except the front brakes that won't reach the wheel, I'm making a rope swing with a board seat for a tree up at the Sally Ann grounds. I got the rope from … yep, the dump. I'm going to put the swing up on my own. It'll be a nice surprise for my friends. There's always lots of things to do.

It's nearly June now and I haven't missed much school lately and the headmaster has stopped threatening to have me sent back to the brothers in Kircubbin. The teachers are telling us to concentrate on learning, 'cos we'll soon be having the early summer exams and the results will decide which classes we will be in after the summer holidays. Mammy has been telling Daddy that we'd be better off if we all moved to England, where there's plenty of work and no one goes hungry. Nearly every week Mammy gets letters from Auntie Mary Murphy and Auntie Edna Reilly, telling her that jobs are available in Keighley and there's lots of flats and houses to rent. They also send the Keighley newspaper so she can read the adverts for herself.

At school I've done the early exams. They didn't seem that hard, except for English and French. I don't like French at all. I can't get interested in it. Arithmetic is easy and I like the art classes. I'm hoping that we won't be moving to England 'cos I'm liking my school friends and my friends up Thorndale Avenue, and especially Bridie from down Dawson Street.

When I get home Mammy's in the kitchen. I tell her that I don't want to go to England and another school, or leave my friends and the army dump that always has lots of interesting things on it. She says that I'd soon settle in any school and make new friends, and if we did go to England things would be a lot better and Daddy could get a job now that he's off the drink and things will be better, please God, and England will be a better place to live. She says it's only the Devil's Country if you stop going to Mass and lose your religion. If we all pray to St Anthony there'll be plenty of jobs for everybody and we'll soon find a place to live, and she's sure there'll be plenty of dumps there too.

"Anyway," she says, "sure we might never to go England at all. So don't worry about anything. With the help of God, things will only get better. God is good, God is good." Then she says quietly "And hopefully the days of your father being a liten bastard are gone, sure all anyone wants is a peaceful life. I don't forget years ago when I wanted us to go to England where your father could have found work. Your Grandad in Dublin turned to me and said, 'No son of mine is going to England to become a labourer for you.'"

Mammy is standing at the big white sink in the kitchen, chomping her teeth and tapping her knuckles on the far edge of the sink washing the clothes.

"Two liten bastards together," she says while she's staring out the window, through the yard wall, into the distance.

*

Two days before the school holidays the exam results are out. My arithmetic teacher is all excited when he gives out the results. I get 100% marks. He says no one in his class has ever got 100% before. The art teacher is also very pleased. He gave me 80% and he says that it's the highest mark he's given anyone since he's been at the school. Then even the headmaster himself congratulated me. I was thinking I bet he's glad he didn't have me sent back to the home last year when he was being rotten to me.

On the way home I meet Roger, who's mad on football, the boy from the kiss catch games who wasn't too sure about who he should have been chasing. He says he heard that I got 100% in arithmetic. I ask him why he's limping.

"Oh it's nothing," he says. "I was playing on a rope swing in the Sally Ann and the rope broke. It was rotten in the middle."

When I get home I'm showing everyone the sheet of paper with my exam results, arithmetic 100%, art 80%, English 60%, geography 50% and French 50%. Mammy glances at the paper, "Very good." Daddy looks and says that's good. Mammy says I have to sit down at the table for something to eat. Then they carry on talking to each other like they were when I came in. They're not excited like me or my teacher. The teacher said I will be put in a higher class after the summer, so I can carry on doing well at school.

After tea I put the exam results in my pocket. I go up Thorndale Avenue where I see Bridie coming up the street on her bike. She says she's heard about my good exam results and says congratulations. I show her the results. Now she's smiling and says she's proud of me. And I'm so proud 'cos she's proud of me. Now it doesn't matter to me that Mammy and Daddy didn't show much interest in my exam result. The paper is stuffed into my pocket. I'm on Bridie's bike, giving her a lift up to the top of the avenue where our friends are waiting by the Sally Ann gates.

Helen is calling for me. Mammy says I have to be in home before the drunks are on their way from the pubs. I'm thinking that it's time I asked Bridie if she really is going to be my girlfriend. I'll definitely have to ask her tomorrow. Tomorrow after school I'll ask her, then she can be my girlfriend all through the summer holidays and we can have longer kisses, like I've seen Raymin and Harriet doing when they thought I wasn't looking. I don't want to have to go home, but I'm still happy 'cos Bridie Gallagher told me she was proud of me.

When I get in Mammy says we're all going to live in England soon. I'm thinking I don't want to go.

"Don't look so sad," she says, "Auntie Edna says I have to tell you that there's a council dump just down the road from her house.

"I don't care about the council dump, I don't want to go!"

*

It's early July now and there's been more serious talking about all of us moving to England. Mammy won't listen to me when I tell her I don't want to leave my new friends, or move to a new school. I'm telling her that the arithmetic teacher says I could do very well at my school, even if I didn't pass the 11-plus examination before. He says the big school has a very good reputation. Some of the former pupils have gone on to become teachers, like Mrs O'Kane's son who lives above their corner shop at the top of Dawson Street is trying to do. Mammy says there's some good schools in England too.

"Now for God's sake, will you hould your whisht, it's all been decided."

Me and Mammy will be going to England first, to stay with Uncle Paddy and Auntie Edna while we look for somewhere big enough for us all. Then we'll go back to Belfast for Daddy, Helen and Baby Mandy. When we're all settled in with somewhere to live, Louise and Deirdre can come to England too. That's the plan, according to Mammy and Auntie Edna and Uncle Paddy, says Daddy.

Most sunny days I see my friends up at the Sally Ann grounds in the afternoon. We play football a lot and when the girls are around we play kiss catch. Bridie doesn't come round as much as before. Maybe she's heard I'm going to England. Maybe she just doesn't want to come round. Maybe she has new friends. Maybe I'll just go to the army dump and let the soldiers catch me and lock me up in Crumlin Gaol.

I'm out in the backyard. I don't want to cry but the tears come anyway. I'm feeling like I felt when we were dumped in Nazareth Lodge and passed on to the brothers in Kircubbin where we knew no one. I won't see my friends from school again. I'm losing my friends up the avenue and I've lost my friend Bridie. I don't want to make things or fix things anymore. Mammy comes out the back door.

“What’s wrong with you?” she asks.

“I don’t want to go to England. I want to stay here with my friends, Catholic and Protestant.”

“You’ll be fine,” she says. “Anyway, the more you cry the less you pee.”

# *Chapter 18*

## Living in the Devil's Country

Me and Mammy are on the boat from Belfast to Heysham. We're on our way to Keighley in Yorkshire to stay with Mammy's brother, Paddy Reilly, and his wife, Auntie Edna, so that Mammy can look for a house or a flat to rent. Mammy tells me that Reilly isn't Uncle Paddy's proper name. His second name is Reale, like her maiden name is. She says that he left home in Hospital village, Limerick, to find work in England to make enough money so he could marry his girlfriend when he'd made his fortune. When he went back home with some money that wasn't a fortune, he found out that she had married someone else while he was away. Mammy says he was brokenhearted, so he went straight back to England, changed his name and never went home to County Limerick ever again. She says I have to hould my whisht about it and not tell anyone what she told me. So I will keep the secret. Well, except for telling you.

The boat travels overnight and in the morning we get the train from Heysham to Keighley. When we get there we call to see Auntie Mary Murphy who lives in Holker Street, across from St Anne's School, on the Skipton road. Auntie Mary has a big terraced house with the cellar made into a kitchen with a big long table, where she feeds her lodgers from the top of the house where they live two to a room. Auntie Mary is in the kitchen cooking the dinner for the lodgers. She's telling Mammy how to find a house and apply for National Assistance 'til her and Daddy find jobs, and that Daddy and Raymin would soon get a job either on a building site or in one of the big woollen mills.

I'm watching her stirring the potatoes and vegetables in big pans on the gas cooker. All the time she's talking, the cigarette she's smoking never leaves her mouth. The ash is bending down over the pan of spuds boiling in their jackets. I'm waiting for the ash to drop into the spuds, but it doesn't. Just when I'm thinking it's finally going to drop off, she turns around and allows the ash to fall on the small piece of carpet on the floor in front of the cooker. She pushes the ash into the carpet with the sole of her shoe and in between giving Mammy lots of advice she says, "That'll keep the moths out." Then she wipes the big stirring spoon on her apron, lifts it over her shoulder and down between her cardigan and her back to scratch an itch that's obviously annoying her. She wipes the spoon on her apron again and carries on stirring the spuds with it.

Two girls come down the steps to the kitchen. Mammy says they're my cousins, Kathleen and Chrissy. Kathleen is about a couple of years older than me, and Chrissy is about the same age as me. She's very pretty and she's nice to talk to. Chrissy tells me that there's two more sisters, Emelda and Rita and some brothers,

Eddie, Tommy, Johnny and Danny. I'm thinking I've a lot more relations than I thought I had.

Mammy finishes talking with Auntie Mary and is wanting to leave, but I'm hanging on as long as I can, watching the ash from another cigarette dangling over the spuds again. Mammy shouts at me to come. I'm telling her that I have to tie up my shoelaces. She says if I don't hurry up she'll give me a good clatter. I'm ready to go, now that I've seen the ash fall from the cigarette, straight down the front of the spud pan and onto the piece of carpet. Mammy says we have to hurry up and go to Uncle Paddy Reilly's, who is expecting us soon.

It's raining and thunder and lightning as we walk up Devonshire Street, where a sign outside number 87 says that the basement flat is for rent, and on up to Guard House estate to Uncle Paddy's council house. Mammy says I have to keep near the walls when I can, so the lightening won't get me. She says that the lightning in England is worse than anywhere else, and these summer storms are the worst and the English lightning is called fork lightning and it would kill you stone dead. When we get to the house, she says I haven't to go out again 'til the lightning has stopped.

Auntie Edna is at home with her daughter Diane. Uncle Paddy is out working as a rag and bone man with his horse and cart. Their son, Stephen, who is fourteen, is at school, and there's a dog under the table. Mammy tells me that Uncle Paddy is famous for having himself and his horse and cart used as film extras in the film

'Room at the top' when part of it was filmed in Keighley and Bradford in the 1950s.

Stephen comes in from school and calls the dog 'Getunder' when it comes out from under the table to meet him. He's asking me if I want to go out with him to meet his friends, but Mammy says I'm not to go out while there's still thunder and lightning. Then she gives me a plate of chips that Auntie Edna has made. Stephen goes out and I sit at the table sharing my chips with 'Getunder' the dog, who's sitting under the table by my legs.

We stay in Keighley for about a week, then we're on our way back to Belfast to tell Daddy all about the flat in the cellar of 87 Devonshire Street that we are going to live in. And about all the jobs advertised in the *Keighley News* newspaper and how he can sign on the dole while he looks for a job.

Back at Kinnaird Street, the dining room is full with all of us and Harriet and Dorothy and Jean from upstairs, listening to Mammy's stories of how things are a lot better in England where no one goes hungry and there's no need to stew the tea leaves or buy stale bread for toast. And in England, everyone toasts the bread on both sides, she says. After lots of cups of tea and smoking smuggled cigarettes, all the grownups have decided that the Devil's Country is definitely the best place to be.

It's soon decided that Mammy, Daddy, Helen, me and Baby Amanda will go over to England with the television and the cat, to Auntie Edna's to sort out the dole and the flat on Devonshire Street. Then when that's all sorted we can send for Raymin if he wants to come, and also Louise and Deirdre who are still with the nuns.

I'm telling my friends up Thorndale Avenue that we're moving to England with the television and the cat. When I look at Bridie Gallagher she wishes me good luck. I'm thinking she doesn't seem too upset that I'm leaving, but then she might not know that she was my girlfriend, and that I had wanted to marry her some day down at St Malachy's, and I'm thinking it's no good telling her now with me going to live in the Devil's Country soon. Helen is calling for me to go in home again. Bridie gives me a backer on her bike down to the house. Now I'm seeing her probably for the last time, riding her bike down the street, and across the Antrim Road and on down Dawson Street, singing 'The night has a thousand eyes'. Now I feel sad.

A few days later Mammy has packed lots of things in cardboard boxes tied up with string, including Tommy the cat, who isn't tied up with string, in a box that has air holes in it. Daddy has checked his watch with the time pips on the radio and we're ready to go. Daddy has the television, Helen has Mandy, Mammy has a suitcase, some bags and the boat tickets, and I have Tommy the cat, a bag of samiches and my old hurling stick that I haven't used since I was in Kircubbin School. Mammy wouldn't let me bring the chariot I made in the backyard. She says Raymin can bring that over when he comes. The cardboard boxes are packed into the boot of a big black taxi and we all squeeze into the back with our bags and the suitcase, to be taken down to the docks.

The boat is packed with people. The only place we can sit together is on the big landing halfway down the wide stairs between the decks. We're sitting beside the cardboard boxes and bags in the corner. Daddy is trying to sit on the suitcase. He won't let me sit on the television. He's telling us to be quiet and saying to Mammy that we must look like a shower of gypsies. Mammy says nothing. She just carries on smoking the cigarettes Top Flat Tommy gave her.

Daddy is looking very uneasy. I'm thinking he's not happy because his clothes are not very smart now, not like when he had a good job at Nutts Corner Airport that suited him and he used to go out looking like a professor, to meet Alice who was a lady. Or maybe he's not happy 'cos he might have found out that before we left Mammy went up the Falls Road to tell Alice's family about her affair with Daddy. I heard her telling Raymin that she left them all fighting and she doesn't care. "They can all go and feck."

There's a woman coming up from the lower deck. When she sees Mandy holding the cat box she says "Hello, little girl."

"Hello, this is my cat Tommy," says Baby Mandy, "and this is my Daddy, and this is my Daddy's telewizion."

The woman smiles at Mandy and then at Daddy. Daddy smiles back, but it's not an easy smile. I can see he feels a bit embarrassed. He's probably remembering his posh Crombie coat with the leather buttons and his dicky bow and matching pale lemon gloves.

It's half past seven in the morning when we're getting off the boat at Heysham docks. We're all grumpy, except Mandy and Tommy the cat who has clean newspapers in his box and had a good night's sleep on the other boxes and coats. Mammy is shouting at me to make sure the cat box is closed properly. She's telling Helen to hold tightly on to Mandy. Daddy is holding tightly on to his precious television as if it's full of money. Now Mammy joins Daddy with his uneasy smiles to the other passengers as we make our way from the boat to the train, where we are going to travel over the mountains that are called Pennines in England, in a steam engine train.

Daddy looks at his watch and then at the big clock on the station. He tells Mammy that the big clock is two minutes fast. Mammy looks at me and sighs quietly.

"I wish he'd look after us as much as he looks after that watch and the feckin television."

On the train, Mammy, Helen, me, Baby Mandy and the cat find seats together in one of the compartments. Daddy is on guard over the television and the boxes outside the parcel cage at the back end of the train. Mammy sends me with cigarettes and matches for him. He doesn't look very happy. He says it's uncomfortable sitting on a chair seat that folds down from the side of the train, and springs back up when you stand catching your clothes, and it's cold and draughty. I'm thinking he's not excited about moving to England, and that he's going to be particular about what jobs are available in Keighley, like he was when we lived in Limerick, where we moved house on a horse and cart. At least this time we haven't to cross the Pennine Mountains on a horse and cart. I bet it'd take about two months on a horse. Clip clop, clip clop. I'm thinking it'd be good fun though.

In Keighley, Mammy leaves the boxes and the television at the left luggage room in the station at the top of the walking out ramp near the exit to the road. We take some small bags of clothes with us, and I'm carrying the box with the cat in it. Helen says it's hard work carrying Mandy. Mammy tells her we can have a rest at Auntie Mary's house.

We turn left out of the station and then right up Cavendish Street, past the Victoria Hotel and the Devonshire pub and turn right onto Skipton Road. We pass a burned down building with just the clock tower left standing. Mammy says it's the old Mechanics' Institute hall that burnt down last year. We carry on to Holker Street to see Auntie Mary, who is down in the kitchen boiling spuds in their jackets for her lodger's dinner, a cigarette in her mouth with bending-down ash. She makes us tea and samiches, and tells Daddy that she's glad we got the cellar flat up Devonshire Street. Then she tells him to go straight away and sign on the dole while he's looking for work. She tells him not to be too particular about the jobs that are available, "'Cos beggars can't be choosers!" Daddy grunts a reply to her. I'm thinking that there's no love lost between the two of them.

Auntie Mary's husband, John, comes down the steps into the kitchen. He says his hellos and sits quietly on his own at the far end of the long table, after getting a piece of meat and a drink of milk for the cat.

Soon we're on our way up to Guard House estate to Auntie Edna's. On the way up Devonshire Street, Mammy goes in the side gate of number 87 and peeps in the flat windows.

"Grand," she says, "that'll be just grand."

At Auntie Edna's, Tommy the cat has to live in one of the bedrooms 'cos 'Getunder' the dog doesn't like him. Me, Daddy, Helen and Mandy wait with Auntie Edna while Mammy goes back into the town to sort out the flat for us. She's back at teatime with the keys. We all have chips for tea with Auntie Edna, who is having a bottle of Guinness that she gets on prescription from the doctor. She says she gets two bottles every week for her illnesses.

The next day, we're moving into the flat. There's a kitchen/living room and a passage to two back bedrooms and bathroom, and an outside toilet in the back garden. Mammy says it's handy having the extra toilet outside, and the side passage with its own gate. She says that we're nice and separate from the rest of the house.

The first job is to put on the electric kettle that plugs in above the small electric cooker. Uncle Paddy gave us the kettle and Auntie Mary gave us extra cups and things to get by with for the time being. Soon we're all having a nice cup of tea and Tommy the cat is out of the cardboard box and exploring his new home, and making sure there's no dog under the table. The table and four chairs and a bed are the only things in the flat.

Mammy sends Daddy and me down to the railway station to collect the television and the boxes. She gives us enough money for a taxi back as there's too many boxes to carry all the way from the station. Auntie Mary has a spare matress and some blankets we can have. She knows a nice young man, a bus conductor called Dennis, who will drop them off to us in the morning, early.

As soon as we're back, Daddy has the television on the table with wires out the window for an aerial, after looking at the aerial on the chimney stack. He has the back of the television off so he can reach inside with his screwdriver to re-tune the coils behind the channel-changing knob to get the BBC TV programmes

We're not in long when there's a knock on the door. It's Johnny Murphy, Auntie Mary's son. Mammy makes him a cup of tea. He's showing me the false tooth at the front of his mouth. He keeps pushing it out with his tongue and then sucking it back in again and laughing. He's telling Mammy that he's getting married soon to a girl called Wendy. He says he's twenty five now and he'll be twenty six next month and it's time he settled down. Then he's telling Mammy that he's getting married in a hurry. Mammy says "Oh is that so?" I'm thinking that he must want to be getting married before he's twenty six.

He's telling her that there's a little old cottage up in Hainsworth Village off the Haworth road. He says that it's really run down and he can buy it for twenty five pounds. He says nobody wants these old run-down cottages these days. Johnny says he can't really afford that kind of money cash, but the man who's selling it says he can buy it on rental purchase. Mammy says that's good 'cos no one wants a mortgage around their neck for twenty years. Johnny says there's a brand new galvanised bathtub in it as well.

After about an hour of talking and joking, Johnny says he has to go down to a pub called The Grapes. He says he's going to see a man about a dog. That's like Top Flat Tommy used to say in Belfast when he was going out smuggling.

Daddy's got the television working. The picture is a bit snowy, but he says it's the best he can do for now. Mammy asks him to move the TV to the end of the table so she can start making some dinner and set the table, when she can remember which box the knives, forks and plates are in. We're having mashed potatoes with fried chopped onions in it and a fried egg on top, and peas. Daddy has a pork chop from the corner shop with his. While we're eating Mammy is making plans with Daddy so that Raymin can come over soon, and Marie, if she wants to. And Louise and Deirdre can come over soon after Raymin if all goes to plan. Mammy's plan that is. Daddy doesn't plan a lot. He just nods his head in agreement when Mammy looks at him waiting for an answer. After dinner, I'm showing the cat the back garden of his new home again so he knows there's no dog around to be frightened of.

*

In the morning there's a loud banging on the side gate. Mammy jumps out of bed.

"Who the feck is that at seven in the morning?"

I go out to the side gate with her. It's a young man in a bus conductor's uniform and there's a noisy single decker bus parked in the middle of the road.

"Morning,' he says, 'I'm Dennis. I have a delivery for Josie." He jumps onto the bus and pulls out a double matress from the aisle between the seats that have passengers on them, and puts it in the passage. Then he picks up a bundle of blankets and hands it to me. One of the passengers shouts "Come on Dennis, I'll be late for work." Dennis jumps on the bus and presses the bell twice. And with a big grin on his face he waves us goodbye. Mammy looks at me. "Well," she says, "I've seen it all now."

Uncle Paddy calls regularly with all sorts of things for the flat. He says that people give him stuff they no longer want and he asks Mammy what kind of things she needs so he can keep a look out for them. I tell him I need a set of big pram wheels to make a bogie cart.

We've been living here about a month. Daddy hasn't got a job yet and I'm still waiting for the pram wheels. There's been no trouble at home and he's getting the dole money every week. Uncle Paddy has been bringing a steady flow of all kinds of furniture for us, and between him and the mad bus conductor Dennis we now have a bed in the back bedroom and a fold-out bed in the dining kitchen and just about everything we need to get by. Marie moves over from Belfast in early August and gets a waitress job straight away at the Victoria Hotel.

The 22nd of August comes and goes without a mention of my thirteenth birthday. At the beginning of September me and Helen will be starting school at St Anne's, across the road from Auntie Mary's. Raymin is still in Belfast and Louise and Deirdre are still with the nuns. Mammy has bought me some black jeans for school. I still have some short trousers but Mammy says at thirteen I'm too old now to wear them. My school blazer with the rip in it must still be in Belfast. That's the last time I saw it. I must have forgotten to pack it. I'm telling Mammy that I'll just wear my three-quarter length overcoat for school, but she says I need a short jacket. Johnny Murphy brings me one of his old jackets. It's miles too big for me. I'm telling Mammy I don't want it, but she insists it'll be alright when she turns up the bottom of it and the sleeves as well. The bottom of the coat is turned up four inches, and so are the sleeves. The shoulders are still huge on me and now the pockets are just one inch deep. The coat looks ridiculous, with wide shoulders and thin pockets and the bottom button nearly on the fold of the turn up. All my complaining does nothing to change her mind. She just says "For God's sake, will you hould your whist, this is the latest Italian fashion."

On the first day walking to school with Helen I make sure my hands are in my trouser pockets with the sleeves covering my one-inch pockets. In the classroom the teacher takes my name and address and registers me for free school dinners. I'm in class Two Trans. I think it means transition two. The classroom overlooks the playground and the side of St Anne's Church. I'm thinking Two Trans is a class where you're put to assess you to see which other class you should be in.

Soon I forget about my wide coat with one-inch pockets when I get to know the two John O'Briens (cousins) in my class, and Dorothy Peterick and her friend Angela. I can see I'm going to like my new friends here. The jacket that will be in fashion some day doesn't really matter much now. On the second day at school we have to go upstairs to Mr Crowther's class for an English lesson. The teacher is telling one of the boys, Colin Richardson, the smallest boy in the class, to behave himself. Richardson stands up and throws all his books at the teacher, who puts his hands up to protect his head. I'm waiting for the teacher to grab him, threaten him, wallop hell out of him with a stick, take him to the headmaster, who will wallop him again in front of the whole school in the assembly hall and threaten him with being expelled. But it doesn't happen anything like that. The teacher picks up all the books off the floor and tells Richardson to sit down and be quiet. I've never seen anything like that before in the schools I've been to.

After a few weeks at the school, the sports teacher Mr Knockton, who also teaches maths and science, picks me for the second year football team. Once a week he takes us on a coach out to Utley Village playing fields on the Skipton road for football practice. I've borrowed some football boots and kit and I've got my overcoat on 'cos Mammy has finally decided that it's not compulsory for me to wear the horrible wide fashionable jacket anymore. After football, in the changing room, Mr Knockton calls me to one side. He asks me if I have my overcoat with me. Now I'm thinking, I hope there's no rules about wearing my overcoat to school.

"Yes," I tell him, "I have." I'm hoping I won't have to wear the short jacket again.

"Listen," he says, "I won't beat about the bush, Jimmy Clark has shit himself and I would like to know if he can borrow your overcoat to go home, because he certainly can't go home in his messed trousers."

"Yes sir, he can."

Mr Knockton says thanks. Now I'm feeling proud 'cos I've helped someone by lending him my coat, and the teacher treated me like a grownup, by saying shit in front of me 'cos he knew I could handle it, and he could rely on me not to go around telling the other boys what had happened with Jimmy Clark. I'm only telling you 'cos I know you won't talk about it.

The bus is late getting back to the school. Helen is out at Auntie Mary's with Mandy when I get home.

Mammy thinks it's very funny when I tell her where my coat is and about the teacher saying shit. I also tell her about Colin Richardson throwing books at the teacher the other week. She doesn't think that is funny at all. She says he wants a good clatter. Later when Daddy comes in smelling of the drink, he says that it's disgraceful for the teacher to say shit. Mammy still thinks it's very funny, so do I.

"It would have been a good idea for the English teacher to have beaten the shite out of the little brat who threw the books at him the other week," he says.

Mammy tells me to get off to the bedroom while she gets Daddy his dinner and tells him about Raymin coming over from Belfast. From the bedroom I can hear Mammy calling Daddy 'Bren' and 'love'. She's worried, I can tell by the tone of her voice. He says something to her, but I can't make out what he says. Then it goes quiet for a long time.

Next day at school Mr Knockton brings my coat to me. He says thanks again, and tells me that Jimmy Clark is at home poorly. I think he means he's sick. When I get home, Helen, Mandy and Daddy are in the kitchen. Mammy's dishing out the dinner. Daddy smells of the drink again. Mammy says Raymin is over from Belfast. Daddy says he saw him in the Cavendish pub with Johnny Murphy today and that Johnny had taken Raymin to the pub to find him a job. Daddy's looking at his watch and saying that Raymin should have been here by now with the pubs closing at three o'clock. Mammy says that Johnny has probably taken him to one of them clubs that stay open after the pubs close. Now Daddy's shouting about the jobs down at the dole office. He's saying that there's only labouring jobs at the building sites and the woollen mills and he's not going to go labouring on building sites with common workmen and louts, or into the mills where, if it's anything like they are in the pubs, they all say things like 'have you owt for nowt' or 'I knew him when he had nowt'.

"They can't even pronounce their words right," he says.

"For Christ's sake, will you sit down and eat your dinner," Mammy shouts at him, then she carries on smoking her cigarette.

He goes quiet for a while, eating his dinner, so does Mammy, smoking more cigarettes. After he's finished the dinner, he's ready to start complaining again. He's taking a deep breath, but Mammy beats him to it.

"It's right what Mary Murphy says, beggars can't be choosers. It's time you stopped being particular and took any old job for now, at least 'til a better one comes along."

He's up from his seat, leaning over the table, resting on his knuckles, shouting at Mammy.

"Feck that Mary Murphy! What the feck does she know about anything? I've got more brains up here in my head than all of them Murphys put together!"

Mammy ignores him. She's sat on the chair staring into the gas fire with her elbows on her knees, and her chin resting on her hands, smoking. She looks totally fed up. She tells me, Helen and Mandy to go back into the bedrooms out of the way. Then she looks at Daddy.

"Sit down for Gods sake, before you damage your dicky heart, and if you've got all those brains you keep telling us about, it's time you started using them! Go on you lot," she says, turning to us, "get off into the bedroom."

I'm in the bedroom a few minutes. There's a loud crash from the kitchen. Helen picks up Mandy while I jump off the bed, over the hurley stick that's leaning against the wall. I run into the kitchen. There's all wet on the wall of the fireplace. Mammy is bending down to the floor picking up pieces of broken cup. Daddy is leaning his hand on the far wall, with his other hand wiping sweat off his forehead. He's staring out the back window. Mammy looks at me and says it's all right, go back into the bedroom.

I leave the kitchen door open a bit so I can hear if he starts throwing things again. Helen is playing with Mandy, telling her not to be frightened, that everything will be OK. It's gone quiet again in the kitchen. I'm lying on the bed looking up at the pink ceiling, listening in case he starts again. I'm wondering who would want to paint a ceiling pink. I'm sure all the ones I've seen are white, or supposed to be white.

There's a knock at the back door. I look out the bedroom window and see Raymin with a small suitcase. I'm looking at him thinking, I knew it, I knew he wouldn't bring the bogey cart! Mammy lets him in and tells him to sit down and she'll make him a cup of tea. Me and Helen and Mandy come out to see them. It's obvious to him that there's been a row. The tea is still on the wall and the small bits of cup are crunching under Mammy's feet as she walks between the kettle, the sink and the table. Daddy's asking Raymin where he's been all the afternoon. Raymin is slurring his words. He says that after the Cavendish closed at three o'clock he went to Auntie Mary's. She gave him some dinner and then Uncle John took him out again to one of the working men's clubs, where Johnny was. When he got there Uncle John said he was going to give Raymin some advice. Daddy tells Raymin that he's too young to be going to the pubs and the clubs.

"Look at you," he says, "You're bloody drunk, slurring your words. You should have been out looking for a job."

"I was," says Raymin. "I'm starting work in the morning, fixing roofs with a friend of Johnny's called Dennis Little." Daddy goes quiet now.

"So what advice did your Uncle John give you?" asks Mammy.

"He says that I'll do well in England, as long as I stay out of the pubs."

"And he took you to the pub to tell you that?"

"Yes," says Raymin.

"What did he do then?" asks Mammy.

"He bought me a drink," says Raymin, "then another."

"Did he give you anymore advice," asks Mammy.

"No," says Raymin.

"Well that's a good one," she says, "he takes you to the pub to advise you to stay out of it, and buys you the drink as well. Mind you, he did get you a job."

Raymin lights a cigarette and looks at Mammy.

"Johnny Murphy gave me some advice too."

"What was that?" asks Mammy.

"Johnny says always listen to the great philosophers who are always right."

"And what do they say?" asks Mammy.

Raymin takes a deep breath. "Confusius says: 'Man who goes to bed at night with itchy bum, wake up in morning with smelly finger.'"

Mammy bursts out laughing, Raymin is nearly falling off his chair. Daddy says it's not funny. Mammy says she thinks that Johnny Murphy's awful, and Helen says 'Huh!' Daddy starts fiddling with the kettle socket on the wall above the cooker. He says it's loose. Raymin goes to bed, still grinning, to sleep off his drink, and Mammy and Helen are talking about Harriet and Dorothy and Top Flat Tommy and Jean back in Belfast.

I'm home from school, Raymin is home from his first day's work, and Marie is sat at the dining table talking to Mammy. Raymin has had a bath and he's nice and clean now, except for the black marks around his eyes from the dust and soot of his new job on a roof. Marie, Helen and Mandy have been laughing at the rings around his eyes. Daddy says he looked like a coalman when he came in and he hopes he is getting well paid. Raymin says it should be worth it, that Dennis Little promised him five pounds a week. Mammy makes him wash around his eyes before he sits down to his dinner of bacon and cabbage and spuds in their jackets.

After dinner Raymin is sitting on the bed talking to me while he's still trying to clean the black lines around his eyes with Mammy's Ponds Cold Cream. We're talking about Daddy and his drinking and him starting his trouble again, and how he can't have a drink without wanting to start on about things that happened a long time before. And how he starts shouting at Mammy, saying that he's not Mandy's father, when he can't think of anything else to shout about.

Suddenly, there's a loud scream from the kitchen. Raymin says "What the feck!" then we hear loud bangs and thuds like furniture falling over. Raymin is on his way to the kitchen, saying the bastard is at it again, and I'm right behind him. I've grabbed my hurley stick. It's time we all stood up for Mammy and ourselves. We're just in time to see Daddy standing by the cooker with his hand on the electric socket above it and Marie taking a flying dive at him, knocking him away from the bare electric wires and making him fall to the floor. Raymin is stood over him.

"Go on, kill the bastard!" I tell Raymin. I push past Raymin and stand over Daddy. Helen is standing in the far corner holding Mandy. There's lots of shouting going on in the room but I'm too focused on stopping the liten bastard from getting up again that I don't hear what they're all saying. The hurley stick is in my hands. I'm ready for him.

"Stop!" shouts Marie. "He's been electrocuted!"

He's lying on the floor. His face is all red and beading with sweat. Marie is opening his collar wide and listening to hear if he's still breathing. Mammy shouts at Raymin to run out to the phone box and call an ambulance. I run back to the bedroom and hide the hurley stick under the bed, then I go back to the kitchen doorway. Marie is helping Daddy up off the floor onto a chair. Mammy is telling Marie it's a good job she was quick thinking when she ran in and pushed him away from the wire in the kettle socket on the wall. When the ambulance men come, they take Daddy out to the ambulance. They check his pulse and take his blood pressure, but he won't go to the hospital with them. We leave him in the ambulance and go back into the kitchen. Mammy says that he had been fixing the wiring in the socket above the cooker when he started gasping and shaking. She panicked and screamed, and that was when Marie jumped up and knocked over one of the chairs as she ran over to push him away from the socket. Marie says that she realised straight away what was happening and knew that she had to push him as quickly and as hard as she could to get him away from the wires.

"Jesus Christ, I thought he was a goner," says Mammy. Then she looks at me. "With any luck, he won't have noticed that while we were trying to save him, you were wanting to kill him."

Now Mammy has her hand over her mouth trying to smother a laugh, a nervous laugh.

"Jesus Christ, I need a cigarette," she says.

Daddy comes back in from the ambulance. Mammy gives him a cigarette.

"I'll put a pan of water on the cooker," she says. "I need a good strong cup of tea."

Daddy says he told the ambulance men that it must have been steam from the kettle that wet the wall socket and made it live, that must have been the problem.

"I thought I was a goner too, and in those few seconds I saw my life flash by in front of me. I'm sure I saw you with a hurley stick," he says, looking at me.

"Yes," I tell him, "I got the stick to push you away from the socket."

"Good thinking," he says.

"You've had an awful shock you know, sit down now and I'll make you a nice cup of tea," Mammy tells him. Within half an hour, he's back at the socket trying to find out what the real problem was. He says he'd taken the fuse out of the main fusebox to make the socket safe, but the black wire was still live, so that means the socket is wired wrong, and that's why he got the almighty shock.

"Thank God Marie pushed me away from the socket", he says. "She probably saved my life."

"Yes she probably did," says Mammy, agreeing with him and looking over at me when she said it. Now all the others are looking at me.

"Now that you're alright," I say to Daddy, "I'll go back to the bedroom and do my homework."

"Yes," says "Mammy, "you get back to the bedroom, out of the way."

*

We're well into November now. Me and Helen are settled in at St Anne's school. Raymin is still working for Dennis Little. Marie is still working as a waitress at the Victoria Hotel near the train station. Mammy looks after the house and does the washing in the bath, and Daddy has a radio that he's fixing, when he's not fixing the television or the aerial.

It's Friday evening, 22nd November, 1963. We're watching Emergency Ward 10 on the TV. There's a newsflash in the middle of the programme. President Kennedy has been shot in Dallas. Mammy is crying. She tells me to sit down and hould my whisht while everyone listens to the news.

The news is being extended while they wait for more bulletins from America. Marie, Helen, me and Mandy are sitting around the telly with Mammy and Daddy. I can feel sadness in the house. Mammy is crying, saying what a lovely man, what a shame. Now I feel sad. It feels like we knew him personally. He's been on the news nearly every day for the last two months, running his campaigns for freedom and democracy and fighting against crime and the Mob. It's a sad, odd feeling. There's only Mandy and the cat acting normal, both sleeping.

The news is still on when Raymin comes in, half drunk, with a black face and clean lips from drinking beer.

"I don't know who would want to kill such a lovely man," says Mammy.

"It'll be the Russians, because of the missile crisis, or Mr Hoover, the CIA man who thinks he runs America," Daddy says.

"It'll be Johnny Murphy, 'cos he wasn't in the pub this afternoon," pipes up Raymin.

Mammy says that's not a very nice thing to say. Raymin says he's sorry, he was only joking.

"You're sounding like the louts you go drinking with," Daddy says.

Mammy gives Raymin his dinner and tells him to take it into the bedroom to eat it and then have a bath. When Raymin's gone out of the kitchen, Daddy turns to Mammy and says it's not right for him to be going drinking he's only sixteen. He says he doesn't know where Raymin gets it from. Later when the news programme stops for a while, Mammy tells Daddy that Harriet wants to come over from Belfast for a week's holiday on her own to see what things are like for jobs over here. I'm thinking it's Raymin who Harriet wants to see. She says that Harriet is leaving her little daughter Elsie with her friend Dorothy and her little one Shirley. Daddy grunts half an agreement. Mammy says, that's fine, I'll write back and tell her it's OK. Then it's back to the news on the television for the rest of the evening. A man called Johnson has taken over the President's job and Mammy says God help that poor Jacqueline, President Kennedy's wife.

*

A few weeks later, Harriet is here. She goes looking for a job during the day and out walking late in the evenings with Raymin, who hasn't been going to the pub much since she came over.

Daddy is back from the pub. He comes in from the outside toilet and slams the door. Mammy asks him what's wrong. He says 'nothing!' Two minutes later Raymin and Harriet walk in. Daddy immediately dives at Raymin, giving him a punch in the eye, shouting 'I saw you out there in the passage. I saw what you were doing!' Raymin is holding his eye, Harriet is holding Raymin and Mammy is holding Daddy by the collar, pulling him away. Daddy's shouting, 'I saw what you were doing out there'. I'm thinking that he must have caught Raymin kissing Harriet. Now the house is in commotion again. Mammy is pulling Daddy away from Raymin. Harriet is pulling Raymin away from Daddy's grip. Daddy is calling Raymin a dirty little bastard. Mammy is calling Daddy a liten big bastard for hitting Raymin. Marie is in the middle telling everyone to calm down and Tommy the cat has run into the bedroom out of the way. Helen is in the corner with Mandy, both of them crying. I'm standing, watching, wishing I'd used the hurley stick last time, even if he was being electrocuted. The arguing goes on 'til two in the morning. Every time he goes quiet and we think the shouting is all over, he jumps up and starts shouting and finger pointing again. I don't go to school the next day, neither does Helen. At dinner time, Daddy is washed and shaved and out again. Now Mammy's worried that there's going to be more trouble when he comes home. Raymin hasn't gone to work. He says he was awake most of the night with a thumping headache. Marie is at the Victoria hotel doing her waitress job.

Raymin is sitting at the table with Harriet, Helen and Mandy. Mammy is sitting by the gas fire getting red marks down the front of her legs from the heat. Raymin says there was no need for the wallop he got last night. He says him and Harriet were only kissing and there's nothing wrong with that. Mammy says she should get Johnny Murphy to give Daddy such a clatter for being such a bully. Raymin says that one of these days he'll give him such a clatter himself, that he won't know what's hit him.

"We should have left the liten bastard stuck to the socket on the wall when he was being electrocuted!" Mammy says.

Now we all start laughing at what Mammy has just said.

"You don't really mean that Josie, do you?" says Harriet. Mammy takes a long pull on her cigarette and looks into the distance with the smoke coming out of her mouth.

"I feckin do!"

I'm telling Raymin that I'll help him give Daddy a clatter if he wants, but he's not listening to me. Harriet is saying something quietly into his ear on the black-eye side of his head.

Daddy's been out a long time drinking. It's after eleven when he comes in. Helen and Mandy are in the back bedroom and I'm in the front bedroom, near the kitchen. I get out of bed, into my black school jeans and go into the kitchen. It's obvious he's been drinking a lot. At first he's quiet, sitting in Mammy's chair by the fire. Mammy is making him tea and calling him Bren again and trying to please him. He looks at Raymin and Harriet sat at the table. Then he starts saying that Raymin deserved the wallop he got last night. Mammy is trying to calm him down. Marie comes in after she's been working late at the Vic. She sits at the table with Raymin and Harriet. Now he's shouting at Marie for leaving home in Belfast and getting a flat with her friend Una, against his wishes. When Marie ignores him, he starts on Mammy. He's pointing his finger at her and towards the back bedroom where Helen and Mandy sleep. His eyes are glassy, his forehead is wet with sweat, and spit flies from his mouth as he shouts.

"That child isn't mine! I'm not that child's father! You're nothing but an effin hoor!"

Now he's out of breath from shouting. Helen comes out of the bedroom to the kitchen door. Mammy tells her to go back to bed. Mammy's telling him to calm down and watch his dicky heart. He's leaning on the table, resting on his knuckles, catching his breath, looking across at Raymin. Raymin is leaning back, ready for the flying fist. I'm getting nearer, ready to grab him from behind if he takes another swing at Raymin. The shouting starts again. He's bringing up the time in

Belfast again, when Raymin wouldn't tell him where Mammy was living, and sent him on the wild goose chase up the Falls Road. Now he's banging on the table again. Teapot, cups, everything's rattling on the table. Helen and Mandy come in from the bedroom. Mammy tells Helen to take Mandy back into bed. She tells me to go to my bedroom too. I don't want to go, but she says I have to. She pushes me out of the kitchen into the hall. I close the door, but not fully, so I can still see and hear what's going on. Harriet, Raymin, Marie and Mammy are having another cup of tea, ready for a long night. Daddy opens the back door and goes out to the outside toilet. Harriet closes the door behind him and says to Raymin that she's glad to be going back to Belfast soon.

"Belfast," she says, "where even with the odd troubles and bombs going off, it's safer than being here with that mad bastard."

Mammy says it's that mad bastard that we should have left in Belfast in the first place. They stop talking when the back door opens and the mad bastard comes back in. Mammy asks him if she makes a cup of tea, will he sit down and drink it. He sits down and says nothing. Mammy is making tea again for everyone. She gives him another cup of tea. He's up on his feet again. The cup hits the wall above the gas fire, smashing into little pieces. I step into the kitchen again from the hall. Mammy moves back over by the window, her hands raised ready to protect herself if he attacks her. He's turned around leaning on the table shouting. Raymin, Harriet and Marie lean back, away from his reach. He's pointing his left hand to the door where I'm standing ready to stop him if he attacks anyone. He's shouting at them.

"I am not that child's father!" His hand is back leaning on the table. There's a short silence.

"I can't be her father," he says. Suddenly they're all looking over at me. I didn't notice little Mandy, lovely little blond-haired Mandy standing beside me, half asleep, wiping her eyes. She walks over to Daddy, pulls on his trouser leg to get his attention. He looks down under his arm to see her. She looks up at him.

"It's all wite, you don't have to shout, you can be my daddy if you want."

Now there's a long silence, I can hear the bits of broken cup crunching under Daddy's shoes as he stands up straight, swaying in front of the table. I move forward and pick up Mandy and check her feet for bits of broken cup, as I take her to the back bedroom and put her into the bed beside Helen and kiss her good night. Mammy sits down in the chair by the fire. Her head is in her hands, she's sobbing. "My God what have I done to deserve all this, all I want is a peaceful life. Jesus Christ, I can't carry on with this much longer."

Harriet stands up.

"Brendan O'Donoghue, you're a disgrace. I'm going home first thing in the morning, and if Josie has any sense, she'll come back with me." Then she goes off to bed in the back room where Helen and Mandy sleep. Next, Marie follows Harriet. Me and Raymin go to bed. I can hear Mammy pulling out the bed settee in the kitchen. Daddy will be sleeping on it. Mammy will probably sleep in the chair by the fire, like she usually does when he's being a liten bastard.

*

In the morning I'm late for school and Raymin is late for work. Mammy says I don't have to go to school, after being up late last night, but I want to go to school. I like the school, and especially my friends, John O'Brien, John O'Brien, and Dorothy Peterick who we call Dot for short. I can't find a clean shirt or socks, so in the end I'm looking through the clothes to find the cleanest dirty shirt and the cleanest pair of dirty socks. I run down the hill in the rain to the school. I get there just in time for the morning break and the free bottle of milk that all the kids get every morning. I'm sitting at a double desk that I share with a girl called Helen. The two John O'Briens are making fun of me, saying that Helen is my girlfriend. I'm thinking they're being funny, but she doesn't. During the lessons, Helen is saying there's a funny smell, like smelly socks, and when she says it again I'm thinking it must be my socks, the cleanest dirty ones. Now I'm feeling really embarrassed. I wait a few minutes before asking the teacher if I can leave the room to go to the toilet. When I go into the toilet cubicle, I take my shoes and socks off. My socks do stink! I didn't notice this morning when I was rushing around. I flush the toilet to make sure the water is clean. I wash my socks in the cold water as best I can with no soap. I flush the water clean a couple of times, then I wring out the socks as tight as I can. They smell a lot better now, so I put them back on after washing my feet as well, in the bowl, and drying them with toilet paper and the half wet socks. The teacher says I've been a long time. "Yes miss," I tell her, "I got belly ache." Later I'm thinking that it's funny how the day seems longer when your feet are cold and damp.

After school when I get home, Mammy and Mandy are there. Mammy says that Marie has gone back to Belfast with Harriet because she can't put up with Daddy anymore and Raymin is at work and Daddy is out in the pubs again. She says that when Helen comes in from school, we're all going down to Auntie Mary's, out of the way of Daddy. I'm looking everywhere for some clean dry socks, but I can't find any. All the dirty washing is piled up in the bedroom and hasn't been washed, Mammy says, because of the upsets of the last three days with 'him' starting his trouble again. I take off my damp socks and wash them in the kitchen sink and put them on top of the gas fire to dry. Mammy says there's no tea ready today. She says we'll get a bite to eat at Auntie Mary's where there's always something cooking, and plenty to eat. When Helen comes in, Mammy is telling her to hurry so we can get out of the house before Daddy comes back. I can see she's worried and being bad with the nerves. Mammy won't let me bring Tommy the cat. She says the cat will be alright for a few days. I'm asking her if we should leave a note for Daddy.

"What for?" she says, "To tell him we're all frightened and fed up with him? You can leave a note if you want," she says, "I just want to get out of here, come on."

I do leave him a note. 'Dear Daddy, don't forget to feed Tommy the cat, from your son Brian.' I grab my socks, still damp, and put them on. We don't go straight down Devonshire Street in case we meet him coming up. We go across the side streets and on to Mornington Street that takes us down by the school across the Skipton Road to Auntie Mary's.

Down in the cellar kitchen Auntie Mary is dishing out big plates of dinner to her lodgers and Uncle John. Mammy is telling them about the trouble at home for the last couple of days and nights. I'm telling Uncle John about my wet socks and having to leave the cat. Auntie Mary tells us to sit down at the long table and she dishes out some dinner, loads of spuds boiled in their skins, splitting open, and lots of boiled hairy bacon, and cabbage and turnips too. After dinner, me, Helen and Mandy move up stairs to the sitting room to watch the television and listen to the latest news on the Kennedy shooting, and make more room in the kitchen. Mammy stays in the kitchen talking to Auntie Mary. Uncle John comes into the TV room and gives me a pair of nice clean warm socks. He says they belong to his son Danny, but it'll be alright for me to have them. When I take off my damp socks my feet are all white and soggy with being wet all day. I never knew warm dry socks could feel so good. But being dry and warm doesn't make me feel happy for long. It makes me wonder if Tommy the cat is warm and dry, and has he been fed yet. Later Mammy and Auntie Mary come up to the television room. Mammy says we'll be stopping a few days, to give Daddy time to cool down. Auntie Mary is telling Mammy she shouldn't put up with that bastard 'Donoghue'. Then she says to Mammy, "I've been with John Murphy for twenty-five years and that man has never as much as lifted a finger against me. We've had our differences and we've had our rows, but he's never raised a hand to me, or my children, and if any man raised a hand to me, like that Donoghue did to you, I'd split him wide open with the poker." Uncle John looks at me and smiles.

Next day at school, my feet are clean and my socks are dry and I'm happy being with John and John and Dot. They're asking me if I want to meet them on Saturday when they're getting a bus to Skipton for a day out. I'm telling them I'll have to ask at home for the bus fare. I'm thinking how I like my friends here and I wish Daddy would stop his drinking and wanting to fight us all every time he gets drunk, and why can't he just get drunk and be happy like most people do, instead of always bringing things up that have happened a long time ago. And now I'm thinking he better not have started shouting at Tommy the cat, just 'cos there was no one else there to shout at last night. After school when I go over to Auntie Mary's house, there's a woman there from the Council's Children's Department.

Mammy says she's sending me and Helen to a foster home in Shipley, near Bradford. She says it's just for a while 'til things get sorted out again and Daddy stops drinking. I didn't even get the chance to find out if she would have let me go to Skipton on Saturday with my friends from school. Mammy gives me a clean shirt and another clean pair of socks from Danny Murphy and some clothes she got from Devonshire Street when Daddy was out. The clothes are in a brown paper shop bag. She says it's only for a while. She says don't worry, everything will be alright, please God. She says she'll write to me. I don't say anything. I can't. I'm trying to swallow the lump in my throat. Now I'm thinking about my thinking, and it makes me think, what's the point in thinking?

# Chapter 19

## Dumped, in a foster home

The woman from the West Riding County Council's Children's Department takes me and Helen to stay with a Mrs Cowgill in a place called Shipley. Mrs Cowgill has a husband and two sons. One is four years old called Tom, and the other is about fifteen and he's called Stephen, her husband is called Mr Cowgill. They live in a nice council house on Greenfield Avenue. The next day is a Friday. I have to go to the Children's Department office in Shipley town centre to see a Mr Mitchell. Mr Mitchell tells me that Miss Green, his boss, has told him to get me fixed up with a school blazer and some grey trousers for when I go to a new school at Cottingley Manor between Shipley and Bingley. He also gets me a bus pass to get to the school. For some reason they say Helen doesn't have to go to school.

On Monday morning I set off to the school with my new blazer and trousers and Danny Murphy's shirt and socks. The blazer and trousers fit me fine, but Danny is a lot bigger than me so the shirt is miles too big, with the baggy collar leaving a big gap that the cold wind blows around in, and the cuffs sticking out of the blazer sleeves and over my wrists down to my knuckles. I'm walking along Crag Road on my way to the main Leeds road where I've been told to get the Bingley bus for

Cottingley Manor School. On the way I'm looking at the steam engines down in the valley on my left, pulling the carriages into Shipley railway station. It's reminding me of Keighley station and I'm wondering how Mammy is keeping, and Baby Mandy, and then looking at my big shirt with the sticking out cuffs I'm wondering how long it will be 'til they are in fashion. I get off the bus with all the other kids at the school. It's a cold foggy morning and as we wait in the playground at the front of the school, there's some big boys walking around smoking. They're hiding the cigarettes behind their backs, but they're blowing out the smoke not caring who sees it, 'cos you can't tell the difference between the smoke and the normal breath turning to steam in the cold of the morning. When they see me they come over and one of them asks me what I'm looking at. I'm not sure what to say, so I say nothing. He leans over me and starts headbutting me on the side of my head. I lean away from him as it starts to hurt. Just then the bell rings and the other kids start going in to the assembly hall. The bully leaves me alone and walks off with his friends. They look back at me and start laughing.

After assembly, I report to the headmaster's office where he was expecting me. He says Mr Mitchell rang him last Friday. He's asking me questions about which schools I've been to and what sums I've been doing and things like that. I tell him about my good exam results in Belfast. I take the folded up piece of paper from my pocket, now coming apart at the folds, and show him the results. After reading it he folds it up again and hands it back to me, asking me if I keep it with me all the time, being as how it looks so raggy, he says. Then before I can answer him, he tells me which class to go to and he says he hopes I settle in well at the school. On my way to the classroom I'm thinking to myself that I'm not too bothered about settling in. I'm hoping I won't be here long enough to settle in. I want to be getting back home to Keighley soon and my friends at St Anne's, who will be wondering where I am.

At dinner time in the playground the headbutting bully is coming over to me. I'm thinking I'm going to have to fight this time, but he says don't worry about this morning, we always do that to a new boy. As he walks away, I'm thinking maybe I should just punch him on the nose anyway. But I don't, even though I really want to.

*

I'm only at the school a few weeks when it's Christmas holiday time. Mrs Cowling is decorating her house with streamers and putting up a Christmas tree and cards she got from her friends. She must have a lot of friends. I've made friends with a boy called Martin who lives a few houses further up the avenue. We are going carol singing. We go down outside the pub on Valley Road. We're stood in the doorway singing carols, but the juke box inside is playing non-stop Beatles records. Nobody is listening to us. Then there's a gap in the music. I open the door and I start singing in Latin, 'Oh come all ye faithful' (*Adeste fidelis laete triumphantes*). That'll make them listen, I'm thinking. The people at the bar stop talking. Everything is quiet, except for my singing. They're all looking at me. I'm feeling myself going red with embarrassment, but I carry on. My shaky voice is getting stronger. I sing it right through to the end. Martin walks around collecting money. The landlord comes over and gives me a shilling. Out loud he says "That was really very good," then quietly he says to me, "Now will you piss off and annoy the customers down at the other pub across the road." That night we made more than a pound each, annoying pub customers.

For Christmas, the woman from the Children's Department has made a special visit to give me a pound Christmas present from the council and tell me to sit up straight on the armchair when I'm watching television. On Christmas day I get some chocolates and a selection of sweets in a net stocking from Mrs Cowgill and her family, a lump on my head from falling on an ice slide on the road, and nothing from Mammy and Daddy. When the Christmas holidays are over I'm back at Cottingley School again, watching the big boys smoking and only occasionally getting headbutted. A week later I'm saying my prayers at night (something I don't do every night anymore) thanking God that tomorrow when Mrs Cowgill is moving to live in Birmingham, me and Helen will be going back home to Keighley and I won't have to go to Cottingley Manor School anymore.

It's been fine staying with Mrs Cowgill, but I'll be glad to get back home to see my friends. The council woman tells me that Mammy and Daddy have a rented house in Thrush Street near Victoria Park down off Lawkholme Lane. I'm asking her if Tommy the cat is there or if he is lodging at Auntie Mary's house. She says that Mr Mitchell from her office hasn't mentioned anything about the cat in her notes.

Mammy, Daddy and Mandy are in the house when we get there. I ask where Raymin is and Mammy tells me he's back in Belfast. Mammy then asks the council woman if she wants a cup of tea.

"No thanks, I've got to get back to the office in Shipley."

Mammy asks me if I want a cup of tea and I ask her where the cat is.

"He's in his box in the outside toilet," she says. The council woman drives off down the road and I go around the corner of the house to the outside toilet to see Tommy. Tommy is happy to see me. He's purring loud, sticking his nails in and out of the front of my shirt when I pick him up. I take him into the house in my arms. Mammy says there's a cup of tea and a sandwich there for me and she says the cat has to sleep out in the box at night. I'm giving tommy some of the boiled bacon from my sandwich. He loves the bacon, but the mustard on it makes him sneeze.

The house is an end back to back. At the top there's an open attic bedroom. Below that there's two bedrooms and below that is the living room that leads to what

Mammy calls the cellar head kitchen. That means that at the top of the cellar steps there's just enough room for a big white sink with a cold water tap above and a gas cooker beside it. Mammy says I can sleep on the mattress in the corner of the attic. I ask her if Tommy can sleep there too. Daddy looks at me and says no. Helen and Mandy can sleep in the other corner.

Mammy asks me to go to the shops for her. She sends me up Lawkholme Lane to the butcher's shop just outside the railway station to get a pork chop for Daddy's dinner. Then on the way back I've to get a bottle of Domestos bleach from the corner shop on Parson Street. When I get back home I'm in trouble. Nobody told me not to put the bleach in the same bag as the pork chop. Now there's a pork chop on the table that smells of bleach. I didn't know the bleach bottle was leaking at the top. I don't suppose it helped when I ran home, swinging the bag around in circles over my head. Daddy is swearing, he's calling me stupid. Mammy is telling him to calm down. She's at the sink trying to wash the bleach off the chop. It's no good, no matter how much she washes it Daddy says he can still smell the bleach. Mammy says it doesn't smell anymore, so does Helen, but Daddy says "It's bollixed, no good, not even fit for the cat." Mammy says she'll cook it anyway and then she'll see if it's OK. When it's cooked, Mammy cuts a bit off and says it tastes alright. Daddy tastes a bit and says no, it still has a smell of bleach on it. Throw it in the effin bin he says. Mammy hands me the chop, telling me to throw it in the bin, and sends me back up to the butchers to get another chop, to keep the peace. When I get back me and Tommy share the bleachy chop. It tastes good.

*

I'm glad to be back at school with my friends and my newish blazer from Cottingley Manor School, that doesn't look like it's miles too big for me, and the shoes that Mammy got me from a catalogue. But on the first day back, at playtime, there's an older girl from another class telling everyone that I've been in a children's home for the last month or two. I'm telling her that I've been staying with my Auntie, but that doesn't shut her up. Even when I threaten to have her done for 'definition of character' she won't shurrup. Only when Angela, one of the girls in my class, threatens to give her a good wallop does she finally stop. Dorothy Peterick tells me if I ignore Loudmouth, she'll go away. My friends probably know that I've been in a foster home, but they never mention it. At home on the Saturday morning Daddy sends me to the scrapyard on Lawkholme Lane to buy some old TV aerials so he can make a 'new' one to pick up the new BBC2 station. He says when he gets a job he'll be able to buy a proper one. He makes an aerial by joining bits together and sticking it out of the little window at the top of the house, in the gable end of the attic. When it's all working and the television is watchable, we can watch a film called 'Androclese and

The Lion.' We all think it's great fun when Androclese is thrown into the arena with a lion who doesn't want to eat him. The lion remembers when Androclese once pulled a thorn from one of his paws. So now instead of being eaten, Androclese starts dancing with the lion all around the arena. The crowds of people are cheering for both of them.

We're all watching the television and laughing out loud, including Daddy. I'm thinking that it seems a long time since we were all sitting and laughing together with Daddy, who seems to have forgotten about me ruining his pork chop with the bleach.

On the Saturday evening, I meet both John O'Briens in St Anne's church while we're all waiting to go to confession. They say they're going to the youth club after, but I tell them I have to go straight home. After telling the priest my sins, he must think I haven't sinned enough 'cos he's asking me things like "Have you had bad thoughts?" and "Have you rubbed your privates?" I'm thinking it's a funny thing for a priest to ask. Maybe next time I go to confession I'd better have a longer list of sins to keep him happy. On the way home I'm walking along the wall of Lawkholme Lane railway bridge. There's a twenty-five foot drop to the lines on my left. As I get to the far side where the wall is only about six-foot high I see some boxes in the grass at the top of the bank, behind a wooden gate that looks as if it hasn't been opened in years. I climb down inside the gate. There's boxes and boxes of cigarettes. I run the rest of the way home to tell Mammy and Daddy.

Daddy says they must be stolen and stashed by a gang of thieves. After about an hour's debating, he still can't decide what to do about the cigarettes. Mammy says the police might be watching the bridge for the crooks to come back. But then when it starts raining outside, she says the cigs might get ruined in the rain. Daddy looks at me. "Come on, let's go," he says.

We're walking up and down the road on the bridge in the rain. It's dark and there's no one around. I pull myself up onto the top of the gate and Daddy pushes me further up and over the wall and I climb down the other side. I grab some packs of cigs and pass them over the wall to Daddy, who shoves them inside his big black overcoat while I rush back to get him some more. Then I shove a load more under my coat and up my jumper, and squash them as I climb back over the wall and chase after Daddy, who is walking very fast off down Lawkholme Lane. When we get near home, we walk around the block a couple of times, to make sure the police are not following us he says. I'm thinking it's not the police I'm bothered about. It's the gang of crooks that I don't want to see running down the road after us. Mammy is delighted when she sees all the cigarettes stacked on the table by the window. She looks at me.

"Don't worry. It's not a sin to save the cigarettes from being ruined by the rain. It'd only be a sin if we were the ones who stole them in the first place."

I'm thinking that the priest up at St Anne's church might not think like that. Well not unless he smokes as well. On Sunday morning, the house is full of smoke when I leave to go to Mass. My cousin, Chrissy Murphy, is there. I don't go to Communion today, 'cos I'm not sure if getting the cigarettes last night was a sin. If it was a sin and I went to Communion with a sin marked on my soul, then that would be a bigger sin, so I don't. After Mass I go to Auntie Mary's with Chrissy. Auntie Mary asks me if 'Donoghue' is behaving himself these days, and what it was like staying in the foster home in Shipley. When I tell her about the bullies there she says they want a good walloping, and so does my father for causing the trouble that sent me there in the first place. Then she's saying again what she would do to any man who lifted a finger to her "like that Donoghue did to you mother, the liten bastard. I'd split him wide open with a red hot poker!" Now I'm thinking about lots of times before when I asked Mammy what a liten bastard is and she told me she'd tell me when I was older. So I ask Auntie Mary.

"What is a liten bastard?"

She laughs and says through the smoke of the cigarette hanging from her bottom lip, "You'll have to ask your mother when you go home, she's the one who's married to one."

So now it sounds to me like Mammy is the only one who knows what a liten bastard is, like in Belfast I thought she was the only one who knew where babies came from, when even the doctor said I'd have to ask that question to Mammy. Now I'm thinking that some grownups make fun of kids and some others just can't tell the truth to save their lives.

On the way home from Auntie Mary's I walk along the railway bridge wall again. The rest of the cigarettes are gone. I don't go straight home, I carry on walking down to the end of the lane, past Victoria Park. There's some engineering works and some spare ground on the left, between the park and the railway line in the distance. I'm rooting around and picking up big tin cans, some round ones and some with pointed tops, bits of bendy pipe and bits of lead piping, plus bits of copper wire and rusty nuts and bolts and nails from the piles of ash where the works people have been burning their rubbish. There's an old pram that's been dumped, so I put all my collected stuff into it and push it home. The pram bits will make a good bogey cart and the tin cans and bendy pipes will make a robot, like I've seen on a television programme.

When I get home the house is full of smoke. I tell Mammy the rest of the cigarettes have gone and I put all my tins and other bits down the cellar. The pram has to stay outside, beside the toilet. Then I'm asking Daddy if the solder used for fixing radios is the same as lead piping. He says that proper solder is made for the job, but it's a bit expensive to use for big joints.

I'm standing at the top of the cellar steps, melting a bit of lead piping in an old frying pan on the gas ring. The melted lead is running around the pan in shiny round balls and I'm lifting the pan making the them form into one big flat circle and then shaking it about to form small balls again. Suddenly, the door to the living room opens and Mammy is asking what's burning. I loose the balance of the lid and some lead spills out onto my arm and sizzles its way through my jumper and shirt and burns a little round hole in my skin before I have time to scream out and shake it off with some wild dancing, and the pan with the rest of my experiment goes bouncing down the steps into the cellar. Mammy grabs my arm and shoves it under the cold water tap above the big white sink. Then she puts her hand over my mouth to quieten me down. Mammy says that castor oil and raw egg white will ease the pain, but I spend the rest of the day in and out of the cellar head running cold water on my arm until finally the pain goes away in the evening. I'm thinking that I'll be using copper wire instead of melted lead to join the robot bits together.

In the evening after school, I spend my time down the cellar. I'm punching holes in the tins with a hammer and nail and sewing the holes together with copper wire. There's a boy from school called Robert who lives on Lawkholme lane. He sometimes comes to help me, by sitting and watching and advising. We have a secret code to let him know if I am at home when he calls. I leave a stone on the doorstep. If it's on the left side it means I'm at home, and if it's on the right side it means I'm out. This doesn't work for long. He can't remember if it was left for in and right for out, or right for in and left for out, or left for in if he was looking in the door, or left for in if he was looking out the door. He said it was easier just to knock and ask if I was in. After about two weeks the robot is taking shape. A five-gallon drum with a pointed top for the body, with the bottom cut out for access. Paint tins for the feet, a bigger paint tin for the head and coiled bendy tubes for the arms and the legs.

When I'm at school one day the gas man calls to read the meter in the cellar. Mammy says that Mandy took him by the hand down the steps, explaining to him that there was a robot down there but he mustn't be afraid 'cos it won't hurt him. Mammy said later that the meter man was in stitches and could hardly read the meter for laughing at how Mandy was so serious about the whole matter. I'm glad Mandy likes the robot. By the time it's finished, his head comes up level with my shoulder. I take him for walks using a stick across my shoulders to support him and my hand on his back to make his legs wobble forward so he looks like he's walking. It's good being back at home making things. Mammy is being happy too with Daddy not being a liten bastard lately, and not saying anymore that little Mandy wasn't his baby.

*

It's March now and there's been no drinking or fighting at home since me and Helen came back from Shipley. At school my friends are talking about going to the St Patrick's night dance at the hall in Victoria Park. Helen has left school and has a job at Peter Black's shoe factory, there's been talk of Raymin coming back over from Belfast and now Tommy the cat is even allowed in the house.

There's a girl that I've got to know. She doesn't go to my school, but she comes around after school. Her name is Maureen Feather. She's good fun to be with and I like her a lot. The robot and Robert don't seem so important to me when she's around. Maureen is twelve and skinny, with streaky fair shoulder-length hair. She wears tee shirts and jeans. She can be a bit of a tomboy. She is a good friend and has a happy face. Lots of my friends from school are going to the St Patrick's night dance and I hope I can go too. Mammy says she'll give me the money to get in. I've got my school blazer to wear and my black jeans, but one of the shoes with buckles on that Mammy got me from a catalogue has the sole coming off, and I've only had them a few weeks. Mammy says the catalogue people can go and feck if they think she's going to pay for shoes that last only three weeks. At school John O'Brien junior (he's two weeks younger than the other one) says he can give me a pair of winkle picker shoes, but there's holes in the soles. On St Patrick's night at the dance I've got on my black blazer, black jeans, highly polished black winkle picker shoes with pieces of cardboard inside to cover the holes and a nice brown striped shirt and brown tie. I wanted a handkerchief for my top pocket and searched the house for something with brown in it to go with my shirt. Mammy was getting mad with me searching through all the drawers in the house. In the end she went to the top drawer of the wall cupboard, took out a pair of scissors, grabbed the back of my shirt, pulled the shirt tail out of my jeans, cut off the tail and stuck it in my top pocket.

"You'll not get a better match than that, now feck off out to the dance and give me some peace!"

The shirt tail hankerchief looks good. Now I'm looking in the drawer for a safety pin to hold the shirt tail in place, in case it falls out and and my friends see what it is.

There's lots of people from school at the dance, including some teachers and some of the kids' mothers and fathers too. There's mostly Irish music being played, but lots of Beatles songs as well and Chubby Checker singing the Twist dance song, and lots of other songs that everyone does the Twist to. It's a good night, but with all the Twisting the bits of cardboard in my shoes keep wearing away and I have to keep going to the toilet to turn them over or find old cigarette packets and stuff them in my shoes. With all the dancing I'm getting hot and sweating, but I can't take my blazer off. If I do, what's left of my shirt might stick out and then I would definitely be out of fashion. It's still a very good fun night. It would have been better if Maureen had come. She hasn't been around all week.

On Saturday morning there's a knock at the door. It's Maureen. She's called to see me and says she's been away at her relatives in Goole, and that's why she hasn't been around. She takes me around to her house, where I meet her Mum and Dad and her brother Ronnie. Now I'm feeling happy again.

For the next two months things are alright at home. Daddy still hasn't got a job, but we're not going hungry or stewing the tea leaves like we used to do in Belfast. School is good too, with my friends John O'Brien one and John O'Brien two, and Dot Peterick. Maureen still comes around, and when she goes to her relatives in Goole she sends me postcards that say she wishes I was there. Auntie Mary Murphy has opened a workmen's café on Low Street. Some times I go to see her on a Saturday morning and she gives me pocket money. Sometimes Chrissy Murphy is there. Chrissy can be bossy but she's fun to be with. She's bossy at her own house too, on a Saturday evening when I go up there sometimes for a bath when other people think I need one. Or even when I think I don't need one, she'll be even more bossy and tell me I do. While I'm there, some of the lodger men say they are going over to St Anne's Church to confession. I'm thinking that I haven't been to confession since the time I found the stolen cigarettes. I'm thinking if I tell the priest about them he might say it was a serious sin to take them home. I think I'm better off not knowing. Anyway, he might ask me more stupid questions like he did last time. I still say my prayers at night and tell God that moving to the Devil's Country didn't make me lose my religion. I also thank God for making Daddy not be a liten bastard anymore, and last night I asked God to help St Anthony find us a house with an inside toilet.

*

It's June now and the summer is here. I'm thinking to myself that I'm a lucky person. There's lots of things that I'm happy about, like Maureen being my girlfriend even if she doesn't know it yet. She can sometimes be romantic, you know, like when she got me a present. She got me a good strong magnet to make it easier for me to get nails and screws out of the works fires down near the football ground. And Danny Murphy never asked for his socks back. And I can tell things are getting better at home 'cos Mammy and Daddy sometimes go for walks through Victoria Park without shouting at each other, and Tommy the cat sits in the house purring and being happy instead of running outside like he did before when Daddy started shouting.

I've got some new shoes without holes in them now. Well, they're not brand new. Mammy got them at a jumble sale at the school. She picked up one shoe as soon as she walked in, but then she saw another woman with the other shoe looking for the match. Mammy says she hid her shoe in a bag and followed the other woman around 'til she saw her throw the other shoe back on the table where Mammy grabbed it. They are brown brogue shoes and they look really nice when they are polished up. Daddy says they'll look better still if I take out the black laces and put some brown ones in. I wear them when I go to the youth club on Alice Street with John, John and Colin Richardson. We do the Twist to the Beatles songs and then the Hippy Hippy Shake to the Swinging Blue Jeans song. We dance to Billy J. Kramer and Lulu and it's good 'cos I don't have to put cardboard in my shoes anymore to do the Twist.

*

Sometimes on my way home from school I go down Grange Street, off Lawkholme Lane, so I can see the men working in a welding shop. The big doors are open because of the heat on sunny days. One of the welders says I haven't to watch the bright welding sparks. He says it can damage my eyes. He lets me watch the welding through a welding mask. I tell him that when I finish school I'm going to learn to weld like him, and then I'll be able to make a proper robot. He says I've to come back when I leave school and he'll take me to see the boss. When I get home I'm ready to tell Daddy about the man offering me a job welding, but I forget about it when I see that Raymin has come over from Belfast. He has Johnny McNeil with him. He says Johnny has just come out of a children's home in Belfast and that he is Harriet's brother and he can't find any work back there. They are both getting ready to go to the pub to find a job. Raymin has a quiff on the front of his hair and he says he wants to look like Ciff Richard. Johnny has waves on the front of his hair and he says he wants to look like a Teddyboy with his long sideburns.

Mammy says Raymin and Johnny can stay, but we'll have to sort out who's sleeping where. She says that Raymin and Johnny and me will have to share the attic, and Helen and Mandy will move down to the small bedroom beside Mammy and Daddy's room. Daddy is sitting at the table, watching the TV. He's not saying much and I'm thinking he's not looking too happy.

Raymin and Johnny soon get a job on a building site up the Haworth Road. I heard them saying that they would use different names, and that way they would not have to pay tax on their wages. Raymin says it's called working on the lump. When they start work, they give false names to the timekeeper, who's called Peter. Later in the day the foreman comes up to them and asks them their names, but they can't remember properly. Raymin says one is Burns and the other is Hicky. The foreman wants to know which of them is which. Johnny and Raymin look at each other.

"I'll tell you what I'll do," says the foreman, "I'll ask you again in the morning and maybe by then you'll remember who you are."

"Right then," says Johnny, and carries on digging a trench. He says the foreman walked off down the site, scratching his head. At finishing time they went to see Peter the timekeeper so that he could remind them which one was Hicky and which one was Burns so that they could have their names put down in the sub book, after 'subbing' the day's wages.

Next day on the way home from school I'm talking to the welder man again. I'm telling him that I'm not happy with my robot's head being tied on with copper wire that breaks easily. He says if it keeps coming loose he can weld it on for me and make it solid. He says he'll do it on Saturday morning when the boss isn't there so he won't get into trouble. When I get home I'm telling Mammy about the welder man, but she's not listening. She seems a bit distant. I think she's being bad with her nerves again. Daddy's being grumpy and Tommy the cat is sitting outside on the window sill and he didn't even try to follow me into the house like he usually does. I gobble down my tea, beans on two-sided toast, then I'm off out into the sunshine to see Maureen with the happy face.

"Don't be late, be in before it gets dark, it's Friday night and there's lots of drunks around on a Friday nights."

She was right about the drunks, Raymin and Johnny for a start. Tommy is still sitting outside when I get home before it gets dark. Raymin and Johnny are in the house after they've been in the Cavendish pub all evening. Mammy has put some boiled bacon and cabbage on the table for them. Daddy is shouting at them for going to the pub and getting drunk, and their dinner being kept warm from six o'clock. I'm stood in the doorway. Helen is at the top of the stairs holding Mandy in her arms looking down.

Now Daddy's leaning over the table pointing, shouting at Raymin and Jonny.

"Who do you think you are, coming in drunk to this house, thinking you can do what you like?"

Raymin and Johnny are eating their tea slowly, keeping quiet and saying nothing. Mammy is trying to calm Daddy down, and calling him Bren, like she always does when she's afraid of him.

"We only went for a drink, that's all, and we don't want any trouble," says Raymin, and Johnny stands up and says he's away out of there. Raymin stands up and says so am I. Mammy looks at them

"Sit down the two of you, it's too late to be going out again, it's nearly ten o clock," Mammy tells them. Daddy goes over and holds the front door closed to block their way. Raymin says if you don't want us here, let us out and we won't come back.

"Calm down Bren love, sit down and drink your cup of tea," says Mammy.

Johnny reaches out to pull the front door open and Daddy grabs his arm and shouts at him.

"Who do you think you are? You're nothing but a Teddy Boy!"

Johnny is getting mad now. He's a bit bigger than Daddy and I'm thinking that Johnny is getting ready to bop Daddy with his head, like Teddy Boys do when they're fighting. Something inside me is saying don't do it Johnny and something else is saying, go on Johnny, bop the bastard! Daddy's hand is still holding Johnny's arm tightly. Johnny looks Daddy straight in the eyes.

"Don't Brendan."

Then there's silence. Raymin steps in between them and pulls Daddy's hand off Johnny's arm. He yanks the door open and pushes Johnny out onto the street into the warm summer evening, with himself close behind. Daddy slams the door behind them.

Now all the shouting and swearing is being directed at Mammy, who's sat down in the armchair drinking her tea, smoking her cigarette and staring into the empty fireplace. Daddy's pacing around the room, shouting, cursing and swearing. He's shouting about Raymin and Johnny, calling them louts and Teddy Boys. Then he starts shouting about things that happened before. He's complaining about Mammy leaving us all in Dublin, about Raymin not telling him where we were living in Belfast. About Mandy not being his child. He's calling her a 'dirty hoor' and lots of things worse than that, a lot worse than that. Really bad words that are not even as nice and friendly as feck. He's shouting at the rate of about twenty five words without taking a breath. Then he's out of breath with sweat beading on his forehead. Mammy is telling him to calm down because of his 'dicky' heart. Finally he calms down and sits at the table, panting, trying to get his breath back. After a while, Helen comes down the stairs. She says Mandy was crying about all the shouting but she's gone to sleep now. Tommy is meowing at the door to come in now that the shouting has stopped. It's not quite ten o'clock yet. I ask Mammy if I can go to the corner shop for a penny chew before it closes. She says OK but to hurry back. I run halfway down Thrush Street, across Parson Street, and at the far end I can see Raymin and Johnny on the park wall. I run down to them and Raymin tells me that they're going to sleep in the park on top of a big pile of grass cuttings beside Victoria Hall. They ask me to get some of their coats and jumpers and throw them out the attic window at the side of the house so that they land on the roof of the outside toilet, and they'll get them later when everyone is in bed. I say OK and tell them I'll see them in the morning. Raymin asks if 'he's' quietened down yet. I tell him yes, about five minutes ago. Johnny says if he hurts any of us I have to come down to the park and call for them. When I get home Mammy asks if I got my penny chew.

"No, the shop was shut and by the time I got to the other one on Lawkholme Lane that was closed too."

Daddy asks is there was any sign of them feckin Teddy Boys. I tell him no, and I go off up to the attic and throw some coats and jumpers out the window, onto the flat roof of the outside toilet.

Mammy comes up to the attic to see if I'm alright. I tell her about Raymin and Johnny staying in the park and that I'm going to see them again in the morning. She says for Christ's sake don't tell your father.

Mammy wakes me up early in the morning and tells me to be quiet coming down the stairs. As I pass Daddy's room I can hear him snoring. She has a tray ready with Raymin and Johnny's breakfast. The teapot is full of tea with milk and sugar in it, and there's lots of toast and jam wrapped up in brown paper and covered with a towel to keep it all warm and two cups for the tea.

It's just after seven o'clock when I step out of the house into the bright sunshine. I balance the tray on the park wall and climb over to the other side, then take the tray over to the pile of grass cuttings by the hall. If it weren't for the three legs sticking out of the grass, nobody would know they were there. One of the boots sticking out is wet. Johnny is snoring. I wake them up and show them the tea and the toast I've brought for them. Raymin says it was nice and warm in the pile of grass. Johnny says his boot is all wet. Raymin takes a smell of the wet boot and says it smells like pee from a tomcat. Johnny says he's a dirty feck.

They scoff their tea and toast and now they're ready to go off to work for the Saturday morning shift. I ask them if they're going to straighten their beds before they go. Johnny tells me to away to Hell. Raymin says I have to be back to meet them at about half past five, to tell them if it might be alright to go home, "if that grumpy bastard has calmed down."

I'm taking the tray and teapot and cups home via Dove Street so I can come around by the back of the outside toilet and hide the tray on the roof. When I sneak into the house Mammy says that Daddy is still in bed, so I dash back out and bring the tray in. I tell her that they're both fine and I'll be seeing them again this evening. She asks if they slept OK and I tell her they slept fine and no one saw them, except me and the tomcat that peed on Johnny's boot. Mammy laughs and says maybe they were sleeping in the tomcat's bed.

I take the robot around to the welding workshop to have the loose head welded on. The man says he'll have to gas weld it because the metal is very thin and the electric stick welder will just burn holes in it. He does a good job of fixing it and I thank him. I tell him not to forget the welding job he promised me for when I leave St Anne's School. Soon I'm back at home with the robot and some green paint in a jar that the welder man gave me.

I'm sat on the doorstep in the warm morning sunshine drinking my tea and eating my toast and jam and painting the robot green. I've never seen a green robot before but it's the only paint the welder man from Grange Street could get for me. Then while I'm waiting for the paint to dry I'm stripping some wheels and axles from the old pram and cutting some wood to make a bogey cart. I'm needing the cart to carry the robot on, 'cos he's no good at walking.

Mammy comes out to tell me to stop banging and making so much noise 'cos Daddy's still in bed and the Pakistani man from across the street will be in bed after working a long night shift. She makes me promise to be quiet. But it's hard to remember to be quiet with such important things to be getting on with, and it's not too long before she's out again telling me to keep the noise down. But it's hard to make things quietly when the only tools I have are a hammer and a pair of pliers and a rusty old saw that the Pakistani man from India lent me. Now I'm thinking that when I get older, about 25, I'll be able to buy lots of tools and I'll be able to make robots and bogey carts quietly without being complained at all the time. And by that time I'll be a welder and I'll be able to make proper things like bogey carts with engines on, and grownup things like that. After dinner, in the afternoon and after another long walk to the spare ground at the bottom of Lawkholme Lane between the workshops and the railway lines, where I've collected lots of nails and nuts and bolts from the ashes of the old rubbish fires with the strong 'magnet present' from Maureen, I'm back at home working on the cart and the robot. Mr Singh from across the street is mending a broken flagstone so I take my chance to apologise for my noisy projects. He smiles and says it's OK.

Soon the bogey cart is finished and the robot is sitting in the driving seat. Now I'm feeling really happy after finishing my important day's work. Mammy comes out of the house and shouts over to me.

"Thank God you've finished banging. At last we can have a bit of peace and quiet now." Then she comes closer and whispers, "Don't forget about Raymin and Johnny in the park," and that made me remember, 'cos the important jobs I'd been doing made me forget about them, and Daddy's shouting last night.

# Chapter 20

## The final bust-up

At five o'clock I set off for the park with a bundle of sandwiches and a lemonade bottle filled with tea and wrapped in a towel, stuffed inside the robot's belly. I'm waiting by the swings beside the hall. There's a boy on the swings, he looks about fifteen. He comes over to me shouting and calling the robot and the bogey cart stupid names. He's swigging lemonade from a bottle and spitting it over the robot. He's pretending to be drunk. I walk away from him with the cart, over to the grass mound, looking for Raymin and Johnny. The boy runs after me and without a warning he kicks at the robot's head. He runs away laughing and swinging the lemonade bottle around in circles over his head. By the time Raymin and Johnny come into the park the boy has gone and I've lifted the robot with his dented head back onto the cart. I undo the wires holding the 'door' onto the bottom of the body tin and out pops the bottle of tea and the sandwiches.

Raymin asks me how things are at home. I tell him that Mammy says Daddy is still awkward and domineering and he's still calling him and Johnny Teddy Boys and louts and all things like that, so it might be as well to stay away for now. Raymin says feckin great, and Johnny says never mind, sure haven't we got Brian to look after us, and his robot that craps sandwiches, sure what more could we want. Raymin gives me a list. Him and Johnny want me to bring them some more clothes from the house, and a towel and some soap and their shoes so they can change out of their working boots. He says there's a tap at the back of the hall where they can have a wash. Johnny ask if I can get a bit of Brylcream for his hair and if not, just to bring a lump of margarine.

Daddy is still being grumpy at home and he keeps asking me if I've seen 'those two louts' and if I know where they are staying. I tell him I haven't seen them, but I don't think he believes me. I manage to get most of Raymin's list of things out of the house by throwing them out of the attic window and onto the toilet roof, including a lump of marge in a matchbox for Johnny. As I'm getting everything off the roof the man from the back house comes out of the toilet and ask what the hell I'm doing up there. I forgot about sharing the toilet with the house at the back. I tell him that some clothes accidentally fell out of the attic window. Now he's watching me as I put the clothes and other bits on the bogey cart and set off down Dove Street towards the park. Raymin and Johnny have a wash at the cold water tap. They hide their working clothes and boots under the pile of grass that is now their bed. They say they'll see me in the morning, and Raymin says I have to tell Mammy that they're both doing fine living in the park.

Things are quiet when I get home. Tommy the cat is at the door trying to get in. It's a good sign that there's no shouting going on inside. Mammy, Helen and Mandy are sat at the table listening to the news about the man who shot President Kennedy, and Jack Ruby, the man who shot the man who shot the President. Daddy goes out to the toilet so that means it's safe to tell Mammy how Raymin and Johnny are doing. I tell her quickly. I tell her that they are OK and about the water tap and their comfy bed made of grass cuttings.

The television is on and we're all watching a play on BBC2. Daddy says that some of these BBC2 plays can be a bit controversial. I'm not sure what that means but it's not long before someone says 'shit'. Me and Helen start laughing at them saying shit on the TV. Then a few minutes later the man in the play says 'bloody shit' and me and Helen are laughing again. Daddy leans over and taps Mammy on the shoulder and says "Turn it off Josie, that language is a bit strong for the kids."

I'm up early again in the morning while Daddy is still in bed, delivering the breakfast to the two Teddy Boys who live in the park. They don't want to get up this morning. I'm trying to get them up, but Raymin says I have to feck off 'cos I'm too early for a Sunday morning. I tell him the sun is shining and it's a nice day. Johnny says feck the sun and go away. I leave the tray on the grass and tell them I'll see them later. When I get home the Pakistani man from India is out on the street. He's mixing sand and cement to fix some more holes in the pavement outside his door again. I give him back the rusty saw he lent me. Then I ask him if I can have some cement mix if he has any left over when he's finished fixing the flagstones. "Certainly you can, no problem Little Boy Brian," he says, with his big white teeth smiling at me.

There's a woman coming up the road with a suitcase. She stops at number 6, our house. It's Dorothy from Belfast. I run over and say hello to her and open the door to bring her in to Mammy. I tell Mammy about leaving the tray in the park for Raymin and Johnny. Then I'm having a cup of tea and toast and jam with Dorothy, while she's telling Mammy about how things are in Belfast and that Marie is coming over in the next few days to visit. Mammy is telling Dorothy all about the troubles of the last two days, and about Daddy wanting the TV off when the man on BBC2 said shit.

"The cheek of him," she says, "when he shouts and swears every word in the feckin' book!"

I'm off out to see the man across the road again to see if he can help me get the dent out of the robot's head and whether we can make it stronger. After we've fixed the robot's head with a hammer, I go back to the park to see if Raymin and Johnny have had their breakfast and finished with the tray. They have. They're both sitting on the pile of grass scratching their heads and arms and other things that they should be scratching in private. Raymin says the grass is making him itch and driving him mad, and the midges have been biting his head all night. Johnny says they've been at him too. I'm thinking that the midges must be attracted to the Stork margarine on his hair. I'm telling them that Dorothy has come over to see us. Raymin says she couldn't have picked a worse time, with all the trouble at home.

"Anyway," he says, "we're going up to Auntie Mary's to see if we can have a bath. We'll see you back here about five o'clock."

It's the middle of the afternoon when Mammy shouts for me to come in for my dinner. We're having boiled bacon and cabbage with mashed potato done with milk and chopped raw onion, "for a change". Daddy is up out of bed in time for his dinner. He doesn't seem to be so grumpy today. He's talking a lot to Dorothy. I think he's trying impress her by being nice to her. I don't think she would have been much impressed by him the other night when he was being a domineering bastard with Raymin and Johnny and a liten bastard with Mammy, when he was calling her a 'dirty hoor'. After dinner Mammy whispers to me to go out to the back of the toilet where the window is open next to the cellar head cooker. She passes out a pan with bacon and cabbage and another with mashed potato and two spoons in it. I put them on the bogey cart with the robot and cover them with a coat while Dorothy is playing her part of the mission by being interested in what Daddy is saying to her.

I'm waiting in the park, but there's no sign of the fugitive 'louts'. By six o'clock the dinner is cold and there's still no sign of them. Just as I'm heading for home, the boy who kicked the robot's head off the other day is coming into the park by the swings. I'm moving faster now, away from him, towards home.

He's running over to me. He's laughing. I know what's going to happen. He does it again. He runs up and kicks the robot's head.

But now he's screaming at me. The robot's head is stronger than before and this time it doesn't fall off with the gas weld holding it on. The boy is lying on the grass holding his leg and shouting that it hurts. The robot is lying on its side. I have to use both hands to lift him back on to the cart. You see, with everything else going on, I forgot to tell you about the Pakistani man helping me to fill the head with the leftover cement. The bully boy is making an awful lot of noise for a tough guy. He's still lying on the grass holding his leg. I think it's time I got out of here.

At home, Helen, Dorothy, Mandy and the cat are watching TV. Helen says Mammy and Daddy have gone up to the Cavendish for a drink. That makes it easy for me to bring in the pots of dinner that Raymin and Johnny didn't eat. Helen says that Mammy didn't want to go but Daddy insisted. I tell Helen that there's no sign of the two Teddy Boy fugitives. Dorothy says she hopes they're not in the Cavendish.

Helen and Mandy are in bed when they get back from the pub. Mammy is making a pot of tea and Daddy is ranting and raving because the pub landlord called him a culchie and a thick countryman.

"It's that feckin landlord who is a culchie and a thick, ignorant, uneducated shite if ever there was one," Daddy shouts. "I'd have given the gob shite a wallop if he wasn't such a big gobshite!"

Mammy is giving Daddy and Dorothy some tea, and trying to calm him down. Then when he's busy telling Dorothy about the landlord being a shite Mammy tells me there's going to be more trouble tonight, she saw it in the tea leaves this morning. Then I tell Mammy that Raymin and Johnny didn't turn up at the park for their dinner.

Daddy won't sit down and drink his tea. He's standing up still with his coat on. He's shouting about Raymin and Johnny again. He says he doesn't believe that none of us have seen them. He says he's going to walk down by the park to see if they're hanging around there. I tell him I've been to the park today and I didn't see any sign of them. He's asks if I'm sure and I say yes, there were just some kids playing on the swings, and a boy, about fifteen, with a sore leg. Mammy tells him not to bother going out again at this time of night. He's banging on the table now and demanding that she goes with him to look for "those two bastards." Mammy says alright and then she looks at me and asks if I'll come too. Mammy is telling him to calm down. She's calling him the usual 'Bren' and 'Love' and I can tell she's getting more frightened of him. She gets her coat on. I've got a jumper on and I'm warm enough without a coat.

When we go down the street, Mammy makes me walk between her and Daddy. We walk down Parson Street, towards Bradford Road. Daddy says we'll walk from the Bradford Road gate through the park and out onto Lawkholme Lane at the other end. When Daddy gets a few steps in front of us Mammy is pulling my arm and mouthing quietly to me and pointing to his back, meaning "Watch him. He's going to start again when we get home."

We walk into the park, side by side. Mammy makes sure I stay in between her and Daddy. The lights from the road are shining on our backs and our shadows get longer and longer until we get far enough into the dark park that there's not enough light to make a shadow anymore. Mammy is saying that it's too dark in here and she's sure if Raymin and Johnny are in the park at this time of night we wouldn't be able to see them at all anyway.

"Come on Bren," she says, "let's go home, we'll come back tomorrow before it gets dark."

We stop walking and turn back towards the gate. Daddy's on my left and Mammy is on my right. We're coming out of the dark and nearer the street lights. Mammy asks him why he thinks Raymin and Johnny might be hanging around the park.

"Something someone said up in the Cavendish," he says.

Now he's shouting about the pub landlord again. He's calling him all the feckers going. He stops walking and turns to Mammy shouting about the "pair of louts" that think they can do what they like in HIS house. Then he starts on Mammy.

"And you, you feckin hoor, I don't forget the time—"

Mammy steps back but he's moving towards her.

"—in belfast when—"

He reaches his hands across in front of me to grab hold of her. She takes a step back. Now he's in front of me. I grab the back of his coat collar and pull backwards as hard as I can. That stops him reaching Mammy who by now has started to run like mad, away towards the gate. Another hard pull from me and before he realises what's happening he's sat back on his arse on the tarmac with his hands stretched back to stop him falling more, and my hands on his shoulders using all my weight to keep him on his arse to give Mammy enough time to get home safely. When I can no longer hear Mammy's footsteps running away back up Parson Street and I realise that the drunken bully of a shite isn't even trying to get up, I leave him there sat on his arse and I run out the gate and back up the street after Mammy. I can't see her. I never thought she could run that fast, what with her bad nerves and her varicose veins in her legs. I stop running and look behind me. There's no sign of the mad bastard. I'm walking, catching my breath back, and now I'm thinking Mammy's tea leaves were right when she saw more trouble in the cup.

At home Dorothy says there's no sign of Mammy. She hasn't come home. Ten minutes later Daddy is back. Now I'm expecting him to want to fight me for putting him on his arse, but he doesn't. He just asks where Mammy is and we tell him we don't know, she just hasn't come home yet. Now he's telling Dorothy about the "shite of a landlord" calling him a culchie, and about Raymin and Johnny thinking they can do what they like in 'his' house when he says they can't. After about an hour of telling Dorothy all about things that she's not really interested in, and Mammy not being home yet, he finally goes up to bed. Dorothy sleeps on the downstairs couch.

*

Mammy is missing all night. In the morning Daddy sends me out looking for her. He says I have to start at Auntie Mary's house. Helen stays off work to look after Mandy. On the way I see Maureen and she says she's going away for a week to her family in Goole again and she'll see me when she gets back. She wants to see the bogey cart and the robot.

Just as I get to Auntie Mary's and knock on the door, there's an ambulance coming off the Skipton Road and down the street. It stops outside Auntie Mary's house as she opens her door. At the same time the ambulance man jumps out and opens the side door wide to show Mammy standing inside leaning on crutches, with a pot on her leg.

"Jesus Christ," says Auntie Mary, "what's happened to you Josie?"

I'm trying to place the bottom of the crutches on the steps to help her but the ambulance man says leave her do it on her own, she has to get used to the crutches by herself. On the way into the house she's asking me what Daddy did after she ran off and I tell her about him landing on his arse and staying there with me leaning on his shoulders. She asks if he hurt me and I tell her no. Then she asks if Helen, Mandy and Dorothy are OK. I tell her they're fine.

Me and Auntie Mary and Uncle John are in the cellar kitchen listening to Mammy. She says when Daddy made a grab for her in the park she was terrified and just ran and ran as fast as she could. She thought he was chasing after her. She hadn't seen him land on the ground with me holding him down. Cousins Kathleen and Chrissy have come down to the kitchen to see what's been going on, and then lodger Jim McGarry is also in the kitchen listening to Mammy's story. Mammy says she ran past Thrush Street and up Lawkholme Lane towards the town. When she came to the gate by the railway bridge where I had found the stolen cigarettes, she scrambled over it and onto the railway embankment, thinking that Daddy would never think she would have gone that way. She knew if she crossed the railway lines she wouldn't be far from Auntie Mary's house, but in her panic, thinking Daddy was still after her, she was running too fast in the dark. That's when she fell on the railway lines and broke her leg. Then she was panicking more 'cos she felt so helpless and frightened. She managed to hobble to the nearest house with a light still on at the other side of the lines. She banged so hard on the window shouting for help that the window broke. The man in the house came out and called for an ambulance for her and then rang for the police. The police told Mammy to go with the ambulance and they would call to see her in the morning at her sister's house on Holker Street. When she got to the hospital and they put a pot on her broken leg, the doctor said she might as well stay in overnight and rest before going home in the morning.

"So here I am," she says, "and well fecked I am too."

Auntie Mary is fuming mad, she's calling Daddy all the 'dirty bastards' going, and telling Mammy it's time she did without that "durty rotten feckin bully." Mammy is asking me again what happened after she ran off. I'm trying to tell her in between Auntie Mary getting more annoyed about "that lousy liten bastard. He needs splitting wide open and his jaw bursting!"

"Calm down woman," says Uncle John, and Auntie Mary looks at Mammy and points at Uncle John.

"That man has never raised a hand to me, in all the time we've been married, not once."

Mammy is smoking, brushing her hair back with her hand and crying.

"If you ever go back to that man there's something wrong with your feckin head," says Auntie Mary. "Jesus, Mary and Joseph, what am I going to do?" Mammy says.

Later in the morning the police come to Auntie Mary's house to see if Mammy is alright and find out more about last night.

"My God, I don't know what the neighbours are going to think with ambulances and police cars coming to my door," Auntie Mary says when they're gone.

There's another knock at the door. This time it's Helen and Mandy. Helen listens to Mammy's story about what happened to her leg. Then she says that

Daddy was shouting about me not going back home after he sent me looking for her. That was before he got washed and shaved and went out, she says. All afternoon, in between the cigarettes, cups of tea and Auntie Mary feeding us all, there's lots of talking about what Mammy is going to do. At teatime, Mammy still doesn't know where to go or what to do. She says she doesn't want to go anywhere near that bastard down in Thrush Street. She's asking Helen if Dorothy is alright and if anyone has seen Raymin and Johnny. Helen says Dorothy is going to Peter Black's factory on Monday to see if there's any jobs going and there's no sign of the 'fugitives' anywhere. Mammy says it's a terrible time for Dorothy to come over, with all this trouble going on.

Just after Uncle John goes out at about half past seven in the evening, there's a knock at the door. I answer it. It's Daddy. He's been drinking. He says he wants to see Mammy. Auntie Mary comes up to the door with her cigarette in her mouth and a big heavy saucepan in her hand and tells him to feck off.

Now we're all up at the door, including Mammy on her crutches. There's a lot of commotion going on. "For Jesus's sake will you all stop shouting and disgracing me in front of the neighbours!" Auntie Mary says.

Daddy says he wants to see Mandy. Helen has Mandy in her arms. Auntie Mary is still telling him to feck off, but he won't. Now she's telling him to feck off before she calls the police. Suddenly, he grabs Mandy, but Helen doesn't let go of her. He's pulling backwards and out the gate onto the street. Mandy is crying, so is Helen. I'm hanging on to his right arm and slowing him down. Mammy is standing at the door crying. With a cigarette still hanging from her mouth, Auntie Mary is out onto the street like a shot, cigarette still hanging from her mouth, grabbing on to his left arm and holding the saucepan over his head. Now he can't go anywhere. I hang on to his right arm with my left hand and take a swing with my right fist to hit him on his right jaw. He looks straight at me. Auntie Mary hits him a wallop on the left side of his head with the pan. He looks straight at her. Mandy is screaming and Helen won't let go of her. I hit him again with my fist on his right eye. He looks back at me. Auntie Mary hits him again with the pan and it rings like a bell. He looks straight at her. He's cursing like mad. In my mind I can hear a crowd shouting 'ABOUT FECKING TIME!' I hit him, she hits him, I hit him, she hits him, 'til he finally lets go of Mandy and Helen runs back to the house with her. He's backing off now, holding the left side of his head. He's walking away, looking back, calling us mad bastards and thugs. He's shouting that he's going straight to the cop shop to tell them that we all attacked him for nothing.

We go back into the house, lock the front door and go back down into the kitchen. Mammy has Mandy on her knee now, they've both stopped crying. Auntie Mary still has the cigarette in her mouth, only now it's broken. She pulls the front bit off and lights what's left on one of the gas cooker rings. She puts the kettle on the gas.

"He won't be back in a hurry," she says, while she's stirring the big pans of dinner she's cooking for her lodgers. There's a knock on the door.

"If that Donoghue's back, I'll finish the fecker off this time," Auntie Mary says as she goes up the steps with the saucepan in her hand again. Mammy is looking worried and passes Mandy over to Helen.

"It's all right," shouts Auntie Mary, "it's Raymin and that other fella."

Auntie Mary tells Raymin and Johnny to sit at the back of the table to make room for the lodgers, who will be coming in for their dinner soon. She asks them if they're hungry. They both say they're starving with the hunger.

"Another two for dinner won't make any difference in this house," she says, putting plates filled to the top in front of them. Raymin is asking me why I didn't come to the park this morning or this evening. I point down to Mammy's broken leg. Mammy gives them the full story from last night when Daddy went for her in the park, and the breaking of her leg on the railway lines and breaking the man's window and right up to less than an hour ago when Daddy came to steal Mandy who he says isn't even his baby, "the durty rotten bastard that he is," she says. When they've had their dinner and after lots more talking, Mammy says she wants to go down to Thrush Street to see if Dorothy is alright, and she needs to get a change of clothes anyway.

"With any luck, he'll be in a pub somewhere, and nowhere near the house."

"Is your head cracked as well as your leg? Don't go near that bloody house! Raymin and Johnny can collect some clothes for you," Auntie Mary says.

Mammy says she wants to go now, while there's a chance that he's not there. She asks Raymin if he has any money to get a taxi down to Thrush Street. Johnny says they've both had a sub from work and they'll pay for it between them. Auntie Mary looks at Mammy from behind the smoke of her permanent cigarette.

"You're feckin cracked in the head, woman."

Johnny looks at Auntie Mary. "Don't yous worry noi. Josie will be 'dandy' with me and Raymin."

Mammy says that me and Helen and Mandy have to stay at Auntie Mary's, she says she won't be long. After about an hour Mammy still isn't back. Me and Helen tell Auntie Mary that we're going to walk down to Thrush Street with Mandy to find out what's going on.

"Go on then, you might as well be all cracked together."

It's about half past 9 when we get to the house. The cat is sitting on the window sill and there's loud talking going on inside. Helen stays outside with Mandy while I go inside. Mammy is sitting at the table with Raymin, Johnny, and now Marie is here too. Daddy is telling Marie, who must have come over from Belfast today, how we all attacked him outside Mary Murphy's house. He's showing her the lumps on the left side of his head. He points at me and says "he attacked me too." Mammy asks where Helen and Mandy are, and when I tell her they're outside on the street with the cat, so she tells me to go out too, away from the shouting. Outside Helen is holding Mandy and talking to Dorothy who says she's been upstairs most of the time, away from the fighting. Now the talking inside is getting louder. There's a big crash and the shadows on the window from the inside light are all moving about and then go into one lump of a shadow, except Mammy's shadow where she's sat at the table with her head in her hands.

I run in and I can see Johnny and Raymin holding Daddy against the back wall and telling him to calm down. Marie comes over to me and tells me not to worry and to go back outside. Mammy is screaming, saying she can't stand it any longer. Marie comes out and tells me Mammy wants me to run to the phone box and call the police, so she can get her clothes and leave. Marie is outside with us when the police car stops at the end of the street. There's a young policeman and an older one walking up. Marie is telling them about Daddy causing his trouble. The younger policeman says he saw Mammy last night in the ambulance before she went to the hospital. The older policeman knocks loudly on the door and walks straight in. I can hear them all talking at once and Daddy's shouting "Who called the police?" The policeman says a neighbour called, because of all the noise and shouting coming from the house and says he's here just to see that everyone's alright. I can hear Daddy telling the policeman about being 'attacked' up on Holker Street and having lumps on his head to prove it. Soon everyone is talking at once again. Outside, the young policeman is listening to Marie telling him what she knows about what's been happening in the house, I'm telling him about what happened last night at the park and today at Auntie Mary's house. Marie is rubbing her shoulders and then folding her arms to keep warm in the late evening breeze. She turns to me and asks if I'm OK. I tell her I'm alright, except I think I'm going to be sick.

It's past half past ten now. I can hear the policeman inside asking Mammy if she's going to stay at the house with Helen, Mandy and me. She says she's definitely not staying in the same house as 'him' ever again. I look into the house. Mammy looks at the policeman.

"This is all his fault," she says, pointing to the pot on her leg. The policeman says he's going to have to call in the Children's Department at the county council office. I'm running into the house.

"Don't call the council woman," I'm begging him. "We can stay here, we'll be fine now won't we?" I'm looking at Daddy now. "Won't we?"

"I'm not throwing anyone out except those two feckin Teddy Boys," he says, pointing at Raymin and Johnny.

"No! I'm not staying here and neither are them kids," she shouts. I'm telling her that we'll be alright staying here.

"No you won't!"

"Well we can stay at Auntie Mary's then," I tell her.

"No," she says, "there's not enough room there for all of us."

I'm telling her that Auntie Mary said we'd never go hungry while she's around. But she says, we're not staying with Mary Murphy and that's that. The policeman says he has no choice but to call in the Children's Department at the Council. It's nearly eleven o'clock when the older policeman says he's leaving and the council woman is on her way to see us. He leaves the young policeman outside the house to wait for her. Helen, Mandy and me are going to be taken away separately by the West Riding County Council Children's Department. It's after midnight when the woman from the council comes to take me away. Mammy says it's just 'til she gets another house away from Daddy. There's no clean clothes in the house for me so I go in what I stand up in.

"It's only 'til my leg is better," Mammy shouts over.

As the car starts moving, I shout back, "Auntie Mary would let us stay with her!" Now I've got a lump coming into my throat again and I'm thinking about my friend Maureen and my friends at school and my other friend Tommy the cat and how long will it be this time?

# Chapter 21

## Back in a children's home

We're driving out of Keighley over the moors. The council woman says she's taking me to a home in a place called Burley-in-Wharfdale. She says it's only until Mammy's leg is better. Then I can go home again. We don't talk a lot. I'm just looking out into the headlights beam and counting how many rabbits I can see feeding on the grass at the roadside. After about half an hour she points at some big rocks on the hillside and says they are called the Cow and Calf rocks because one is big and the other is small, like a big cow and a small calf. Then, pointing down into the valley at all the lights, she tells me that it's Ilkley town down there. She asks me if I've heard of the Cow and Calf rocks on Ilkley moor. I ask her how much further we have to go to get to the home and she says about three miles.

"Nearly there," she says when she turns left off the moorland road and down a steep hill for about a mile. Then just before the street lights start, she turns right onto a dark bumpy road, past a bungalow on the left nearly hidden by a tall hedge. Then left through two big stone pillars that have a black patch like a dinner plate painted on each of them with the words 'The Court' in the middle, written in gold. The sound of the car changes now, as she drives slowly to the big wood double front door, with the gravel driveway crunching loudly under the wheels. She asks me if I'm all right.

"No, how can I be? I'm being dumped and losing all my friends again, and 'specially my friend Maureen, who my friend John O'Brien junior described as a 'doll' in pop music talk."

When we get out she leaves the engine running and the headlights on so we can see where we're walking. She rings the doorbell and waits. She rings again and waits, and waits. There's a movement at one of the front downstairs windows. It's a big spotty Dalmation dog looking out at us. I'm thinking it must be the guard dog. Its paws are up on the windowsill and the curtain behind it is moving. The council woman says it's OK, there is someone there at last but I'm telling her there isn't, it's only the dog's tail wagging like mad that's moving the curtain. She rings the bell once more, waits, and then she says you'll have to stay at my house tonight. I'll bring you back in the morning. We crunch our way out through the front gate and onto the bumpy road, past a sign on the left that says Burley-in-Wharfdale Railway Station. She turns right onto the main road, into the village. There's a telephone box a hundred yards down the road.

"Why don't you ring them?" I ask her.

"I never thought of that," says the council woman, so she does.

This time there's a light on in the hallway and there's a man standing in the doorway in his pyjamas with an overcoat on top. The council woman tells me this is Mr Watson and that he's going to look after me. I wave at the guard dog in the window and it swishes the curtains around with its tail again. Inside the house there's a big open hallway and sitting area with seats and settees facing a big television. The council woman and Mr Watson move further into the house, away from me, and are talking for about five minutes. There's a pendulum clock on the wall. The clock says its just after half past one.

The woman is gone now. Mr Watson takes me up the staircase and into a bedroom with about eight beds in it. He points to an empty bed in the middle of the room and says that's your bed. Then he shows me into the bathroom and asks if I need to use the toilet, I tell him no. He hands me some pyjamas and says to put them on. When I get to taking my socks off, I can see my feet all dirty and dusty. I try to hide them away from Mr Watson because I'm feeling ashamed for not being clean, but I'm sure he's seen my mucky feet. I climb into the bed, in between the crispy white sheets that are so crispy that they feel hard to me. Mr Watson turns out the light and it's pitch dark, probably because we're somewhere up in the Pennine Mountains. I'm looking around to see a bit of light somewhere. I'm not used to it being so dark. I see a bit of light around the edge of the curtains on the window. I keep looking at the edges of light 'til I fall asleep.

I can feel myself crying. I'm sobbing. I'm pulling the curtains back so I can see. The light goes on. There's a boy standing beside me holding my arm asking if I'm alright.

"You've been peeing on the radiator in front of the curtains," he says. I'm still half as asleep. He leads me to the toilet where I finish a long pee. He then leads me back to my bed and asks me if I'm alright, before he gets a cloth from the bathroom to clean up the pee by the radiator and turn off the light. I'm looking for the bit of light around the curtain 'til I fall asleep again.

*

In the morning Mr Watson comes into the room shouting that it's time to rise and shine. He tells me not to get dressed yet. He runs a bath full of soapy water and tells me to have a good scrub. He's giving orders to everyone around him. I'm thinking he sounds like an army man. He brings me a full change of clothes. Then when we're alone in the bathroom he tells me that he saw me trying to hide my dirty feet while I was getting into bed last night. He says he understands that with all the trouble at home I wasn't being looked after properly.

"We won't be washing your own clothes. I've burnt them in the central heating furnace," he says.

I'm thinking of telling him that I usually have a bath at Auntie Mary's house every Saturday, even if I don't need it, but then I'm thinking that maybe he would think that a bath once a week is not enough, so I just say nothing. When I'm dressed I join the queue of boys in the long hallway downstairs waiting to go into the dining room for breakfast. There's about twenty boys, aged from about six to fifteen. Mr Watson leads me to the front and tells the boys my name and says that I'll be staying here for a while. He then leads me over to one of the boys saying, "This is Roger. You'll be sitting at his table."

There's lots of small tables in the dining room with four chairs at each table. There's white napkins rolled up in plastic rings. It's like being in a restaurant, like Brother Ignatius once took me and Raymin to in Belfast on the way to see Mammy. There were more knives and forks on the restaurant table though. Brother Ignatius told us that if we didn't know which knife and fork to use we have to just start on the outside and work our way in on the different courses. That day I had just waited, and then did the things the brother did first. I won't have to worry about that today though, 'cos there's only one knife and fork and spoon at each place. At the top of the dining room by the door there's a big table where the staff sit. There's Mr Watson, Matron Watson and two women staff that are called aunties. Mr Watson makes us all say grace before meals. It's the Church of England grace before meals and Mr Watson makes a point of telling me it means the same as the Catholic one. Today the breakfast is cornflakes, toast, boiled egg, tea, marmalade and grace after meals. After the breakfast I am put in the small kitchen with Roger and two other boys. It's our job to wash and dry all the cutlery and crockery from the dining room. The other boys all have their own jobs to do. Some clear away all the tables and sweep the dining room floor and reset the tables for the next mealtime. Others work in the big kitchen and others in the main house. Every boy has his own job to do, and when all the work is done we can play out on the lawns at the side of the house.

Mr Watson takes me through the TV lounge and the playroom that looks out on the gravel drive and into a small office at the far end. He's asking me about what happened at home and he's making notes. Then he asks me if I wet the bed. I tell him no and that I was sorry about peeing on the radiator last night. We go back into the playroom across the noisy floor made out of rectangle pieces of wood that Mr Watson says is called 'park' flooring, or something like that. He then shows me one of a stack of square wooden lockers by the wall and says I can put my belongings in that one. I tell him I haven't got any. He says when I get some I can keep them in there.

I go out past the little lawn and on to the big one where some of the boys are playing football and some are playing cricket. I don't try to join in. I'm sitting there thinking about what might be happening at home and thinking about Maureen calling for me when she gets back from Goole. One of the boys comes running down to me.

"Mr Watson wants to take you to the barber shop in the village to have your hair cut. He says it looks like you're six months overdue for one and he doesn't want you looking like one of those idiots on the top of the pops show."

In the evening, bathtime starts at seven o'clock for the smaller boys and follows on for the big boys. The small boys are eleven years downwards and the big boys are twelve years upwards. Small boys go to bed at 8pm and the big boys go to bed at 9.30pm, except for the little boy called George who is only six years old, he goes to bed at 7pm. 'Auntie' Carol says I have to have a bath even if I did have one this morning, and I'm thinking this is serious clean, having two baths in one day. She says I have to wash my hair too. She says she can tell if I just wet it 'cos then it won't squeak when she pulls her fingers along it. After my bath I ask Auntie Carol if I have to wear a night gown on top of my pyjamas like the other boys. She says yes, and it's called a dressing gown, not a nightgown. Then she tells the other boys standing around to stop laughing at me for calling it a nightgown. We can go downstairs then to watch TV or go in to the playroom with the park floor if we want. At twenty five past nine the big boys go into the small kitchen for a glass of milk and some biscuits before going to bed. I'm put into a different room tonight with only one bed in it. I'm thinking Mr Watson wants to see if I'll pee on the radiator again and he doesn't want any of the other boys to see me in case they start doing it. I'm in the room on my own. The door is closed. It's dark, I'm thinking of what might be happening at home. I'm getting frightened. I don't know why. I'm thinking something is going to happen to me. I can't explain it.

Maybe the Devil is in this room. I'm starting to panic. I'm getting short of breath. I don't want to be in here. I get out of bed and out of the room. Being in the corridor makes me feel a bit better but I don't want to go back into the room. I go down the big stairs where I can hear talking coming from the big kitchen. It's Matron and Mr Watson. I go to the doorway and Mr Watson is looking at me as if I've done something wrong.

"Mr Watson ... I'm ..." My voice is going, I can't stop myself from crying. "I was in bed and suddenly I got frightened and—" now I'm sobbing "—I got afraid, and I don't know what I'm afraid of and I think something bad is going to happen to me."

I'm sure Mr Watson will be an understanding person. He looks at me with a scowl on his face.

"Don't be so stupid boy, get back up those stairs and into bed. Nothing is going to happen to you here." "But I'm frightened Mr Watson."

"My God boy, you get thrown out of your own home for us to take you in and look after you. Is this the thanks we get? Get back to bed, boy, and stop your stupid crying!"

I'm back in the bedroom. I don't feel too good. I'm thinking Mr Watson doesn't care about me. That was a bad thing to say, that I was thrown out of my own home. It makes it sound like it's my fault that I'm here. I hear footsteps coming up the stairs and on to the landing. Mr Watson looks around the half open door.

"Are you alright, boy?

I try to swallow my sobbing. "Yes Mr Watson."

The next morning Mr Watson is not my friend. I'm standing in the queue for the dining room. He's telling me off in front of the other boys for what happened last night, and saying that none of the other boys act like that. Some of the boys are looking at me as if I've done something bad. Other boys look at me half smiling, as if to say 'Don't worry things will get better – for God is good.' He's not my friend the next day either. Matron is ignoring me too, and most of the boys don't talk to me when Mr Watson and Matron are around. In the dinner queue Roger Seamour is whispering to me. He says that's how they treat you here if you get into trouble. They send you to a place called 'Coventry.' Now I'm feeling worse than I did before. I don't want to be sent to Coventry, I want to go back to Keighley. Roger doesn't talk to me all through dinnertime. After, when we're in the small kitchen washing up all the plates and things from the dining room, we can talk when there's no staff around. I'm asking him how far it is.

"How far is what?" he says.

"Coventry," I tell him.

"You don't go to Coventry," he says. "It's a figure of speech. It means they won't talk to you, it's just like a punishment."

"Oh!" I say. "It must be quiet there."

"Where?" asks Roger.

"In Coventry," I tell him.

*

Every day during the summer after the housework jobs are done, we all go out to play on the lawns. The little lawn is at the side of the house and has a big hedge across the bottom edge that separates it from the big lawn where the football and cricket games are played. At the bottom of the big lawn at the far right corner there's a small wood. In the middle of the wood is a big oak tree. The boys call it the fat tree. I climb to the top and I can see across over the rooftops of the village and on to the hills about four or five miles away. When I turn around I can see the big house and the Dalmation dog called Peggy looking out the window of Mr Watson's sitting room on the corner of the house. It's good being up here on my own in the sunshine. I wish I had some binoculars or a telescope. I climb back down the tree. Mr Watson is standing there.

"Don't you know it's against the rules to climb trees here, especially the big ones?" he says.

"I'm sorry, I didn't know," I tell him.

Now it looks like I'm falling further down the hole of trouble.

"Get out of the woods," Mr Watson tells me. "You've only been here a ruddy week boy and you can't keep out of trouble."

I'm thinking he says ruddy instead of bloody so that it's not a proper swear word he's using.

*

By the end of the week I'm finally no longer invisible, I'm being talked to. Even Matron has spoken to me. It's a Friday teatime and I'm in the queue for the dining room. Mr Watson walks up to me and hands me a letter. He says there's a photograph in it and he wants no more like that sent to me. He says he doesn't agree with things like that. I'm thinking I could be in trouble again. At the dining table I'm dying to look in the envelope, but if I do everyone will be watching to see what the picture is. After tea, and after washing up in the small kitchen, I'm in the playroom. The letter is from Maureen. She says she's back from her holiday and when she called to the house in Thrush Street she met my sister Marie who told her what happened at home and gave her this adresss. The photo is of her and some of her family on holiday on the beach. The others all have their clothes on, Maureen is wearing a bikini. I'm looking at the photo to see what's wrong about it. I can't find anything wrong. It must be just the bikini that Mr Watson doesn't agree with. I'm thinking it's a good photo and it's not rude at all, but I can't say that to Mr Watson. Maureen says she misses me and she hopes to see me soon when I go back to Keighley to stay with Mammy, without Daddy, like Marie told her the other day. She say's she's doing fine and she hopes I like the photo of her on her holidays in sunny Goole and she wished I had been there, and now she wishes I was in Keighley.

Mr Watson walks through the playroom as I'm looking at the photo.

“We don’t want things like that here, boy! The best thing you could do is send it back and tell that young girl to send no more.”

I’m really glad to get the letter and the photo from Maureen and to know that I’ll soon be going home, where I can see her again. And I’m glad she wishes I was there. But for now I think I’d better go along with Mr Watson and send the photo back with the reply letter, or I’ll be back in ‘Coventry’ again with the quiet people. Mr Watson will read the letter any way. I send the photo back and tell Maureen not to write to me here and don’t send anymore photos and that I’ll see her soon when I go home. I’m thinking that’ll keep Mr Watson happy and keep me out of trouble. And when I see Maureen again I’ll tell her about Mr Watson thinking her photo was rude and that he was just being domineering like Daddy, but Mr Watson does his domineering by sending you to ‘Coventry’ and Daddy does it by bullying and swearing and hitting. Now I’m thinking that when I got into trouble with the brothers at school in Kircubbin I got a wallop and that was it done with, but ‘Coventry’ punishment goes on and on. I think I’d prefer the wallop. I go for my bath at eight o’clock. Mr Watson and Matron are ignoring me again. Auntie Carol isn’t. She’s telling me to cheer up.

*

After breakfast I'm sat on the small lawn with Roger Seamour and a boy called Paul. Paul has a really small transistor radio. He's listening to pop songs. He's singing along with a song that goes 'Riding along in my automobile, My baby beside me at the wheel.' He knows all the words. He has the front of his hair in a quiff, and he's shaking his head from side to side as he's singing. I'm thinking he's practising to be a Teddy Boy like Raymin and Johnny at home, or a long-haired lout like them on Top Of The Pops.

Me and Roger go down to the big lawn. I'm wanting to join the game of football, but one of the boys won't let me join in. The others don't mind when I join the game. The boy, called Trevor, goes up to the house to complain to Mr Watson. Mr Watson sends a message back that I have to sit on the small lawn by myself, where he can see me. After about half an hour, Mr Watson calls me in to his sitting room. There's a tall man there with black hair. It's Mr Mitchell, from the Children's Department in Shipley. Mr Watson leaves the room and Mr Mitchell starts asking me about why I'm getting into trouble all the time. Mr Watson has told him all about me, everything. I tell Mr Mitchell that I was half asleep when I peed on the radiator, that I didn't know that you could get into trouble for being frightened at night, that no one told me we weren't allowed to climb trees, that I didn't think a picture of a girl in a bikini that I didn't know was coming was rude and not allowed, and that I only wanted to play football with the boys when nine out of ten of them wanted me to join in. Mr Watson comes into the room. He looks at Mr Mitchell.

"That last complaint about spoiling the football game, cross that one off. Apparently most of the boys wanted Brian to join in."

Mr Watson leaves the room again. Out of the window I can see Roger Seamour and David Hudson walking back down to the big lawn. I'm thinking it's them who told Mr Watson that I wasn't causing trouble. Mr Mitchell's tone of voice changes. He's telling me to try and keep out of trouble. I'm telling him it's that 'Coventry' thing that makes you get into trouble in a place like this, and that Mr Watson said I had been thrown out of my own house, when I hadn't. No one talks to you all day 'cos they're saving it all up to shout at you for the least little thing. He changes the subject and starts talking about Mammy. He's telling me that there's a court hearing in September at Keighley Courts to see if I'm going home. He says try to keep out of trouble 'til then. I ask him if he'll get me my hurley stick and the brass cross that Brother Ignatius bought for me from the house in Keighley. He says he'll try. I'm thinking about missing being at home with my family and Tommy the cat so I ask him how the cat is getting on.

Mr Mitchell calls Mr Watson back in and asks me to wait outside in the hall. After about twenty minutes he comes out again with Mr Watson who says, "Go on lad, go back down to your football game."

Mr Mitchell says goodbye to me. I go out the side door, through the small room, that Mr Watson calls the gun room, where we all keep our shoes. I go down to the big lawn and sit on the edge by the path. I don't feel like playing football anymore. I wonder if Raymin and Johnny are still living in the park, with the weather being so good.

# Chapter 22

## A little taste of a happy home

On Sunday morning after breakfast all the boys have gone to the village to the Church of England service. Mr Watson says he's not making me go to the Catholic church on the Menston Road because I haven't got any good going out clothes at the moment. Then he says that on the next Saturday, all the boys will be going to Blackpool with him on a coach for a two-week holiday like they do every year. He says that it's too late to make arrangements for me to go, so I'll be spending the two weeks in another home in Otley. He gives me two shillings pocket money. He says that each week every boy gets two shillings from the Children's Department, and most of them just take sixpence of the money and save the rest for the summer holidays.

When the following Saturday comes, after breakfast and me not being in 'Coventry' for the whole week, the council woman's car crunches onto the drive beside the holiday bus. All the boys are excited and looking happy 'cos they're going to a place called Blackpool at the Lancashire end of the Pennine Mountains. Mr Watson told me they are not big enough to be called mountains so I'll have to start calling them hills. She's taking me to a home in Otley with a change of clothes that Mr Watson got for me and four shillings pocket money for the two weeks I'll be there. She says that she's arranged for me to be going to a farm on each week day. She says she thinks I'll like it. She says the farmer's grandson will be there and that we can help on the farm in the mornings and play around the fields in the afternoon. The farmer will pick me up from the home in the mornings and take me back for teatime. I ask her if Mr Mitchell has managed to get my brass cross and hurley stick, and found out how Tommy the cat is doing. She says she'll ask Mr Mitchell on Monday when she sees him.

The home is a big old terraced house joined onto another one, on the main Ilkley road before Otley town. She tells me about the big hill at the back of the house. It's called Otley Chevin hill. She says lots of people walk up to the top and back down again on the weekends, and maybe I would like to do the same sometime. The house is big, but not as big as the one in Burley in Wharfdale. When we go inside the house the first thing I notice is that there's girls here as well as boys. I didn't know it would be a mixed home. The council woman introduces me to the matron and some of the kids, including two girls that are older than me. The matron in charge is very nice. So are all the kids and the two older girls. One of the older girls says that it's good to have someone their age to talk to. She asks me how old I am. Thirteen I tell her, fourteen in two weeks, on the twenty second of August. They want to know all about me, if that's OK with me, one of them says. I tell them why I'm here and that I'll be going back home in September. I'm thinking that everyone here is really friendly. All the kids seem close to each other, like proper brothers and sisters should be. Matron is nice and kind looking, and kind acting. She doesn't act as if she's been an army woman, like Mr Watson acts like an army man.

*

On Monday morning the farmer man picks me up from the home in a noisy, smokey truck that he calls a pickup. He takes me through Otley town and out the other side near a small village called Pool, to his farm on Castle Lane, where I meet his wife and his grandson Johnny. Johnny is a bit younger than me but I soon learn that he knows a lot more than me about farming things. We spend the morning pulling weeds up in the potato fields. Then after dinner we go over the cowfields to the little stream that he calls a beck, Riffa Beck. Johnny has a bit of fishing line and a small hook with a piece of worm on it. He catches an ugly little fish that he calls a bullhead, then he lets it go, back into the stream. I'm asking him if there's any bigger fish in the stream and he says no, the bigger fish are in the River Wharf across the fields on the other side of the road. He says we can't go fishing there without a licence.

In the late afternoon at milking time, Johnny runs out to the field to get the cows in. As soon as he starts calling they start coming over to the gate and into the milking shed. Johnny shows me how to chain the cows up in the stalls, and keep away from their hind legs in case they kick out or do their mess on top of you. There's about thirty cows and each one has its own stall and its own name. There's one cow called Bonnie that's having a calf and she's kept inside a small cowshed all the time now. Me and Johnny clean out her dirty straw and give her some clean straw for her bed. We feed her, and when she's lying down and resting she likes to be stroked, like a dog. Johnny's all excited when I get there one morning.

"Bonnie has had a calf, and cow and calf are doing fine," he says. His Grandad is complaining about the weeding not being done. He's telling us that the cow and the calf will still be there in the afternoon, after weeding.

The next day there's no weeding to do. The farmer says that we can go with him to the cattle market in Otley, where he goes every week if he can manage it. There's lots of things being sold besides cattle and sheep. It's a good day out. When we get back to the farm we run straight into the barn to check up on Bonnie and her new calf. Johnny gets me some chalk and I do a drawing of the calf on the wall. I'm thinking it's about one of the best drawings I've ever done. I like being at the farm during the day, and I like going back to the home in Otley in the evening. I wish I was staying in Otley 'til September instead of going back to Burley, where they send you to Coventry a lot, for nothing.

On Sunday I go for a walk up the Chevin Hill with some of the boys and girls at the home. There's two little girls who are sisters at the home because their mother has gone blind and she can't look after them anymore. The council are trying to find permanent foster parents for them both. They say that the council might find them homes separately, but they don't want to leave each other. One of them says the council might be putting them in the Bradford paper to see if anyone wants them so they can stay together, with someone who is kind and would take them to see their mam sometimes. I'm smiling at the little girl, to show her that I agree with her. I can't talk to her, the lump in my throat won't let me, and I don't want her to know it's there anyway. One of the older girls is looking at me. I think she knows it's there. She smiles at me, and looks away.

Later in the evening when I go to bed I don't sleep too well. I'm thinking of going home next month, and going back to the other home at the end of the week. I'm thinking about the two little girls, very polite with good manners, aged only eight and nine years old, whose mam is blind and can't look after them, and about my mam who isn't and doesn't want to look after us.

On Friday the twenty first, the farmer and his noisy pickup truck take me back to the home in Otley for the last time. In my pocket is a birthday card with five shillings in it. At teatime there's another card on the dining table from Matron and all the boys and girls. It's a nice surprise. Matron asks me why there are no cards from my family. I tell her they'll be at the home in Burley waiting for me when I go back tomorrow, my birthday.

Saturday dinner time and the council woman is here to take me back to Mr Watson and the other boys in Burley. It's been good fun at the farm and better at the home. All the kids and Matron come out to wave goodbye to me. I'm thinking that this home in Otley is really good. It would be a good place for me and Mandy to stay while we're waiting to go back home. I'm thinking there's a big difference between here and Burley in Wharfedale. The difference is that this is a home and Burley is an institution. On the way back in the car, I ask the council woman if Mr Mitchell has the cross and the hurley stick for me, and she tells me no but that he hasn't forgotten.

*

I'm back at 'The Court' home in Burley. The council woman has gone and Auntie Carol is in the house waiting for the boys to come back from Blackpool. Soon it'll be back to school in early September for all the boys. I don't go to school here 'cos I'll be going home soon.

When the boys go back to school I have a week of being on my own during the day and doing my best not to be sent to Coventry. The council woman is here to take me back to Keighley. It's the first Monday in September.

"Do you have all your belongings? she asks.

"Yes."

She's looking around for them. "Where are they?" she asks.

"They're in my pocket," I tell her.

"Good luck lad," Mr Watson says. I think he means it.

We crunch out of the gravel drive, onto the bumpy road, left up the hill to Burley Woodhead and on past the Calf and Cow rocks on Ilkley Moor where Mr Watson said you should never go without a hat. The wind is blowing so hard off the moor that the council woman has to drive slower than she normally does.

Mammy, Marie, Helen and Mandy are in the courthouse corridor. Mammy still has a pot on her leg. Marie has a friend called Peter with her. Uncle John Murphy is here too. Daddy comes in late and stands on his own, away from the rest of us. The council woman is talking to Mammy first. Then she goes and talks to Daddy. When she comes back over to Mammy she says that Daddy says we can all go back to live in the house at Thrush Street. Mammy says she's going nowhere near that liten bastard and neither are any of us. She asks Mammy where she's living now. In Bradford with her nephew, Eddie Murphy, she says, adding that he only has enough room for her, and her leg is still bad and she doesn't know what she's going to do. Now she's crying. Uncle John says him and Auntie Mary can look after the kids 'til she gets sorted out. She's not crying for long. She says no to Uncle John.

"They'll be fine where they are for now, 'til I get a place of my own, 'til then they'll be fine."

When the court starts, Helen, me and Mandy have to stay in the corridor with the council woman. Mammy comes out first, wiping her eyes and saying, "What can I do?" When Marie comes out she says that she's told the man in there that Helen can stay with her in her bedsitting room in Holker Street near Auntie Mary, as long as Daddy stays away from them. I'm telling Mammy that me and Mandy can stay with Auntie Mary and be near Marie and Helen.

"You're not staying at Mary Murphy's house to be made into skivvies for her lodging house and her café," Mammy says when she's sure that Uncle John can't hear.

"I'd rather stay with Auntie Mary and be a skivvy and help her than go back into a home where it's against the rules to be frightened!"

She says it'll only be for a few weeks 'til her leg is better, then she'll bring us home.

Me, Helen and Mandy are put into a small room off the main corridor. There's bench seats against the wall, but there's no window. The council woman is outside the door telling Mammy that the court is waiting for a doctor to come and see her before they decide what to do.

Helen is telling me that she's been staying in a home in Penistone. She says she ran away when they first sent her there and came back to Thrush Street. She went back to work at Peter Black's shoe factory, but she was taken back to the home the day after. She says if they send her back to the home she's going to run away again.

Little Mandy says that one of the 'aunties' at the home in Bradford where she was staying was telling them all a story and hit her a wallop behind her left ear that started her head bleeding down onto her dress. She says the 'Matron woman' told the auntie, who said it might need a stitch, that she's not to go to the hospital. Mandy says they cut some of the hair around the cut and put some stuff that looked like frying pan fat on it to stop the bleeding. She says she got the wallop just 'cos she wasn't listening to the story.

Mammy comes into the room. She says we have to keep quiet and let her do the talking. Just then the doctor comes in and Mammy starts crying and saying "Whan can I do?" and "I can't cope anymore," and things like that. She says she's frightened and can't look after any of us with her bad leg and bad nerves, and anyway she has nowhere to take us home to. She starts to cry and scream hysterically. The doctor turns around and looks at us. Then he leaves the room. He's been here less than three minutes. When the door closes behind him, Mammy stops her crying.

"Don't worry, you'll only be going back to the homes for a few weeks, just 'til my leg is better and I can find another place to rent."

Helen tells her that Uncle John would keep us at his house for a few weeks. Mammy says no, I told you that Mary Murphy is not having you for skivvies.

Out in the corridor the council woman says she's ready to take us back. We're walking towards the main door. I look back and see Daddy at the other end of the corridor. I shout back to him.

"I hate you, I hate you 'cos we're all back in homes again, it's all your fault!"

My words are echoing all around the building. He doesn't reply. I don't really expect him to. I've seen scenes like this in films and on TV sometimes and I've always thought that the kids were wrong acting like that. Now I can understand more how they felt.

Mandy is in a car and is being taken back to the home in Bradford. We wave our goodbyes. She's sobbing her eyes out calling for her Mammy. Me and Helen are put in another car together. Mammy is standing in the doorway with Uncle John. Mammy isn't crying anymore, she's done her job. She's convinced the court that we'll be better off in homes for now. Uncle John Murphy has tears in his eyes, just like my Grandad in Dublin had, when Mammy dumped us all that time. Mammy is lighting a cigarette.

Soon we're passing the Calf and Cow rocks again and three miles later the car goes from the bumpy station road to the crunching gravel on the drive of the home. I get out and leave Helen crying in the car. I walk past Mr Watson and into the playroom and wave out to Helen as the council woman takes her on her way back to the other home in Penistone.

*

I'm sitting by the window watching little birds playing in the bird bath in the garden between me and the wooden driveway gates. Mr Watson comes in.

"Are you alright lad?"

"Yes thanks, I'm alright Mr Watson."

I know I'm not alright, and so does he. Mr Watson tells me that I have been placed in the care of the local council authority for the forseeable future. Permanent he says, not temporary like before. I'm still looking out at the bird bath. There's all sorts of things going through my mind. Why didn't Mammy let us stay with Auntie Mary? Will Helen be back at the home in Penistone where she'll be planning to run away again? Is Mandy back in the home in Bradford yet, where someone walloped her and cut her head? Does Mandy understand what's going on? She can't, she's only three and a half years old, and if I can't understand what's going on, how can she? Will some bad tempered 'auntie' hit her again, or even again and again? Who was the man called Peter who was with Marie? How can I let Maureen Feather know the real reason I sent her photograph back with an abrupt letter? What about Louise and Deirdre still in the home in Belfast? They have been promised, not long ago, that Mammy was going back to bring them over here to England. Now they'll be wondering what's going on over here in the Devil's Country, and the two John O'Briens and Dorothy Peterick will be wondering why I'm not back at St Anne's school. Now I'm wondering how the little girls in the home in Otley, who's mam is blind, are doing, and I'm feeling sorry for them. And now maybe everyone should be able to see that I'm entitled to think 'feck it' now and again.

Mr Watson says he'll sort out some clothes for me for going to the Catholic school in Ilkley. He says the Church of England school that the other boys go to is Ben Rhydding on the way to Ilkley. He says I'll be going by train with the other boys each morning, but that'll only be for a while 'til the new St Mary's school opens at Menston. It should have opened for early September, he says, but the building work was behind schedule. I'm only half listening. I'm thinking maybe I'll just run away like Helen did.

# Chapter 23

## I get a new name

Over the next few days 'permanent' things start to happen. Mr Watson says that now I'll be staying here, I'll have to have my name sewn into all my clothes, including underwear and socks. Like the other boys, so they don't all get mixed up. He says it's a lot of sewing to put O'Donoghue on all the clothes, so he asks if it is OK if he calls me 'Irish' like the tramp is called in the Arthur Haynes show on the television. "No offence meant," he says, but it'll save a lot of work for Auntie Carol who does all the sewing. I tell him it's fine with me. Now I'm thinking it really is OK with me for him to call me 'Irish' if it helps Auntie Carol. Anything is OK with me today. If he asks me if it is alright if they take me out to the backyard put me up against the wall and shoot me, I'm thinking that'll be fine too, no offence taken.

In the evening after tea I'm in the small kitchen with Roger Seamour and two other boys and my new name. Mr Watson says I can be in charge of this kitchen and make sure that all the cups, plates, dishes and cutlery are all washed, dried and put into the cupboards nice and neat. When the work is done I'm in the lounge area watching the television waiting for bath time. Auntie Carol is shouting for 'Irish'. One of the boys is nudging me. She hands me a pile of clothes with my new name stitched into them, including school clothes that I'll be needing next Monday when I start going to St Mary's school in Ilkley. I take them upstairs and put them into the small wardrobe, in the bottom drawer, beside my bed. Then I have my bath and have my hair pulled to see if it squeaks before putting on my pyjamas and dressing gown to go downstairs. I stop a while at the television lounge. 'Top of the Pops' is on. Peter and Gordon are singing a song about a world without love. Then Billy J. Kramer and the Dakotas are singing a song about little children. It reminds me of being at home and singing the song to little Mandy. I go into the playroom and sit by the window looking out into the rain. It looks cold out there, but I'm nice and warm in here, sitting over the brass grate that lets the heat rise up from the central heating pipes underneath. Then for no reason, I think about Tommy the cat and wonder if Daddy allows him into the house, or if he has to sleep in the outside toilet, in a cardboard box, being cold. Roger is playing a game with a dice and some other boys. He asks if I want to join in. I tell him no, but thanks anyway. At 9.30pm it's time for a glass of milk and some biscuits, then upstairs to join the compulsory queue outside the toilet and then into bed and lights out in ten minutes.

*

On Sunday morning I go to Mass by myself, across the field footpath and on to Menson Road, where the St

John Fisher and Thomas Moore church is. I put a penny in the collection plate and bring back the paper with this week's bible story, for Mr Watson. He says he likes to read it, but I'm thinking he wants to make sure I've been to Mass and not just gone for a walk. When I get back and change out of my school clothes and into my house clothes – shirt, striped jeans, and sandals instead of shoes – Matron says I can help in the big kitchen where she's making Yorkshire puddings for the Sunday dinner.

Matron makes me wash my hands and gives me a big bowl with the Yorkshire pudding mix and a big wooden spoon. She says I've to stir the mix clockwise and try to trap big air bubbles in it, and whatever I do, I mustn't change the direction of the mix. If I do, she says the puddings won't rise in the oven and the whole dinner will be ruined, and I have to stir it without stopping for exactly ten minutes, not nine minutes or eleven minutes, but ten. Now I'm thinking that I never knew that mixing for a Yorkshire pudding could be such an important part of the Sunday dinner. I'm hoping it turns out alright. There's a big pudding for each boy and each member of staff. The puddings are so big when they come out of the oven that they have to be put on side plates with gravy on them to be eaten before the roast beef and potatoes, 'cos they won't fit on the plates with the rest of the dinner. Now maybe Mr Watson and Matron won't be sending me to Coventry again, not after I've helped them cook the dinner.

On Monday morning I'm at the railway station with the other boys. Roger jumps down to the track and puts a penny on it. Then he jumps back up and waits for a diesel train to run over it. When he gets it back after the train has gone, it's been squashed and flattened out a lot bigger than it was. He says if Mr Watson found out, he'd be sent to Coventry for a long time. We go to the other side of the station and wait for the school train. When the next diesel-engined train comes I go to step on, but Roger holds me back and says the next train, in about ten minutes, is better. He says it's older and is pulled by a steam engine. He says we'll get that one instead. He's right, the next train is pulled by a proper steam engine. When we get on we stand at the doors and pull down the windows so we can lean out and see the big engines pumping out the steam that drives the wheels that are clattering along the lines. It's making me think of Mammy breaking her leg on the railway track in Keighley. The other boys get off the train at Ben Rhydding and five minutes later I get off at Ilkley station. I follow Mr Watson's directions out of the station and down Brook Street. I'm wondering if waiting for the steam train has made me late. I'm thinking it's about a quarter to nine. I ask an old man if he knows what time it is.

"Aye lad, it's just leaving five and twenty to," he says. I say thank you, but I haven't a clue what he meant and I still don't know what time it is. Left onto the Skipton Road, past the semi-detached houses, some with apple trees overhanging the pavement, tempting me, and right on to Stockled Road. And down to the tiny school just before the Church of the Sacred Heart.

The nun in charge shows me around the school. Two classrooms and a changing room next to a small yard. The nun looks older than my mother, more like Nana's age. She asks me lots of questions about my family, and where we come from and things like that. She's nice. She shows me a new statue of the Virgin Mary in the church, carved out of oak, and asks me how much I think it cost. It's a hard thing to guess. I'm thinking about how much a week's pay was for Daddy at the airport to help me figure out the cost. He was paid about £20 a week and the price of a good-sized cooking apple is sixpence. I'm guessing to her that the statue cost about fifteen pounds. It cost eighty pounds, she tells me. Eighty pounds! That's a month's wages for Daddy when he was at Nutts Corner Airport, and he was on a very good wage, Mammy used to say. Now I'm thinking that I'll have to learn how to do carving when I leave school instead of being a welder and making robots that can't walk and things like that. And anyway, a wood-carver can make things quietly, and won't keep getting shouted at by his mother or his wife when he's making nice things like statues, instead of making bogey carts and things like that.

At breaktime out in the playground, there's a tall boy called Ian and his friend John. They're making fun of me, asking me questions, silly questions that don't really need an answer. I'm trying to ignore them. I'm thinking I won't be making friends with them two.

After school I'm on the train. The other boys from the home get on the train at Ben Rhydding station. It's a diesel locomotive train, not a steam one like in the morning. The boys are pushing each other for a place by the door so they can lean out the window. Roger is telling me about his science teacher, who makes his science experiements more interesting by turning them into magic tricks when he can. He says today the teacher covered a glass of water with a cloth and when he pulled the cover off the glass, the water had turned red. I'm sure I've heard about that somewhere before. He asks me what my school is like and I tell him it's OK. But his question only makes me think about my friends in the Keighley School.

By Friday afternoon I'm thinking that the best part of going to school is the morning ride on the steam train. Ian Braithwaite and John O'Connor have stopped making fun of me and I've given in to temptation. I've had two of the overhanging apples on the Skipton road. I'm sure God will forgive me for this small crime, though I'm not sure Mr Watson would if he knew.

*

On Saturday morning it's pocket money time. Mr Watson wants to know how much of the two shillings I want to spend and how much I want to put into savings. I tell him I'll have sixpence to spend snd I'll save the other one and six, like the other boys do. I go down to the village and buy a big cooking apple for sixpence from the grocery shop on the main street, where the girl in the shop tells me off for holding the sixpence in my mouth before I give it to her.

I'm walking back up to the home, eating the cooking apple that reminds me of Grandad's house in Dublin. I meet Ian Braithwaite from school. I didn't know he lived in Burley. We stop and talk a while, then on my way back up to the big house I'm thinking maybe he's alright after all. Anyway that's the pocket money gone. Never mind, I'll be getting another sixpence next week.

Back at the house, David Hyam comes over to me in the playroom. He says he's seen me in the grocer's shop buying a cooking apple.

"It's not against the rules is it? I'm asking him.

"No," he says, "it's just that I know where there's lots of cooking apples, not far away, across the field behind the fat tree. There's an orchard at the bottom of Langford Lane." He says we could go apple raiding at night, when everyone's asleep. I'm telling him I'm not so sure, it's a big risk, and I know how easy it is to get into trouble here and it's not easy at all to get out of 'Coventry' when no one will talk to you. He says he'll take the chance if I will. I tell him I'm still not so sure. All week long before bedtime David keeps asking me about the apple raiding. He says he's never done anything like that before because of all the strict rules, and I'm the only one he trusts. I tell him I'll think about it.

Next Saturday it's the monthly haircut time again. Mr Watson pays the two shillings for the haircut, a short back and sides. We can have a different hair cut called the square neck if we want, where the barber cuts off less hair and charges sixpence more. If we have the square-neck haircut we have to pay the extra sixpence out of our pocket money. So I give up my Saturday cooking apple and go for the square-neck haircut. David hyam is still asking me about the apple raiding, which he says will be an adventure. I tell him it'll be an adventure lasting a month if Mr Watson finds out.

It's Saturday night and all the boys are in bed. The other boys in my bedroom and David's room are in on the apple-raiding plan. Some of them want to come with us but that would make it too risky. It's foggy and very dark outside, just the right weather for going on a quick and simple mission. We're going to do it like we've seen at the pictures, with sheets tied to the radiator so we can climb out the window and lower ourselves down to the drive. I'm telling David we'll go at midnight, and for now I'm going to do what I'm good at, going to sleep. He can come to my room later to wake me up. Secretly I'm hoping that he will fall asleep and the raid will not happen. But he wakes me up at quarter to twelve. I'm tired and I don't want to go, but he keeps telling me I've promised. I get dressed and put on my school shoes that should be downstairs in the old gunroom in their pigeonhole boxes. I take a pillow case to carry the apples in and sneak out of the bedroom and along the corridoor past Mr Watson's room, doing my best not to make the old floorboards creak. David is ready with two sheets tied to the radiator beside Johnny Hird's bed. We have to take two more sheets from Johnny's bed to reach far enough down. The bottom sheet is now about four feet above the gravel on the drive. I'm first out the window and I lower myself down with one foot on the stone at each side of the lower window, sliding down the window pillars, being careful to keep my feet away from the glass on the way down. At the other side of the big front doors there's a face at the window of Mr Watson's sitting room. It's Peggy the Dalmation dog, wagging her tail. David is climbing out the window.

"Come down slowly with a foot on each pillar," I tell him. Halfway down his right foot slips and grates across the leaded part of the fancy window. We're lucky it's not broken. He slides down the sheets with his back to the window. Peggy the dog is getting more excited because David takes her out for walks and she thinks she's going now. We spend a few minutes trying to calm her down with sign language. Johnny pulls the sheets up and leaves the window open so he can hear when we come back. The gravel under our feet sounds like the rumble of thunder in the quiet of the night. It takes a full five minutes to get across the gravel to the beginning of the lawn without making much noise. The Dalmation is watching us from the window all the time, with her tail wagging the curtains.

We go down across the lawns, into the small wood, past the fat tree and across the field to the bottom of Langford Lane. The orchard is on the left. There's some houses nearby with lights still on. We climb over a low fence and sit quietly, listening to the silence for a while.

Then it starts to rain heavily. We half fill the pillow case with apples, put a load more in our pockets, and walk back up the lane. We are soaked to the skin. We go back across the field and lawns and now we're soaked to the socks. Our socks are as wet as our school jumpers. We quietly crunch across the drive and I shout up to the window. It's hard to shout in a whisper. Peggy the dog is at her window with the curtains moving side to side behind her tail. There's no sign of Johnny Hird at the bedroom window. I throw a stone up and the dog starts yelping a bit. She thinks it's a game. I'm telling her to shush. Johnny opens the window and lowers down the sheets. We tie on the bag of apples and he pulls them up. Then I climb up, pulling myself up with my arms, my legs walking up the stone pillars that are now very wet and slippy, at each side of the TV lounge window. I go head first into the room and onto the floor. David climbs up a little bit and says he can't manage to climb up any further. I tell him to pull up with his arms and walk up the pillars with his feet. He tries. His right foot slips and nearly goes through the ground-floor window again as he spins round on the sheet and slides down to the ground. I climb back out the window and down to the drive. He has another go at climbing up the sheets with me pushing him from underneath, but he only succeeds in spinning around again and hitting his foot off the window pane. He's down on the drive again. The simple mission is now turning into a nightmare. I tell Johnny to pull up the sheets and close the window. We walk away from the dog, who is still watching us and wagging her tail. We walk around by the playroom to where Mr Watson's office is with a flat roof. I climb up the corner of the building and onto the roof that is level with the window in the wet-beds room. David has a leg on the windowsill down below, but he says he can't pull himself up any further. I climb back down and try to push him up again, but it's no use. We'll have to call Johnny again and get him to go downstairs and open the side door in the old gunroom. I'm throwing stones up at the window but there's no sign of him. The dog is growling now, a playful growl. I'm telling her to shush in case anyone hears. We're trying to crunch quietly around the corner of the house. The dog is following us from window to window. I try the handle on the door to the gunroom. *Thank you, God, it hasn't been locked tonight.* We put our wet shoes in the pigeon boxes and take off our wet socks and wipe our feet on the other boy's coats. We creep our way up the staircase, which takes a full five minutes 'cos the old stairs creak a lot more than the corridoor does. David goes back to his room. I'm making my way quietly back to my room when I hear Mr Watson moving around in his bedroom and his door handle is turning. I turn quickly into the toilet and into the cubicle. He comes out onto the corridor and calls into the toilet.

"Who's in there?"

"It's Irish, Mr Watson," I tell him.

"Is everything all right, lad?" he asks.

"Yes Mr Watson," I tell him.

"Good," he says, as I hear him walking back along the corridor at the side of his bedroom to the private toilet that's for him and Matron only.

I rush back to my room, strip off, put the apples from my pockets into my wardrobe drawer, then jump into bed in my nice dry pyjamas.

In the morning I'm fast asleep, doing what I'm good at. Auntie Carol is waking me and saying I'm the last one to get up and asking where my pillow case is. She says all the other boys are nearly dressed. I'm getting dressed slowly 'cos I'm still half asleep. She comes back into the room and folds up my pyjamas to help me. She opens the bottom drawer of my small wardrobe to put them away. She looks at the apples and then at me, and quickly shoves the pyjamas over the apples and closes the drawer.

"Hurry up," she says.

After breakfast and the washing up, I'm in my school clothes and wet shoes ready to go to Sunday Mass. Roger Seamour lends me a penny so I have something to clink into the collection plate when it comes round in the middle of the service. As I'm leaving the house Auntie Carol comes over and shoves an apple into my coat pocket.

"I found it on the front drive," she says. "I don't think Mr Watson should see it."

"Thanks!"

Ian Braithwaite from school is at Mass. We're talking a lot as we walk back through the fields on the footpath. I'm thinking he might be my friend after all, but I don't tell him about the apple raiding last night. He's not that good of a friend, yet. Back at the home Matron says Mr Watson wants to see me in his office when I've got changed, and when he's done with me, she wants to see me in the big kitchen. He must have found out about the apples. Auntie Carol won't have told him, I'm sure of that. I'm thinking that it looks like I'm in for the 'not talking to me' treatment again. And he'll be calling me 'Boy' instead of Brian or 'Irish'. The silence will probably last about three weeks, and even the things I do right will be wrong, and when the staff are around (most of them) the other boys will pretend they're not talking to me. I wish I was back in Keighley. There's plenty of apples there, and I wouldn't have to look for them at night, in the rain, when I should be sleeping, doing something that I'm good at, that doesn't get you into trouble, unless you can't wake up in the morning that is. I knock at the glass door to Mr Watson's office.

"Come in. Your mother has phoned this morning [phew, relief!] she's coming to see you next Sunday [no going to Coventry!]. She'll be here just after dinner [thank you God, I'm not in trouble after all!] you can show her around if you like, and take her for a walk into the village, weather permitting."

"Yes Mr Watson, thank you".

I go into the big kitchen. Matron, Auntie Carol and David Hyam are there.

"Come in Irish, I've got the Yorkshire pudding ready for you to mix. Just wash your hands first," says Matron. She is talking to Auntie Carol, telling her how Irish has settled in well and doesn't keep getting into trouble anymore. Auntie Carol looks over at me, so does David. Auntie Carol looks at Matron.

"Yes Matron. Irish asked me if there's any chance he can have a go at making apple crumble."

"Which way round do I do the stirring, Matron?" I'm asking.

Me and David move the apples and hide them in one of the sheds at the back of the house as soon as we can. I tell Him, Johnny Hird and Roger Seamour that if any of the other boys want an apple they can have one, but only one apple at a time, and only tell the boys that they can trust.

*

After school the next day there's a new boy at the home. I'm talking to him in the playroom. His name is David Brennan, he says he's fifteen. I'm thinking he's small for his age. Mr Watson says he's putting him in my bedroom. He says he wants me to look after him and show him what to do if he's not sure. Then Mr Watson calls me to one side and tells me that the new boy's family has split up, just like mine. On the first night in bed, David Brennan is crying. He doesn't want to talk to us. He's still crying when I fall asleep.

The next day after school, I let him join the apple club when he promises he can keep a secret. At night in bed, he's telling us about his mam and his stepdad fighting and splitting up, and the council taking him into care. He says he comes from Leeds where he lived in a block of flats, but he can't now 'cos his mam is in hospital. The next night he never shuts up. He knows everything about sex and girls and things like that. He's telling us how to have sex with rubber johnnies. He says when you do it you have to be careful that your stuff doesn't creep up inside the johnny and down the outside and make a girl pregnant. He says that girls like you to know what you're doing and go straight for the sex. He's still talking when I go to sleep. As a matter fact, he's still talking when I wake up. Mind you, I'm always the last one to wake up, even when I go to sleep first and haven't been out apple raiding, or staying up late talking. As another matter of fact, I think I'm the best sleeper in this home. David Brennan can talk the leg off a donkey. Every night for the next week he talks me to sleep. By Friday night, I've learnt a lot about sex and Leeds girls and periods and things like that. I'm thinking that now I know why my mother called Leeds 'Sin City'.

On Sunday morning I meet Ian Braithwaite on the way to Mass. I'm telling him that my mother is coming to see me today. When we get to the church we decide not to go to Mass. I go in to pick up the piece of paper with todays bible story on it so I can give it to Mr Watson so he'll think I've been to Mass. We walk up to Menston village phonebox and back down to Burley as there was nothing else to see up there. I have to keep a look out for Mr Watson's red mini car, in case he sees me.

At dinner time I still have my school clothes on from going to Mass, so I'm ready to go out again when my mother comes. After, when I'm in the small kitchen washing up I have to wear an apron so my school clothes don't get wet. Just as I've finished the washing up and putting away Mr Watson calls me out of the kitchen. I'm thinking she must be here.

"I've just had a phone call," he says, "your mother can't come today. She says she'll come next week and she'll ring again before she comes. He says never mind lad, better get off upstairs and get changed."

I get changed and lie on my bed. I don't want to go downstairs and see the other boys. All week I've been telling them that my Mam was coming to see me, and maybe she'll tell me when I'll be going home. I don't want them to see me nearly crying. It's got me thinking about wanting to go home to Keighley to see all my friends. Now I'm feeling upset again and confused. Last week I wasn't confused. I was happy pinching apples and hiding them and giving them out to the boys who could be trusted to keep a secret. I don't care about anything anymore. I'm finding it hard to stop myself from crying. Mr Watson comes into the room.

"Come on lad," he says, "come downstairs, it's not good for you to be up here on your own."

I go down to the playroom and sit on my own. When I look out the window at the birdbath, it reminds me of the day of the court case when I was waving Helen goodbye. David Hyam comes over to me. 'Hey Irish' he says quietly I've got a plan to raid the kitchen tonight for a midnight feast. No, I tell him, I'm not interested.

At night before bed David Hyam asks me again about raiding the kitchen. I tell him no. David Brennan is quieter than usual. He just asks me if I'm alright. I tell him a lie. I say yes I am thanks. Soon I'm settled back into the routine of the home, probably because there's been no letters and no phone calls and no being let down with promised visits to remind me to get upset.

At school I learn about arithmetic, English and religion. After school I learn how to do things so I don't get sent to Coventry, and at night I learn about the birds and the bees and a lot of bullshit as seen through the eyes of David Brennan who is back to talking the leg off a donkey. I never tell him to shurrup though. I don't want to upset him.

*

Around the end of November, Mr Watson leaves a catalogue book in the playroom. He says each boy can pick a Christmas present from the toy section, up to the value of one pound ten shillings. The boys are telling little six-year-old George Kershaw that Santa sent the catalogue. The boys pick out things like board games, plastic footballs, guns and swords and things like that. I pick out a pocket watch on a chain, it costs one pound ten shillings. That'll do I'm thinking, Grandad used to have one of those. If a pocket watch was good enough for Grandad then it'll be good enough for me. Now I'm thinking, at least the Council People make sure that everyone has something for Christmas.

The new boy, David Brennan isn't new anymore. He's been here talking for nearly two months. There's another new boy now called Martin. He's only thirteen, but he's very tall, he looks about fifteen. Mr Watson has put him in David Hyam's bedroom. The big boy, Martin, doesn't talk much to us. He's a bit of a bully. On the first night in bed he's threatening David Hyam, and Johnny Hird, and wanting to fight them. At breakfast time Mr Watson is telling us all, in front of the new boy, what happened when he was in the army and there was a big bully in his platoon. He said the other soldiers got together to give him a 'good ruddy thumping' and that sorted him out. He tells Martin to watch out, because that could easily happen here. It's after lights out when David comes into bedroom seven, he says that Martin is threatening them and wanting to pick a fight. I tell him that I was nearly asleep. He tells me that the bully boy says he's going to 'knuckle' them. Me and Roger Seamour follow him back to his room. Martin is stood beside his bed, calling the other boys names. He's getting excited now. He doesn't think we're going to stand up to him. When I see him standing nearly a foot taller than me, I'm not too sure myself. He's mouthing off and calling us names. I'm thinking we'd better do something now that we're here. I tell him that we don't want any trouble. That seems to give him more confidence to threaten us. His fists are up ready to fight. I put my hands up and half turn away.

"Look, we really don't want any trouble." I turn back, giving him one good punch with all my strength to his belly, which knocks the wind out of him and he falls. He falls onto his bed with me under him. The other boys are pulling me out from underneath him and telling him if he starts picking on them again, they'll all jump on him. Mr Watson walks in and turns on the light. He looks at Martin lying on his bed holding his stomach with both hands.

"Is everyone alright?" Mr Watson asks. "No black eyes? Good," he says, "everyone back to bed."

In the morning we're all lined up in the hall waiting to go in to breakfast. The new boy isn't here, he's run away. Mr Watson says he's stolen some money from the boys' lockers and a pair of shoes from the gun room.

"Well that's one bad penny gone for good," he says.

During breakfast I'm thinking that Mr Watson wanted Martin to run away, and he used me and the other boys to help make it happen. I'm thinking maybe I should have stayed in bed last night instead of helping him get rid of the problem boy who obviously wouldn't fit in with his army routine here.

On Saturday afternoon when I come back from buying my sixpence worth of sweets in the village Mr Watson is shouting at David Hyam. He's got hold of David by his collar and he's pinned him to the wood-panelled wall in the long hall. There's blood on David's lip. Mr Watson turns around and sees me watching. He lets go of David.

He says "Some boys can be hurt just by words, and there's others that can't." Then he walks away through the playroom and into his office. David walks past me. He has his wellies on. He goes into the gun room and takes them off. I know you're not supposed to wear your wellies in the house, but he must have done something worse than that to get a wallop. I'm also thinking that Mr Watson wouldn't have said anything to me unless he thought that he was in the wrong too.

After dinner on Sunday David Brennan tells me his mother is here to see him with her new boyfriend. The three of them go out down to the village. They come back in a couple of hours. His mother and her new man soon leave. David is in the gun room changing his shoes for his sandals. He's crying. He's crying a lot. He can't stop. Mr Watson is asking him what's wrong. In between the crying he's telling us why he's so upset. He says he doesn't like his mam's new boyfriend. He says when they went into the tearoom in the village he was just about to ask his mam when he'd be going home, but before he did she asked him where he will be staying when he leaves the home when he's sixteen. He says it was then he realised that she wasn't asking him to go home. Mr Watson takes him into the TV lounge and sits him down. He tells him that this is the first in a long line of kicks in the teeth that he'll get throughout his life.

"You'll get over it, lad," he says. "Life isn't easy."

Mr Watson asks me to stay with David to make sure he's alright. I sit down beside him. He's still crying. I'm thinking how could his mother do this to him? At least my mother is looking for a place so that I can go home again, isn't she?

*

November has gone and I never did find out why David Hyam got the cut lip. The new St Mary's secondary school at Menston is finally open. Mr Watson says that the nun at the Ilkley school has given me a 'glowing' report. He says she told him that she thought I was an angel and she wished all the children were as good and mannerly as me. I'm asking Mr Watson if he's joking. He says that's exactly what she said. I'm feeling a bit embarrassed. I don't think he should have told me in front of the other boys. Mr Watson says I'll be getting a new blazer for the new school. I'm telling him the one I have is fine. He says it is fine, except for the colour. The new one will be purple. Now the boys are pulling faces and saying things like 'very nice' and trying to be funny. In bed at night I'm trying to count up the number of schools I will have been to when I start at St Mary's Menston. It comes to eleven different schools, but if I count the times that I went back to schools I'd been to before, then it'll be about fourteen.

The headmaster is Mr Dalton. His first job is to tell us the rules and show us how strict he is. There's to be no talking while moving around the school from class to class. At the end of each playtime in the schoolyard, a whistle will be blown twice. Once for everyone to stop what they are doing, and the second for everyone to line up silently in their separate classes, before walking silently into the school. Mr Dalton is Irish. I'm thinking he's going to be very strict. I bet he's been taught by the brothers in Ireland and been beaten with leather straps and the stick, and he'll do the same to us if we step out of line. He says he's noticed that not everyone is wearing the purple blazers of the school uniform and he wants to see 'all purple' by next week. I'm glad I'm going to Guiseley after school to the school uniform shop to collect my new blazer. Not because I want a purple blazer but because I'll stand out if I don't have one.

There's a nun at this school too. Her name is Sister Mary Carmel. She's a lot younger than the nun at Ilkley school. She teaches English and she's very nice. I'm thinking she won't have been beaten with straps and sticks when she was going to school in Ireland like Mr Dalton probably was. She's too nice for that to have happened. During the first week I'm getting to know some of the boys and girls in my class. There's Raymond Hezelgrave and Trevor Scales and two girls, Barbara Jackson and Angela Dickinson. I'm thinking that they are going to be my friends.

It's nearly Christmas and David Brennan has heard nothing from his mother since she visited him. I've heard nothing from mine since she didn't visit me. There's a Christmas tree in the TV lounge and the presents that have come from Father Christmas's catalogue are wrapped up and put under the tree. At school there's preparations going on for the Christmas party in the assembly hall before the school holidays. Raymond Hezelgrave, Trevor Scales and me have brought some mistletoe to save for the party. Mr Mulvahill, the deputy head, takes it off us in case we want to try kissing any of the girls. When we finally have the party a week before Christmas it isn't that good anyway. The school is too strict to let us have any fun.

On Christmas Eve the boys in the home are sorting out the presents into different piles with their names on them. Some can't remember exactly what they asked for. Right at the front there's a small box with 'Irish' written on it. I'm not really bothered about not getting anything from home, wherever that is. I didn't really expect anything. I got some cards at school, but I've left them in my desk. One of them was from Sister Carmel. Now I feel bad, 'cos I didn't get one for her. On Christmas day, after breakfast and after doing our housework jobs, we can open our presents. The other boys are excited and making lots of noise.

I'm in the playroom with David Brennan. I have my watch and he has a football and some books. We're talking about not hearing from our mothers. We're finding reasons for them not even sending a card. He says his mam is probably sitting at home with no money. I'm telling him that mine is probably at home stewing the tea leaves and then trying to read them to see if things won't always be like they are now. But really I'm thinking we're just making excuses and trying to make each other feel better. It's not working for either of us. It makes me think about the day at the courts in Keighley. That day I blamed my father for everything. Now I realise that my mother is just as much to blame for me being in here as he is. I'm thinking that my mother and David Brennan's mam would get on well, and so would Mr Dalton and the brutal brothers in Ireland.

The weather outside is dry but very cold. It makes me think of my cat, Tommy. I have a feeling I'll never see him again. I hope he's warm, wherever he is. I'm thinking too about little Mandy and wondering why the council woman never brings her to see me. And I'm remembering about Raymin telling me that he had his worries but didn't worry about them. He won't be sitting somewhere worrying and thinking. He'll be sitting somewhere drinking. I don't say my nightly prayers like I used to. What's the point of asking St Jude to help my hopeless parents. They are both useless. I just have to accept that I'm on my own. Just like David Brennan.

# *Chapter 24*

## A phone call and a visit from my mother

I've been back at school three weeks since the end of the Christmas holidays. Some of my school friends are going to the pictures in Ilkley next Saturday. They want me to go with them. I have to make an excuse because the Saturday sixpence isn't enough to get me to Ilkley and into the pictures. After tea I'm in the small kitchen washing up and eating the leftover bread with real butter on it from the staff table. I'm washing a glass in the warm water when it breaks and cuts my thumb. Mr Watson says I'll have to go on the bus to Otley Hospital to get the cut stitched. He says Auntie Carol will go with me. When we get back Auntie Carol tells Mr Watson that we would have been back a bit sooner, only we had to wait twenty minutes to see the doctor. Mr Watson tells me that my mother rang to see how I was while I was at the hospital. He says she rang because she got a funny feeling that something was wrong with me so he told her that I was fine and that I was outside playing football with the other boys. He says he didn't want to worry her by saying I was at the hospital. She left a message for me to say she'll be coming to see me tomorrow.

"Bit of a coincidence that, don't you think? All this time with no news from her and she decides to ring when you're at the hospital."

"Yes Mr Watson," I say in agreement with him, but I'm not really surprised. I'm just thinking she'll have been reading the tea leaves again and getting another 'funny feeling.'

*

After dinner on Sunday I'm in the small kitchen wearing an apron over my school clothes, drying the plates and cutlery, and keeping my stitches away from the sink water. Little George Kershaw comes in shouting for 'Brian Irish.'

"Brian Irish, Mr Watson says your mam is here to see you."

Mr Watson is standing in the hall talking to my mother. There's a man with her. He's just a bit taller than me, about forty years old, with thick black hair. He's Irish. I know he's Irish before he even says hello. He just looks like an Irishman, like he's not happy wearing his suit and tie. He looks like he'd be happier with his tie in his pocket and his sleeves rolled up, so his arms could match his suntanned face that he's probably got from working outside in all weathers.

"Hello, this is Jack," my mother says, and he says hello and so do I. He shakes my hand.

Mr Watson is telling my mother that I was really at the hospital the night before when she rang but he didn't want to worry her and that's why he said I was out playing football. He's telling her now that I've been doing fine here in the home. He tells her that I got into a bit of trouble when I first came here and that he gave me a good telling off, but it was for my own good, and I'm doing fine now. He says I can show her and Jack around the house if I want to.

We go for a walk down to the village. It's a bit cold so we go into the tearoom on the main street after I've shown them the sights around Burley. I showed them Nobby Clark's barber shop, the greengrocer's where I sometimes buy my Saturday apple, and the garden where we raided apples one night. Jack buys some tea and biscuits for us all, while my mother is looking in her handbag for her cigarettes and matches, and I'm fiddling with the plaster on my stitches. When Jack sits down, my mother says his full name is Jack Maddigan. He's a friend of Raymin and Johnny. She says she's known him for three months, and he's a good man, nothing like that liten bastard in Keighley, God blast him! She says she's told Jack all about the troubles before at home and especially the time she broke her leg, that still hurts sometimes on a very cold day.

"Haven't I?" she says, looking at Jack.

"Oh yes you did, Josie," he says.

"Jack thinks he's a proper bastard, your father. Don't you Jack?" she says.

"Oh yes, oh yes, a proper bastard," says Jack.

"And you know how to deal with someone like that don't you?" She asks.

"Oh yes, Josie," says Jack.

"Well tell Brian what you'd do," she says.

Jack looks at me and says, "Your father wants tying to a wagon with a long rope and towing up and down on the road 'til he wears away on the tarmac and there's only the rope left."

"Now then," my mother says to me, "what do you think of that? Jesus, that's a good one isn't it!"

I'm not sure what to say, so I just smile and nod my head at Jack in agreement. Then Jack says, "Oh yes, lad, that's what he wants alright."

My mother says she's living in a room at Tennyson Place in Bradford and Raymin and Johnny have a room in the same house, and so has Jack. She says she's trying to find a bigger place so that me and Mandy can go home, and later Louise and Deirdre too, who are still with the nuns in Belfast. She says Helen is OK, living with Uncle Jimmy Reale who is my mother's brother, in Bury in Lancashire.

After lots more cigarettes for my mother and Jack, and lots of talking that didn't really tell me much, we're on our way back up Station Road and onto the footpath that leads past the lawns and up the steps in the rockery to the big house. My mother gives me a pound note, ten shillings from her and ten shillings from Jack. She touches the top of my head when she says goodbye, saying she'll write soon.

I'm upstairs changing into my house clothes, and when I look out the window I can see my mother and Jack going through the gate at the corner of the big lawn and onto the footpath that curves to the left, where they disappear back out onto Station Road. I don't think I'll be going home soon, and I'm not going to be waiting for the post to come in the mornings.

When we were out in the village I didn't even call my mother Mammy or Mam. Mammy or Mam is for someone who you live at home with, not for a mother you might see twice a year. It just doesn't feel right calling her Mam. When I wanted her attention, or to ask her a question I said "excuse me" or "by the way." In my brain, when I was thinking about her, I was still thinking of her as Mammy, but by the time the thinking got to my mouth it changed to "excuse me" or "by the way." Sometimes I just think of her as Josie.

*

I'm lying on my bed. I'm thinking about when David Brennan's mother came to see him and he got all upset when he realised she wasn't making plans to bring him home. I'm thinking now I know a little more about how he felt. I don't want to go downstairs yet. I'll try to forget about not going home. I'll think about Ann Mahon, a girl from school. We're going out with each other. There's not much actual 'going out' though, because with me being in this home and her living in Ilkley, we only see each other at school. I can't even afford to take her to the pictures on a Saturday, with only sixpence to spend. But now I have a pound in my pocket and I'll be able to afford to take her to the pictures next Saturday. Now I'm not feeling so sad anymore. I think I'll go downstairs and get some advice from David Brennan for my first proper 'going out' with Ann, who looks a bit like Bridie Gallagher in Belfast, with shoulder-length hair, except Ann is a bit taller than Bridie, about six inches. She's taller than me too. She has a smiling, pretty face, like Maureen in Keighley. I find David Brennan in the playroom. I'm feeling a bit better now.

On Monday morning I'm on the bus going to school. I can't wait to see Ann to ask her out to the pictures next Saturday, now that I can afford to. Sam Renton is on the bus. I know Sam from going to the Ilkley School. He knows all about car makes, and he can tell you the name of every make of wagon on the road. Sam knows I've been going out with Ann. He asks me if I'm still going out with her and I tell him yes and that I'm taking her to the pictures next Saturday with the money my mother and Jack gave me yesterday.

"I've something to tell you," Sam says.

"I bet you've got another one of those wagon models that you collect."

"No," he says, "it's about Ann. I saw her in Ilkley on Saturday, she was with Trevor Scales from your class and they were kissing at the pictures. I'm sorry to have to tell you, but I just thought it wouldn't be fair if you didn't know."

The second half of the fifteen minute bus journey to school seems to take an hour. I end up thinking it doesn't really matter. How could I be going out with her properly, with me being in a home in Burley in Wharfdale and her living in Ilkley and only seeing each other at school breaktimes? It wasn't her fault I didn't have enough pocket money to go to see her in Ilkley on a Saturday or a Sunday to take her to the pictures, where she would have been kissing me instead of Trevor Scales. Trevor Scales is supposed to be my friend. He's smaller than me and she's taller than me. He'd have trouble kissing her if they both stood up. And I'm better looking than him. I'm feeling hurt now, but if it wasn't Trevor it would eventually be someone else who could afford to take her out at the weekend. I'm not going to say anything at school, there's no point.

I'm in the locker room when Trevor comes in. I don't say anything about Ann, I'm just acting normal. He starts fooling about, as usual.

"I hear Ann Mahon is pregnant," he says.

I'm thinking that's a really stupid thing to say, but then he does say lots of stupid things. The head girl is standing in the doorway. She looks at me and asks if it's true. I'm just feeling embarrassed. I tell her it was what Trevor just said. We go to the classroom on the top floor of the school and I try to forget about Trevor and Ann, and the stupid thing he said. I'm looking out the window over the playground and the sports field to the railway line. The occasional steam train reminds me of Keighley and my friends there, and St Anne's School. There's a knock at the classroom door. The head girl sticks her head in and says that the headmaster wants to see me and Trevor. We go to Mr Dalton's office with her. The door bangs a bit as it closes behind us. It hasn't got a cushion closer on it like all the other doors in the school. The head girl is telling him what was said in the locker room. Mr Dalton says he's not having talk like that in his school. Trevor says it was only a joke. The headmaster gets his cane out and gives Trevor two wallops on the hand and sends him back to the classroom. He then gives me two wallops of the cane on my hand. I tell him that I've done nothing wrong. All I did was say to the head girl that it was what Trevor had said, it wasn't me who said it in the first place. Now Mr Dalton is getting annoyed.

"So if you did nothing wrong, why did you put you hand out for the cane?"

"Because you told me to. And it's not true about Ann Mahon," I tell him.

"I didn't think it was true for one minute, now get back to your classroom!" he shouts.

I leave the office. I haven't got more than four steps away from his door when he runs out after me and belts me two hard blows to the side of my face with his hand. I'm really surprised by the wallops he gives me. I can't think fast enough to figure it out. He's shouting at me.

"Don't you ever slam a door on me and show your temper in this school!"

I'm telling him I didn't slam the door, but his temper is up and he won't listen to me.

"Get off to your class!" he shouts at me.

I go back to the classroom. I've got my left hand up to the side of my face. It feels red hot and sore. The teacher, Mr Bramer, says he's just been talking to the class about voluntary staying on at school for another year, starting in the autumn. He says he's been taking names of the people who might want to stay on. I'm trying to talk to him but it's hard because I'm shocked and on the verge of crying. I don't want the class to see me crying so I manage to get the words out.

"I won't be on your list for next year," I tell him.

"I don't think now is the right time for you to make up your mind," he says, "I'll ask you again later."

I don't have much to say to Trevor Scales for the rest of the day and I don't go to see Ann at breaktimes anymore. I'm thinking today must be one of the 'kick in the teeth' days that Mr Watson talks about. When I'm leaving school at about a quarter to four the head girl comes up to me.

"I'm sorry'" she says, "I never thought you would get into so much trouble. If I knew what was going to happen, I wouldn't have told Mr Dalton."

"It's OK," I tell her, "it wasn't you who hit me."

When I get back to the home I go to see Mr Watson. I tell him all about what happened at school. I tell him that I didn't do anything wrong and I got the cane and walloped as well. I'm getting upset and something inside me is wanting to burst out crying, but I won't let it. I'm telling him about it being a kick in the teeth day, like he says life gives you, when you don't expect it.

"Leave it with me," he says, "I'll be ringing the headmaster first thing in the morning."

After tea I'm in the playroom with some of the big boys and Auntie Carol. They're wanting me to join them in practising for a show they want to put on for the rest of the boys and the staff. Most of it is just miming to record songs. I tell them no. The next week at school seems a very long one.

Auntie Carol is asking me again if I will join the show they want to do. Each evening I can hear them practising their show in the laundry room with a record player on. On the second week I join them. I'm getting over the wallop at school and the problems with my love life, or the love life I nearly had. Auntie Carol wants me to mime to a Rolling Stones song. She gives me an oversized jumper to put on and a piece of stick to use as a microphone. The other boys have cardboard cutout guitars and are the Rolling Stones band. I have a mop head tied to my head and I have to be Mick Jagger and dance around the 'stage' like he does. All goes reasonably well until the middle of the song, "Because I used to love her" – ba bum bum – "but it's all over now." I burst out crying. I'm wailing out loud. I sit on the old armchair that's full of clothes waiting to be ironed and pull off my mop head. The backing group stops playing the cardboard guitars. One of the boys turns off the record player. I'm sobbing into my hands. Auntie Carol comes over to me.

"What's the matter, Irish?" she asks.

"Nothing's the matter," I sob back to her.

She tells the other boys to go into the television lounge while she has a talk with me. She tells them not to say anything to the other boys or the staff. Then I blub it all out to her. My mother came to see me and it looks like it'll be a long time before I'll be going home, my ex-girlfriend's been kissing my classmate at the pictures, the head girl got me into trouble even though she didn't mean to, Mr Dalton gave me the cane, and then the walloping for banging his door shut when I didn't, and the new girlfriend I have at school who I got on the rebound has finished with me today and given me no reason.

"And I thought I was going to be alright until Mick Jagger reminded me that 'It's all over now,' with Ann Mahon and made me break down and cry, 'cos it's been another kick in the teeth day, and now here I am sobbing my eyes out, with a broken heart, and it's all Mick Jagger's fault!"

Auntie Carol has her arm around my shoulder. I'm trying to catch my breath and stop crying.

"What are you crying about most?" she asks me.

"Everything," I tell her.

"But what's the worst one?" she asks.

"Ann Mahon kissing Trevor Scales," I tell her.

"You'll soon get another girlfriend," she says.

"Not like her," I'm saying, "I really liked her, I loved her."

"How long had you been going out with her?" she asks me.

"Four weeks," I tell her.

"And have you kissed her?

"Of course I have."

"How many times have you kissed her?" she asks me.

"Once."

"Just once?" asks Auntie Carol, smiling at me.

I'm thinking for a minute.

"Yes once."

"Where did you kiss her?"

"In the playground"

"No, where did you kiss her?"

"Oh, you mean *where*?"

"Yes," says Auntie Carol.

"On the bottom lip."

"On the bottom lip?" she asks.

"Well she's taller than me," I tell her.

Auntie Carol is smiling. Now she's making me smile too. I'm wiping the tears away from my face now.

"So it wasn't really such a serious love affair," she says.

She's making me smile again.

"No."

"And you're going to be alright now?"

"Yes, thanks," I tell her.

"Right," she says, "I'm going to call the other boys back in."

When they come back into the room Auntie Carol tells them that Irish is OK now, but they mustn't tell anyone about me getting upset, not even Mr Watson.

"Right," she says, "let's try a different record. How about Peter and Gordon's 'World without love?'" That does it, now I'm off again wailing into my hands.

# Chapter 25

## Adventures in Blackpool

The next day at school, Sister Carmel is asking me about getting into trouble with the headmaster the other week. She's asking if I'm alright. When I tell her exactly what happened, she doesn't look too happy about Mr Dalton walloping me. When I see her again later in the library, she doesn't mention anything more about it. It's only then that I realise Mr Watson hasn't mentioned anything about ringing the headmaster like he said he would about the walloping thing. I don't think I'll bother asking him. (It would be many years later when I found out that Sister Carmel had gone to the headmaster to protest on my behalf, only to be told that if she persisted with her complaint she would be putting her job on the line.) Sister Carmel asks me to help in the library each afternoon during breaktime. I have to stamp the books out or in, and keep track of the names of the pupils who use the library. I'm thinking it's me she really wants to keep track of, and not the books. I think she's trying to keep me out of trouble.

I've found a book about Darwin's theory of evolution. I've been talking to Mr Bramer in the maths class about it.

"How can the Bible be right about the world being created by God in seven days, if evolution is true?" He says that Darwin is right and that the stories in the Bible are symbolic, an easy way to explain to young people how God made the world and the universe. I'm asking him about the stories of Adam and Eve and Cain and Abel, and saying that they couldn't have existed if Mr Darwin was right. I'm saying that all the priests, brothers and teachers have been telling lies since I first started school.

"No, they haven't been telling you lies, not really. The stories were just symbolic," says Mr Bramer.

"So they are symbolic lies then?" I'm asking him.

"How did we get onto this subject?" he asks. "Let's get on with the sums on the board."

But I can't get on with the sums. I'm still thinking about the story of Adam and Eve in the Garden of Eden and Darwin's story about evolution. They can't both be true, not if one of them is symbolic. Now I'm a bit confused, and now for no particular reason I'm remembering that when Mr Dalton was walloping me he said I had a chip on my shoulder, and now I'm wondering what that means.

"And when you've done the sums on the board," Mr Bramer says, "we'll be doing some logarithms." God I hate logarithms, and Mr Dalton for walloping me when I didn't deserve it, and calling me a chip on the shoulder, when I don't even know what he meant, and Trevor Scales too, for kissing Ann Mahon and saying something stupid and getting us both into trouble. I don't hate Ann, though, I just don't. By the next day, I don't hate anybody. By the next week, we're all talking to each other again, except me and Mr Dalton.

A few weeks later we're all on a school trip to Malham Cove in the Yorkshire Dales. We go from the school on coaches to Malham village, and then for a walk along the river and the waterfalls, along the top of the cove and then back down to the village where we have sandwiches, fruit and cold drinks. We're allowed to look around the village before it's time to get on the coaches to go back to the school. Those of us who live somewhere on the route back can ask the teacher to get the bus to stop when we're near home. Just before we get on the bus, Raymond Hezelgrave tells me that Ruth Copsy wants to go out with me. He says he's serious, she's asked him to ask me if I will go out with her. I know Ruth Copsy and she's very nice. Raymond reminds me that she has a good figure, especially the top half. I remind him that she lives a long way from the school near Otley, miles away from Burley in Wharfdale. She even has to leave school early every day to get home at a reasonable time. What's the sense in me saying yes, with her living far away, and me living in a home that doesn't let me out, only on a Saturday afternoon, and sometimes for a walk on a Sunday? What's the point in going out with her if I can't 'go out' with her?

We're on the bus. We've come through Ilkley and we're just getting into Burley in Wharfdale. Mr Bramer is asking why Ruth Copsy is crying at the back. Raymond Hezelgrave says "She's lovesick, sir." I get off the bus with Ian Braithwaite. We walk up Station Road together 'til he turns off onto Midgley Road. I'm walking up to the big house thinking about Ruth Copsy. I'll see her at school tomorrow. She'll be alright by then. And when I do see Ruth at school, she waves and smiles. I wave back to her. She's fine. Like I was after Mick Jagger and Peter and Gordon upset me.

It doesn't seem long 'til school is preparing for the inter-house competitions in June. I'm entering in everything I can think of. I'm not great at sport, but I give it a good try. I enter for the long jump, the high jump, 100 metres and 800 metres. I even borrow a bicycle from a boy called Alan Field and enter the cycle race around the sports field. The high jump was the one I really tried to win. I tried so hard that I landed hard on the sand and hurt my back when I cleared the bar at 5 feet 3 inches. I came second in the school. The head boy, David Walker, won. I really wanted to win him, not the competition. Later, Sister Carmel told me that I had, as an individual, entered the most competitions. She said she had suggested an award for the best individual effort of the day, but the headmaster didn't seem interested. I tell her I would have been happy just to have beaten the head boy at the high jump.

At the end of term and the start of the summer holidays some of the pupils who won't be back next September are saying goodbye. Mr Watson has told me that I'll be staying on 'voluntarily' next year. Ruth Copsy won't be coming back. She puts her arms around me and she's crying. Tears are streaming down her face.

"I might never see you again!" she cries. I tell her she can always come and see us all at school.

I didn't expect it to be like this. I didn't think anyone would be crying. I can't remember pupils crying about leaving other schools. I'm trying to think about when I left the other schools I've been to. But then I didn't know I was leaving most of them, it just turned out that I didn't go back. I'm not the least bit sad that I'm leaving for the summer holidays. I'm not looking forward to coming back in September either.

We finish early today for the holidays. The sports teacher walks out onto the main road and puts his hand up to stop the traffic so that we can cross the road safely. The car coming up the road stops. The wagon behind it doesn't. I don't think the teacher will be finishing early today like we are.

*

By the end of the first week of the holidays, there's another boy come to the home. His name is Alec Cunningham, he's aged sixteen. The weather is good and most days we're out on the lawns playing football or cricket. Me, Roger Seamour, Johnny Hird and Alec Cunningham climb the fat oak tree and nail a big plank of wood to the top y-shaped branches so we can sit up there and look out over all of Burley in Wharfdale. Mr Watson can't see us because of all the leaves on the trees, so we don't get into trouble. Matron Watson even lets me take Peggy the Dalmation for walks across the fields and back through the village. Some days we get the big empty fruit tins from outside the back kitchen door and 'borrow' sausages from the fridge to go 'camping' behind the fat tree. We have to keep the fire small and inside one of the tins, so Mr Watson doesn't see the smoke. Three other boys have started a gang. They call themselves the Black Knights of the Court. They even have a flag with B.K.C. on it, with a big B and the K and C written inside the top and bottom of the B. We let them use the top of the fat tree for their meetings.

We're all lined up in the hallway one dinner time when Mr Watson has a word with us all.

"I hear there's a gang operating in the house. I hope this gang is for playful purposes and not for going down to the village and causing trouble. If it's just for fun, then you can have as many gangs as you like."

I'm thinking Mr Watson doesn't miss much.

"And I hope there'll be no lovesick boys jumping into the river Wharfe. Love," he says, "you haven't a clue what love is. Have they Irish?"

"No Mr Watson," I reply. Now I'm thinking someone has been doing a lot of talking.

*

There's a new auntie in the wet-bed room one morning. She's not sure if one of the boys has wet the bed or not. He says that when he woke up his pyjamas were a bit wet. He says it's what the boys call a wet dream. The auntie calls Mr Watson. He says leave the sheets, just change the pyjamas. At breakfast time the boy has a big yawn at the table. Mr Watson stands up at his table, points at the boy, and shouts across the dining room.

"Look at that, I'm not surprised you're tired, boy! You go to bed at night to sleep! Not to play with yourself! You'll be going blind as well as being tired, boy!"

Mr Watson's face is red. The boy's face loses its colour and goes pale. He bursts into tears and runs out of the room. The breakfast is finished in total silence, including the staff. I'm thinking that what Mr Watson just did is not right. Any of us older boys could have been in that position. It's just not right. Mr Watson was wrong to do what he did. He was totally wrong. Mr Watson is a dirty liten bastard, I'm thinking. The boy was in Coventry for nearly three weeks, for doing nothing wrong. Me, the new boy Alec, Roger and the Black Knights didn't send him to Coventry though.

*

It's the end of July and I've been here nearly a year. It's over six months since I've heard anything from any of my family. We're all going to Blackpool in about a week for a fortnight's holiday. Mr Watson has got the pocket money ready for us. It's what we're been saving all year. It will be divided by fourteen and each day we will get the daily pocket money from our savings. I'll be getting seven shillings a day pocket money when I'm at the seaside.

We have to have the monthly haircut early for the holidays. Mr Watson says we can have the square neck haircut if we want and sort the extra sixpence out with him later. Most of us have the square neck haircut because David Brennan says the girls in Leeds go for boys with modern styles, and there's sure to be some Leeds girls in Blackpool.

We're sitting in the barber's shop in a queue when a local man comes in. Mr Clarke lets him jump to the front of the queue. When he's leaving he asks Mr Clarke for a 'packet for the weekend'. The barber is laughing and having a joke with him as he takes a packet of something out of a drawer at the back of the shop and gives it to him. I'm thinking that they are cigarettes and the man must only smoke at the weekend, probably when he's out drinking in the Malt Shovel.

The next Saturday the sun is shining and we're on the coach to Blackpool. After about two and a half hours, Mr Watson says there's sixpence for the first person to see Blackpool Tower. I'm asking him what it looks like. Like a smaller Eiffel Tower he says.

"There it is!" I'm shouting.

"No," he says, "that's an electricity pylon."

"There it is," I'm shouting again, when I see a fatter-looking pylon.

"Yes," he says, "that's it." Then he says, "Did you have a square neck haircut?"

"Yes sir."

"Right then, we're straight with the sixpence you owe me," he says.

We go into Blackpool past a small airport and over a railway bridge beside a field with lots of horses with bushy, hairy legs on them. Mr Watson says we're on the South Shore. We stop outside a house on Withnell Road, number 46 is on the stone door pillar. 'Mil-dene' is written under the 46. The sun is shining. We're on holiday. I've heard a lot about Blackpool, but I've never been here before, so I'm excited. We take our bags and small suitcases into the rooms that Mr Watson tells us to go to. Then we go to the dining room for some dinner and the first day's pocket money that Mr Watson gives us, after he's taken out the sixpences for the square-neck haircuts from the other boys.

After dinner we can all go out to explore the town. Me, Roger and Alec Cunningham set off together. The first place we go to is the Pleasure Beach, where we stand laughing at the laughing policeman that's in a glass box. Then we go into the Fun House where we get lots of bumps and bruises from falling down inside a big rolling barrel. Back outside the Fun House we have lots of tries at winning things on the stalls, but we don't win anything. Pocket money doesn't last long at Blackpool.

On the way back to the boarding house, there's a man on a corner with a suitcase selling bits of sponge that looks like fried eggs. There's a crowd around him and he's telling them that the sponges will cure any ailments you have just by rubbing them on your body. He's selling them for 10 shillings each. Alec says he's a confidence trickster, he says there's lots of them around, you'd have to be stupid to buy one of those. Back at the boarding house Colin Metcalf says he's bought something special today. He takes it out of his pocket. It's one of those miracle sponge eggs.

After tea we're back out around the seafront. Mr Watson says we have to be back at the house for nine o'clock at the latest. We've spent today's pocket money in the afternoon so tonight we're just walking around looking at everything. There's the open-air swimming pool on the seafront before you get to South Pier. I think we'll go there tomorrow for the afternoon. It'll be cheaper than going to the Pleasure Beach.

There's posters everywhere advertising the shows. Charlie Cairoli the clown is on at the Tower Circus, Thora Hird is at the Grand Theatre, the Black and White Minstrels are at the Opera House and Jimmy Clitheroe is at the Pavilion. Gerry and The Pacemakers are on at South Pier and The Beatles were on the 'Blackpool Night Out' television show in the first week of August. On some other posters we find out that we can go to Liverpool to look for The Beatles if we want for twelve shillings return on the train, and if we have a car we can buy a new tyre for two shillings down with nine months to pay the rest. Alec says he would like to go to see Gerry and The Pacemakers sometime, but at six shillings and sixpence for the cheapest seats he's out-voted. He'll have to go on his own if it's going to be that expensive. At night in bed after the usual glass of milk and biscuits, Mr Watson tells us all to try to keep the noise down. He says he knows we're all excited about being on holiday, but we mustn't be talking too late. He has let some of us swap beds so that me, Roger and Alec are in the same bedroom. It was hard work trying to convince Colin Metcalf to swap with Alec. Colin wouldn't let us have a go with his miracle sponge, but that's no surprise to us. He never shares anything. He's a bit selfish. As a matter of fact, he's a lot selfish. We had to give him some money to swap beds.

We're planning what to do tomorrow. The decision goes to the vote. In the morning we're going to find the field at the far side of the railway line where we saw the horses with the hairy legs. After dinner we'll go to the South Shore open air baths for the afternoon and we'll still have some of the daily pocket money left for the evening. Now I'm thinking I'll leave it 'til tomorrow to explain to the others that I've never learnt to swim.

In the morning the three of us set off down the road to the railway line and the fields. There's about six ponies in the field. We go over to them slowly. They let us get close to them and pet them. It's not long 'til we're sitting on three of them and they're walking around the field giving us a free ride. Then it's not much longer 'til we're running like mad back to the main road with two gypsy men chasing us off their horses and their field.

After dinner we go to the outdoor baths. It's got big pillars and a part glass dome on top of the entrance. It's the biggest swimming pool I've ever seen. We change into our swimming trunks and start sunbathing on our towels. I tell the other two that I can't swim. Alec says that it's OK cos he can't either. We spend most of the afternoon in the water. I keep practising swimming and bit by bit I'm getting better. By the end of the afternoon I can swim about twenty feet without putting my feet onto the bottom of the shallow part, I can hold my breath and sit on the bottom of the pool, and our backs are getting red with the sun. After tea we go to the Pleasure Beach where we meet some Scottish girls. We pay to take them through the Tunnel of Love, where they let us kiss them in the dark. Then we take them into the Fun House where we get lots of bumps and bruises and grazes on our knees and elbows from falling down inside the big turning wooden barrel again. We're spending our money on the girls and getting lots of kisses from them. We think we're big 'men' now 'cos we have money to spend. Then when the money is all gone and we try to kiss them again outside the Fun House, the biggest of the girls pulls the younger ones away and turns and tells us to get lost. Now I'm thinking about something my mother would say: "When little boys have money they're men, but when it's gone they're boys again."

A bit later we see the girls again. I persuade Roger to approach them. He goes over to them and talks to the big girl.

"Irish wants to see you."

He comes back with a message for me: "Tell Irish to get lost!"

Now I'm thinking maybe it's time to go back to the boarding house where Mrs Love who owns it will be getting the milk and biscuits ready.

The days are going too fast and the weather is great. Blackpool is crowded, the sands and the pavements are crammed with people. The loudspeakers at the Pleasure Beach are blasting out all the pop songs. 'Hey Mr Tambourine Man' by The Byrds is topping the charts, along with The Beatles and lots of other bands from Liverpool. Back at the boarding house, Mr Watson hears us talking about the pop bands and he says that they are all just a bunch of bigheaded show-offs. He says it's nothing like the good music from the 1940s.

By the second week of the holiday we're saying that spending money on girls only gets you a few kisses and empty pockets. David Brennan says that's because we haven't met any Leeds girls yet. So now we're listening out for girls with a Leeds accent and spending the pocket money on things we can keep, like footballs, cricket bats, cowboy hats, water pistols and John Bull printing sets. Alec Cunningham has more savings than the rest of us. He buys himself a good accoustic guitar so that he can try to be a bigheaded show-off when Mr Watson is around, he says.

Roger Seamour says there's another swimming baths, not an open air one, somewhere behind the Queen's Hotel across from South Pier. So on Thursday, two days before the end of the holiday, me, Roger, Alec and David Brennan go to the indoor baths. We go along the front past the Queen's Hotel where all the posh people go for their holidays and down Waterloo Road. We're asking a shopkeeper where the indoor swimming baths are. He sends us further down the road and right onto Lytham

Road where we find it. After a while in the baths, and me practising my swimming in the not-too-deep end, Roger comes running up to us from the other end of the pool. He's telling us that a girl came up and stood beside him in the water. Then without saying anything she put her hand under the water and squeezed his privates through his swimming trunks. I'm telling him I don't believe him. Watch this he says. He goes back to the girl, who looks to be about fourteen. He stands beside her in the water. He's leaning against the side of the pool. She's looking away from him. Her hand goes down under the water. He's looking at us, his eyebrows are raised and he's got a smile on his face as big as the first quarter of the moon. The girl gets out of the pool and says something to him. He comes sliding up the side of the pool.

"Told you," he says, "and she says she'll be back tomorrow morning and she wants us all to come back then, when she'll bring her friends."

"Is she serious?" I ask him.

"Is she from Leeds?" David Brennan wants to know.

"Come on," I tell them, "it's time to go back for dinner."

Me, Alec and David climb out of the pool.

"Come on," I'm telling Roger.

"I can't just yet," he says, looking down under the water at his trunks, "I'll be out in a minute."

*

At teatime, most of the boys are outside the house sitting on the walls and the steps waiting to be called in for tea. David Brennan is telling them about the girl at the baths. Suddenly everything goes quiet as Mr Watson opens a first-floor window and shouts down.

"If there's any boy down there who haven't paid me their sixpence for the square-neck haircuts, will you please let me know so that I can take it out of Friday's spending money?"

The window closes and David finishes telling the boys all about the girl at the swimming baths. He makes sure not to say anything in front of Colin Metcalf, 'cos he might tell Mr Watson, or in front of little George Kershaw 'cos he's too young to know 'big boy' business.

Later when Mr Watson is collecting the three sixpences still owed to him for the haircuts, he says he's noticed that some of the boys are in the house, hanging around either to save money or because they've spent it too soon.

"If you've spent your money early, then get off down to the beach and enjoy the sunshine. Play football or cricket on the beach, do something positive, don't hang around the house being miserable and getting in Mrs Love's way. Get out and enjoy yourselves for the rest of the evening."

*

It's Friday morning, the sun is blazing down. After breakfast, most of the boys are outside the house. There's footballs, cricket bats, kites, towels and trunks, everyone is outside and ready to go except Colin Metcalf who is looking after little George Kershaw. Colin 'volunteered' to look after George today. He volunteered after the rest of us chipped in enough money for him to buy himself another fried egg. So now he can cure twice as much of everything. Mr Watson says it's good to see us all together and taking his advice about going to the beach. Colin and George are soon ready. We all set off up Withnell Road towards the front. When we get to the promenade, I tell Colin that we'll all be down on the sands if he wants to join us. He says he's not bothered about playing football or cricket. He says he's off to find the man on the corner with the suitcase.

We all go to the road crossing. When we're sure that Colin and little George are out of sight, me, Alec and Roger run up towards the Queen's Hotel, then turn right onto Rawcliffe Street, with most of the other boys following us down to the baths on Lytham Road. When we get to the baths there's a board outside on the pavement. It says 'Welcome to the adult swimming lessons for beginners, over 18s only.' On the way back to the seafront and the beach, David Brennan is explaining to us that girls like the one at the baths yesterday, who didn't come back today, are called prick teasers in Leeds. I'm thinking they're probably called prick teasers in Blackpool too.

The day is spent on the sands playing football and swimming in the sea. The evening is spent at the Pleasure Beach and in the Fun House again, collecting more bumps and bruises from the turning barrel and the spinning circle on the floor that you can't manage to stay on no matter how hard you try, and all the other things you can go on for free after the entrance fee is paid. In the evening me, Roger, Alec and David Brennan try one last time in the Fun House and on the prom listening out for girls with Leeds accents.

On Saturday morning after breakfast we're on the coach heading for the A62 going over the Pennine hills on our way back to the home in Burley in Wharfdale. I'm thinking about the two weeks in Blackpool. I've got a sunburnt back, bruises on my elbows and knees. We've been cheated by the Scottish girls who only kissed us so we spent our money on them. We've been chased by the gypsies who owned the horses with the hairy legs. We've been fooled by the girl at the baths who was a prick teaser. The promenade is full of conmen selling things that don't work properly, and I've nearly learnt to swim.

Blackpool is great. I can't wait to come back again.

# Chapter 26

## A running away adventure

Mr Watson calls me into his office. He gives me a letter from my mother that's come while we were in Blackpool. I read it in the games room. The letter is from Brighouse, a small town between Bradford and Huddersfield, where she is living with Jack Maddigan and my brother Raymin, and a dog called Bunty. She's asking if I've left school yet or will I be staying on the extra year that's just come in with all the schools. The letter is two pages long and doesn't tell me much, or mention anything about me going 'home'. My 15th birthday is tomorrow and she doesn't even mention that. She signs it love from your Mam. In my head I'm not thinking of her as Mam. I'm thinking of her as Josie, just someone I know. I'm thinking about her not mentioning my birthday. But then I'm realising that I didn't remember her birthday on the 20th of June either. Mr Watson calls me into his office again.

"There's another letter here for you," he says.

It looks like a birthday card. Now I'm thinking to myself, maybe she did remember my birthday after all. I open the card: 'To Brian, happy birthday and God bless, from Sister Mary Carmel.'

The day before school starts in September Mr Watson hands me an old leather briefcase. He says it's called a Gladstone bag and he's had it all through his military service and I have to look after it at school. He says that the council woman in Shipley is going to get me one of those new plastic briefcases for my schoolbooks, and he'll have his Gladstone bag back when the briefcase comes.

I'm on the bus to school. I feel the odd one out regarding my clothes. Winkle picker shoes are in fashion, but I have lumpy round-toed shoes that look like working boots. Tight slim trousers are in fashion, mine are baggy and grey with turnups, and the old battered Gladstone bag will never ever be in fashion again if I was to wait for twenty years. I wish the other school kids wouldn't keep calling me 'doctor' and telling me their ailments. When I see Sister Carmel I thank her for the birthday card.

On the second day back at school, Raymond Hezelgrave puts me forward to be captain of Dickinson House. Him and Trevor are handing out the voting papers and telling everyone to vote for me. When the votes are counted, I've won and I get my blue house captain's badge.

Mr Dalton sends for me to go down to his office. I make sure the door doesn't slam shut this time. He congratulates me on being voted house captain. Then he brings up the conversation we had a year ago just after I moved from the school in Ilkley when the nun there gave me a glowing report. He said if things work out well at this school there's a chance I might be put forward for head boy. But then he says, unfortunately, because of the trouble I got into last year, it won't be possible for me to be put forward. He says he hopes I understand his position.

All summer I haven't been looking forward to coming back to school. I haven't done any of my holiday homework and I never expected to be put forward as a candidate for head boy anyway. Yet now that Mr Dalton tells me I won't, it just makes me realise how much I don't want to be here at this school, or at the home in Burley. It's just another 'kick in the teeth' day.

*

In the evening after tea, Alec Cunningham is in the games room playing his guitar. Most of the other boys are either having their baths and compulsory hairwash, or watching TV in the big lounge, or complaining about Alec playing songs that he can't play. I'm talking to Alec, telling him how much I hate being at school and that I'm seriously thinking of running away. Alec stops playing the guitar that he can't play properly yet anyway.

"Where are you going to run to?" he asks.

"I don't know yet."

"Right," he says, "I'm coming with you."

Mr Watson comes into the games room. He hands me a soft plastic briefcase. Look after it he says, it cost one pound ten shillings. Just as much as my pocket watch, I'm thinking. I'll need my Gladstone bag back he says. In my mind I'm thinking 'Thank God for that'.

Me and Alec are saving any pocket money we get. Alec gets some money from his savings that was left over when he bought his guitar in Blackpool. After about two or three weeks we've got three pounds fifteen shillings, most of it from Alec's savings. I've written a letter to my mother in Brighouse telling her not to worry about me when I run away, that me and Alec will be fine. My friend Ian Braithwaite has left school and is working in Guisley, where he is going to post the letter so if the police look for us, they'll think we're in Guisley.

It's a rainy October day and I'm at school for the last time. Me and Alec are running away tomorrow, Wednesday. Wednesday because it's Ian's day off from work, and I can give him the letter to post for me. Sister Carmel is at school. I feel bad about not telling her what I'm doing. I can't tell her, because it will put her in an awkward position if I do. So I don't tell her. I don't tell anyone at school, even my best friends Raymond Hezelgrave and Trevor Scales. I'll leave my house captain's badge pinned to the timetable on the underside of my school desk. When they find it, they'll know I'm not coming back.

Wednesday morning I set off down station road. It's a dark morning with drizzling rain falling. I have my blue gaberdine raincoat on over my purple blazer and the one pound ten-shilling plastic briefcase filled with socks, underwear and a couple of shirts. My pocket watch tells me that I have over two hours to wait for

Alec who is doing his house jobs. I turn right onto Langford Lane and then I walk across the wet field to the wood copse just below the big lawn and the fat oak tree, where I'm meeting Alec at about eleven o'clock.

At five to eleven I see Alec walking down the path at the far side of the big lawn. He has a small duffle bag over his shoulder. I climb up the wet, slippy oak tree from where I can see Mr Watson's red Mini on the gravel drive outside his sitting room. It looks like it's safe. I'm glad it's time to go, I'm damp and cold from waiting around in the little woods. I meet Alec on the corner of Station Road and Langford Lane. We cross Station Road, keeping a look out for Mr Watson's car, and on to Midgley Road to Ian Braithwaite's house. I give Ian the letter to my mother for him to post tomorrow. After getting warm by the fire in his front room and having a cup of tea, we're ready for off. Ian takes Alec's duffle bag and my briefcase and sets off down Station Road to the bus stop on Skipton road across from the grocer's shop where I usually get my Saturday cooking apple that always cost sixpence even when it was bigger than normal. Me and Alec walk around the long way to the bus stop, away from Station Road so Mr Watson and the Aunties won't see us if they happen to be walking or driving into the village. Now I'm thinking, 'I would have liked to be able to say goodbye to my close friends at the home, and especially Auntie Carol who is the best out of all the staff there, and Roger Seamour too.'

At the bus stop we get the briefcase and the duffle bag from Ian. He waits with us until the Skipton bus comes along, then he says goodbye and good luck. We go through Ilkley and on to Skipton and then get a bus to Keighley. We're going to find my father. That's the last place anyone will think of looking for us. We pass the playing fields at Utley on the left where Jimmy Clark from St Anne's school had his accident. We get off the bus across from St Anne's, where the school kids are going back into the school after the dinnertime break. I turn up my coat collar and walk quickly down Holker Street to Auntie Mary Murphy's house.

Auntie Mary opens the door. She has a cigarette in her mouth. She looks at me then at Alec and then back at me.

"Are you out of the children's home now?" she asks.

"Yes," I tell her.

"When did you come out?"

"When we ran away today."

"Oh Jesus Christ almighty," she says, as she pulls the two of us into the house and closes the door behind us.

She waves us down to the cellar kitchen. There's two damp-looking lodgers sitting at the long table eating bowls of stew and peeling floury boiled spuds to add to it. Auntie Mary's fur coat is hanging on a hook on the wall, ready for the cold winter days spent cooking for her lodgers down here.

"Sit down," she says.

She doesn't ask if we're hungry. She just puts two bowls of stew in front of us and, pointing to a huge bowl of spuds steaming in the middle of the table, she tells us to help ourselves.

"You know that we offered to take you all in, that day at the courts, don't you? But your feckin mother and Donoghue couldn't agree on anything. That was a sad day for all of you, and me and your Uncle John too," she says. "Where's the little one, Amanda?"

"As far as I know she's still in a home in Bradford," I tell her.

"And where's Helen?"

"She's in Bury living with Uncle Jimmy.

"And what about the others, Louise and Deirdre?"

"Still in Belfast with the nuns."

"Jesus Christ," she says, "what a sad state of affairs this has all come to. And where's your mother now?"

"She's living in a place called Brighouse," I tell her.

"Where's that?" she asks.

Then one of the damp workmen at the table joins in.

"It's down in a hole between Bradford, Huddersfield and Halifax," he says. Auntie Mary looks at him.

"No one's asking you Jim McGary, so just hould your whisht and eat your dinner." Auntie Mary looks back at me. "So what are you going to do now?"

"We're looking for my father," I tell her.

"And what would you want to see him for anyway? Sure he was never any good to you before, what good do you think he'll be now?"

"That's just it," I tell her, "no one will think of looking for us there."

"Your father is living at 15 Sandywood Street, a couple of streets on from here, and your sister Marie is living at the bottom end of the town on Grape Street off Dalton Lane down past the railway station. Marie is married to an English man called Peter and they have a little baby girl," says Auntie Mary. "And if you take my advice you'll keep away from Donoghue, who'll probably be in the Cavendish Pub by now anyway."

We finish the stew and spuds and thank her, then we go around to 15 Sandywood Street. There's no answer, so we go to the Cavendish Pub on the corner of Cavendish Street and Lawkholme Lane. There's a man coming out of the side door of the pub. He looks drunk. I tell him I'm looking for my father, Brendan O'Donoghue, and I ask if he knows who he is. The man looks at me. He's swaying and trying to stand up straight. His mouth opens but nothing comes out. It closes again. I'm just going to ask him again when he answers me in a strong west of Ireland accent.

"You're looking for your father?" he asks.

"Yes," I tell him.

"Well if you don't know your own father," he says, "how the feck am I going to know who he is?"

Now he's grinning at me, as he leans against the wall with his shoulder, to help him stand nearly straight. We walk away and leave him holding up the side of the pub with his shoulder.

"Let's go and have a cup of tea in that café we've just passed," says Alec.

"Which one?"

"On Cavendish Street, where there's two people sitting inside the front window, drinking tea and reading the newspapers."

Alec has his head down, leading the way in the rain. He goes inside and puts his bag on one of the two tables by the window. I'm thinking it's good to get inside, out of the cold. Alec is sat down. I'm looking around. There's people sitting on a long bench. They're looking at us. Alec asks me if I want a cup of tea. "Haven't you noticed anything?" I'm asking him.

"What?"

"The people at the table are drinking tea from a flask and the people on the long bench are sat in front of a row of washing machines!"

We find a proper café and spend an hour there with two cups of tea. Then we go around to Sandywood Street again. A man opens the door. Alec digs me in the ribs and nods his head at the doorway. It's only the same man from outside the pub. I ask him if Brendan O'Donoghue is in.

"Oh yes, it'll be 'Up stairs Brindin' you'll be wanting. He's up in the attic at the top of the house."

"But you said, outside the pub, that you didn't know Brendan O'Donoghue," I tell him.

"I don't know any 'Brindin Donohu' but I do know 'Upstairs Brindin' alright."

We go up the stairs. There's a small landing with a gas cooker and a sink on it. I knock at the only door beside the cooker. My father's voice answers.

"Who is it?"

"It's Brian," I tell him. He opens the door.

"Oh Jesus, what are you doing here?"

The room isn't very big and isn't very tidy. There's an unmade double bed in the corner with a woman about the same age as my mother sitting on it, a table full of dirty cups and plates, a chair with an old black and white TV on it, with wires going up and sticking out of the window in the roof. And the carpet looks like it hasn't been swept for three months. There's a fireplace beside the TV with an electric fire with one bar glowing in front of the fire grate and a clean mirror sat on the mantle piece. The room is full of cigarette smoke.

"We've run away from the children's home," I tell him. He doesn't know what to say.

"You better sit down," he says, as he pulls two chairs out from the table, lifting newspapers from one and some clothes from the other. He calls the woman Anna.

"This is Brian," he says, ignoring Alec. Anna comes over to us and shakes my hand and then Alec's. I tell him we'd like to stay for a few days.

"Why did you come here? he asks.

"Because this would be the last place the police would think of looking for us," I tell him.

He's not looking happy.

"There's not enough room here," he says.

"We'll sleep on the landing," I tell him. "We'll be missed by now and the police will be looking for us. We're 'hot' and the police will probably have put out an all points bulletin and put us on a wanted list, 'cos we're so hot," I tell him.

"Stop using those gangster words," he says, "and talk properly." Anna looks at him.

"They'll be alright for a day or two, Brendan, they can sleep on the landing, there's plenty of blankets," she says in her northern Irish accent. My father grunts.

"Oh alright then." Anna takes some cups out to the sink on the landing and then puts the kettle on the gas stove. My father has a wash and a shave at the sink and checks himself in the mirror over the fire before he goes out with Anna. His shoes are not as highly polished as they used to be. And the seat of his pants is shiny, with little or no creases in the legs. It's a long way from when he used to go out to the bars in Belfast looking like a professor.

In the morning he's up and out to work as a TV aerial fitter for a shop down Cavendish Street.

"Keep quiet and don't answer the front door," he says.

Anna goes to work later somewhere in the town centre. Before she goes, she tells us that my father wanted to call the police last night and have us taken back to the home, but she managed to talk him out of it. She finds me a needle and some thread before she goes so that I can alter my school blazer, and she leaves a front door key in case we go out anywhere. Me and Alec are talking about what we're going to do. We don't trust my father. He doesn't want us here. One more night here and we'll go and see Marie down at Grape Street. I spend a couple of hours turning in the collar of my school blazer. I want it to look like the coats that are in fashion, the ones with no collars, like The Beatles and the Dave Clark Five wear when they're on the TV. There's not much I can do about the vivid Catholic purple that can be seen for miles. I unpick the breast pocket also, to remove the St Mary's school name. I ask Alec if we have enough money for me to get some peroxide from the chemist so I can make my hair blonde, so the police won't recognise me when we go out. Alec says we do, but he's not doing his hair.

"I might buy a hat though!" he says. I'm thinking he's just joking.

I go to the chemist across the road from St Anne's Church. The bottle of peroxide costs one shilling and sixpence. The cost of three cooking apples seems a fair price for a blonde disguise, I'm thinking.

I'm at the attic sink sprinkling the peroxide on to my hair and rubbing it in with my fingers. I'm rubbing it in as fast as I can and then washing my hands so the peroxide doesn't burn them. The peroxide stinks. It smells like vinegar mixed with ammonia, Alec says. After twenty minutes I wash my hair with plenty of cold water at the sink. Alec is laughing at me. I go to the mirror on the mantlepiece. My hair is streaky brown and gingery. Alec is laughing more now. I wash my hair again, but it's still the same, streaky brown and ginger.

"I think it's you who'll need the hat now, and not me!" laughs Alec.

I put my purple blazer on and look in the mirror. Purple blazer and brown and ginger hair. I look at Alec.

"How long do you think it'll be 'til this'll be in fashion?"

"Never," he says.

Now I'm back at the sink washing my hands, my fingers have gone white and they won't stop itching. We go out into the town to buy the *Keighley News*. Alec says he wants to see if there's any jobs in it. I'm thinking it's a bit soon to be looking for a job seeing that we don't know where we'll be living yet. We walk down Cavendish Street around by the Victoria Hotel and up Low Street, where Alec points to a cheap woollen hat in a shop window.

"I think we'll buy you that to cover up your hair, then people won't be looking at you so much."

I don't argue with him.

We're back in the attic room when Anna comes in. She's brought some sausages for tea. I keep my new hat on all the time. She makes sausage sandwiches for me and Alec. She says she's got a pork chop for my father's tea. As soon as he comes in, my father is asking us if we've decided what to do. He says we can't stay here all the time. He says we can't just hide here indefinitely. He washes his hands and sits at the table waiting for the pork chop that's sizzling in the pan on the cooker, where Anna is watching over it. He turns to me.

"I don't forget when you hit me outside Mary Murphy's house."

I tell him that I don't remember, but of course I do. I can clearly remember hitting him with my fist and Mary Murphy hitting him with the cooking pan when he was trying to steal Baby Mandy. But now I've got to pretend I don't remember.

"You did hit me," he says, "you and that mad bastard, Mary Murphy."

Anna puts a plate in front of him, pork chop with a fried egg and garden peas. She starts talking to me and Alec, changing the subject. He's finished his food and he's asking us if we've decided what we're going to do.

"Yes," I tell him, "we're going back to the home in Burley in Wharfdale. We're going back tonight, aren't we Alec?"

"Yes we are, that's what we've decided."

"Maybe we'll come and visit you there, what do you think Brendan?" Anna says.

"Yeah, OK," he says, with a sincere lack of enthusiasm.

Me and Alec get our things together.

"We're off back, then," I tell them. Anna says goodbye, my father says OK. Anna says they'll visit us, but my father says nothing.

Me and Alec are out on Sandywood Street. He's got his bag and I've got my school briefcase with my bits and pieces in it. I see a police car on Skipton Road indicating to turn onto Sandywood Street. I grab Alec and pull him into a garden at the other side of the street and behind a hedge. We watch the police stop outside number 15 and knock loudly at the door. My father finally answers. They are asking him about me and Alec. He tells them that they have missed us, and that we are on our way back to the children's home. The police say they'll check later at the home, and they thank him for letting them know. I look at Alec and we both whisper the same thing: "Bastard!"

The police have gone and we're on our way to find Marie's house. Halfway down Alice Street there's a doorway with music pounding out. It's the Swinging Blue Jeans record, 'The hippy hippy shake.' Me and Alec look in. It looks like a youth club. Three boys come over to the door. It's the two John O'Briens and Colin Richardson, from St Anne's School. John O'Brien junior says they missed me a lot when I was sent into the home in Burley. He says there's many a time they've been talking about me and saying how it used to be good fun when we were all together before. I tell him that we're on the run from the home and that we're going to look for my sister's house, down Dalton Lane. He says that him and John come to the club most evenings, so now I'll know where to find them. I show him my purple blazer and my streaky ginger hair and he has a good laugh.

"Feckin hell Brian, you're picking up the Yorkshire accent, you'll be needing to watch that!"

We find Dalton Lane down the side of the railway station, and Grape Street that runs off it. We ask some kids on the street where Marie and Peter live and they show us which house to go to. The houses are small terraced back-to-backs, like the one on Thrush Street by Victoria Park where we all lived one and a half years ago in the summertime when Raymin and Johnny were living in the park. Marie answers the door.

"Come in," she says, "the police have been here looking for you two." I tell her we just missed them at my father's house. She introduces us to her husband Peter, who is sat at a small dining table. Peter is a lot older than Marie, and he's got a beard. He looks a bit like the ship's captain on the front of Senior Service cigarette packets. Then she introduces us to a man called Ernest. Ernest looks about 55 years old. Marie says Ernest lodges with them and that he's happy as long as he's got his pint pot of tea and his cigarettes. Marie then shows us her new baby, sleeping in a pram beside the television.

"Her name is Joanna," she says, "and she's four months old." Peter says he calls the baby 'Boo' because she likes to look at Yogi and Boo Boo bear on the television. Marie asks us if we would like a cup of tea and Ernest says, "Yes please."

Me and Alec sit at the table with Peter. I take off my woollen hat and tell them not to laugh at my hair. Nobody takes much notice of it. When I tell Peter about trying to make my hair go blonde, he says it was a bit of an extreme thing to do, but he doesn't think we'll be on the six o'clock news. Now I'm thinking Peter talks very posh. I bet he sounds just like the ship's captain on the cig packets. Ernest talks broad 'Yorkshire.' I'm betting he's good at saying things like 'Have you got owt for nowt?' and 'I knew him when he had nowt,' and things like that. Peter leaves the table, puts his coat on and kisses Marie.

"I'm just going for my usual pint of Timothy Taylor's, my dear," he says.

I'm telling Marie what we've been doing since we ran away. She's telling me that my father hasn't changed. She's tells me and Alec that he caused a lot of trouble the night of Boo's christening. She says that my mother and Jack Maddigan were invited, so were my father and Anna, as long as he didn't cause any trouble. Anyway, they didn't bother coming, him and Anna. Later in the evening Marie, Peter, my mother and Jack went out for a drink. Boo was being looked after by a neighbour and the house was being looked after by Ernest and his pint pot of tea. My father had been drinking all day when he called at the house demanding to see Marie. He pushed his way in, shouting loudly, demanding to know where she was. Ernest told him he didn't know, but my father walked around the house, knocked over Ernest's pot of tea, threw the radio on the floor, danced on top of it and kicked in the television cabinet, before leaving the house and slamming the door behind him and leaving poor Ernest in the middle of all the mess. Marie looks at Ernest.

"Tell Brian what you did next, Ernest." Ernest looks over to Me and Alec.

"I checked that my pint pot wasn't broken and put kettle on."

I tell Marie that me and Alec have been talking on the way to her house about what we're going to do. Alec has decided to go to Wakefield tomorrow, where he has some friends. I ask her if it's OK for him to stay tonight. She says it'll be alright, so I ask her if it will be OK with Peter.

"Yes," she says, "Peter won't mind. Peter is easy going."

*

On Saturday morning Alec leaves for Wakefield. I go up to the train station with him. I'm wearing the purple blazer with its turned-in collar and my woollen hat. On the way back down Dalton Lane a car passes me and then slows down. The woman driver is looking in the mirror. It looks like the council woman from the Shipley office. I run off down a side street. I can hear her car reversing fast, so I run into the first passage between the houses, out onto the next street, through another passage and to the far end where I can peep up Grape Street and see Marie's front door. I'm panting and out of breath. It's not long 'til the car comes around the corner and stops outside Marie's house. The woman is in the house for about five minutes before she leaves. I wait another five minutes before I go in. Sure enough, the council woman has been asking Marie if she's seen me and Alec. Marie told her she hadn't seen us, but the council woman wanted to know how she knew about them running away from the home. Marie told her that the police had also been there looking for them.

"Did that shut her up?" I'm asking.

"No," says Marie, "she says she wants the plastic briefcase back, she said it cost two pounds ten shillings." "Mr Watson said it cost one pound ten shillings," I tell her.

"It doesn't really matter what it cost now, does it?" says Marie.

"No," I tell her, "I suppose not."

I go out for a walk up into the town in the afternoon, with my hat on. When I get back at teatime the milkman is in the house. He's having a long chat and a cup of tea with Marie. I'm having my tea at the table and then I get my blazer and my hat and tell Marie I'm off up to the youth club to see the John O'Briens. Before I go, the milkman asks Marie if she realises that I've been sitting at the table eating non-stop for twenty minutes, and asks whether she can afford to keep me. I'm thinking he's joking. I hope he's joking.

On the way up to the youth club I bump into Maureen Feather on Cavendish Street. I tell her about running away from the children's home, and why I had to send her holiday photo back to her because Mr Watson said it was rude. We arrange to meet tomorrow at the little café on Dalton Lane that's run by a Pakistani man. I go on up to the youth club on Alice Street and meet John O'Brien junior, and Colin Richardson. John O'Brien senior hasn't turned up. There's more kids at the youth club tonight. We're all dancing to the pop songs, with the reflected spots of light shining on us from the silver ball hanging and spinning in the middle of the ceiling. John then leads me and Colin around the edge of the dance floor, "Looking for dolls," he says. Blue lights from the side walls light up the dandruff on people's shoulders. At half past nine we leave the youth club, with not a 'doll' left in sight.

On Sunday morning I'm outside number 3 Grape Street wearing my purple blazer, and my hat, talking to Tony, the boy who lives there. Marie is outside her house at number 1. None of us expect to see the council woman coming down Dalton Lane again so soon after yesterday, but suddenly Marie is shouting.

"The council woman is here!"

The car is coming round the corner on to Grape Street. I lean into the open doorway of number 3, but I think she might have seen me. Tony's mother sees what is happening. She pulls me and Tony into her house, pulls my blazer off, quickly puts it on Tony and throws him out onto the street.

"Make sure the council woman sees you!" she says to him. Then she turns to me: "Cup of tea?"

When the council woman is gone Marie comes into number 3 with Tony.

"What's she said this time?" I'm asking.

"Not a lot," says Marie. "She doesn't believe I haven't seen you, and the cost of the plastic briefcase has gone up to three pounds and ten shillings. That's a good investment, an asset and a good investment!" Tony's mother looks at me and tells me not to look so worried. Now we're all laughing about the council woman coming so close to catching me. But my laugh isn't a belly laugh, it's more of a nervous laugh of relief.

It's getting dark and frosty when I go to the Pakistani man's café. Maureen and two of her friends are there and two boys are with them. I'm telling them about the council woman nearly catching me. I'm telling them about the price of the plastic briefcase that goes up each time she calls, and about how Marie says if it keeps going up at that rate how it'll be a good asset.

Then I'm asking them whether if it went down in price it would be a bad asset. But they're not really interested in investments and assets. They're more interested in finding out who watched Elliot Ness and the Untouchables on the television. I'm thinking that I'll shurrup about the difference between a good asset and a bad asset 'cos it might make me look stupid.

"Who's Elliot Ness and the Untouchables?" I ask one of the girls. They all go quiet and stare at me.

"You don't know who Elliot Ness and the Untouchables are?" one of the boys says.

"Of course I do," I tell him, "I'm only joking."

Me and Maureen tell the others we're going for a walk. We go down a side street and we're leaning against a wall under a street light. I'm glad she's my girlfriend again. We're kissing long kisses. I'm thinking about what David Brennan in the home told us about what girls like you to do, and that they like boys to know what they're doing. I'm kissing Maureen with longer kisses. I'm pressing against her. It feels so good. I put my right arm around her and bring my left hand up and grab her chest. This is how to do it. This is what girls want you to do. This is the bit when she tells me that she loves me. My heart is beating fast.

Now my face is burning.

She's slapped my face so hard that it's stinging and I have a ringing in my ear.

She's walking away from me, back to her friends. I'm calling her but she's ignoring me. Now, thanks to that little shit, David Brennan, I've blown it. I'm thinking it must only be the Leeds girls in 'Sin City' that like the boys to know what they're doing and not the girls in Keighley. Now I feel bad about what's happened. I suppose I deserved a slap in the face, but so does that David Brennan.

I go back to Marie's house. I don't tell her why I'm back early. I'm asking her all about Elliot Ness and the Untouchables, who everyone knows about except me. Marie says the programme is on late at night, that's why I wouldn't know about it. Being in the home I wouldn't have been up late enough to see it. "Don't worry about it," she says, "there will be lots of things you know that your friends won't."

Yes, I'm thinking to myself, like the good assets and the bad ones.

At least now when someone mentions Elliot Ness, I'll know what they're talking about and I won't feel so stupid, or the odd one out. I'm looking at the clock. It's half past ten. David Brennan will have been in bed an hour by now. I bet he hasn't stopped talking yet. He'll be giving the other boys advice on how to handle girls, the little shit.

*

I stay at Marie's house for another two weeks. I've only seen Maureen once since the night I tried to do to her what girls want you to do to them, only she didn't. When I saw her again I got the feeling she wasn't my friend anymore. I'm going to leave Keighley. Now I've blown it with Maureen, I don't want to be in the same town as her if she's fallen out with me. I'm not making any excuses for myself. I'm leaving, I getting away from the hurt I'm feeling. I've never been lucky in love. I'll go away as far as I can from her. I'll go to the 'hole' in between Bradford, Halifax and Huddersfield, where my mother lives. Where, according to Auntie Mary's lodger Jim McGarry, people can go and never be seen again. I'm off to a place called Brighouse, where no one will ever think of looking for me.

It's a Sunday afternoon and I've got my bits and pieces in the plastic briefcase. Marie has given me the bus fare to get me to Brighouse. At the top of Dalton Lane I meet Peter on his way home after having his pint of Timothy Taylor's beer. I tell him that I'm leaving. He offers his hand for a handshake and we say our goodbyes. I'm just about to go when he turns to me.

"That handshake of yours is like a wet fish, never shake a hand like that again!" He grabs my hand and with a firm grip and a firm shake he says, "That's how to do a handshake, and always look the person straight in the eye, never offer a hand like a floppy cod again!"

We say goodbye and I make my way past the railway station, up Cavendish Street and into the bus station. I never realised a good handshake was so important. As I walk through the bus station I get a big wave from Denis the bus conductor mattress delivery man. It's dark and raining. I'm thinking about 'My Maureen,' who isn't mine anymore. I get on the bus for Bradford and try to accept my life situation, like I've had to accept being dumped in homes lots of times. In the distance I can hear a pop song playing. It's the Everly Brothers. They're singing 'Love Hurts.' The bus sets off … "Love hurts, love hurts" … and goes past Victoria Park near Thrush Street … "Love hurts, love scars" … and on through Bingley … "Love wounds and mars" … and on through Shipley ... "Takes a lot of pain, takes a lot of pain" … past the foster home and on to Bradford … "Love is like a cloud, holds a lot of rain." Them Everly Brothers have a lot to answer for. Like that Mick Jagger fella has, writing songs and not caring about people's feelings.

I change onto the number 64 bus for Huddersfield that goes through Brighouse. When I get off at Brighouse opposite the Albert Cinema, I ask directions for Birds Royd Lane from the bus driver. He tells me to get back on the bus and wait for the next stop that's at the top of Birds Royd Lane. I walk down the lane and eventually find Woodlands Grove on the left, across from the Woodlands pub. There's a house halfway along the street with an Irish rebel song blasting out the open door. This'll be my mother's house, I'm thinking. She'll be on one of her 'rebel' trips, that's usually sparked off by a row. It doesn't matter who the row is with, it could be with one of the neighbours or Jack or Raymin or the dog. She'll get it out of her system by blasting out the songs on her old record player and joining in when she knows the words, or sometimes she'll join in even when she doesn't know the words. The last time I heard her as loud as this was in Keighley when one of the neighbours used up all the communal washing line.

I knock hard on the open door. A mongrel of a dog, black and brown and skinny, about three quarters of the size of a greyhound, comes to the door barking at me and showing his teeth, followed by my mother.

"Oh it's you!" she shouts over the music. "I see you've met Bunty. Are you still on the run?"

"Yes."

"You better come in then. I heard you were in Keighley. Do you want a cup of tea?"

I nod my head.

"Well get in there and make it yourself," she says, "and make us all one while you're at it."

I walk into the house, past Jack and Raymin sitting in front of the coal fire on an old two seater-settee. Over in the far corner there's a gas cooker at the top of the cellar steps with steaming pans on it. There's a sink inside the cupboard door on the wall by the front window. I find enough of everything to make tea for the four of us and persuade my mother to turn the record player down.

"Them two feckers don't lift a hand to help me in this house," she says, pointing to Jack and Raymin. Jack looks at me and then at her.

"Sure, when I try to help you, you tell me I'm in the way!"

Raymin gets up off the settee. He says he doesn't want a cup of tea, he's taking the dog for a walk down by the canal. My mother tells him not to let the dog eat anymore grass when they're out walking. Jack looks at me and says that the dog was running around the house this morning after his early walk, with long bits of grass hanging out of its backside. He says him and Josie had an awful job trying to hold the dog still while they pulled the grass out with the coal tongs.

"With them old tongs, it's hard enough to pick up a piece of coal, never mind a blade of grass!"

My mother looks at me. "You'll have to sleep in the same bed as Raymin if you're staying."

"That's if we don't get thrown out because of the loud music," Jack says.

"I'll play my feckin music as loud as I want," she says, "and if the neighbours don't like it, they can go and feck, and so can you Jack Maddigan!" She turns to Jack. "Where's the feckin fags?"

Raymin comes back in about an hour.

"Has the dog been eating grass?" my mother asks him.

"No," says Raymin, "is there any tea in the pot?"

"No there feckin isn't," says my mother, "you'll have to make some more, and tomorrow you and Brian can get out early in the morning and look for a job, the pair of you. I'm not having Jack working hard all day in his demolition job in all weathers to keep you two."

No one asks me about the clildren's home or what I've been doing since I ran away.

At night, my mother is shouting for everyone to go to bed early, ready for an early call in the morning. I've found out which of the outside toilets across the cobbled open yard is ours, and I've been told there's a bucket on the landing for emergencies only. I'm sharing a bed with Raymin. It's a three-quarter-sized bed with two blankets and an overcoat on top to help keep us warm. The bedroom is freezing. I'm lying in bed trying to figure out how we ended up in a place like this after leaving Belfast, to come to the Devil's Country for a better life. In the morning I can hear Jack downstairs. He's shouting up to my mother that he's lit the fire, and her cup of tea will be ready soon, and he's let the dog out onto the spare ground. I look out from under the blankets. Raymin's alarm clock says it's a quarter to seven. It's freezing cold. I can see ice on the inside of the bedroom window and my breath is turning to steam. Jack comes up the stairs.

"There's your tea, Josie," he says.

"Go and wake them two feckers up and tell them to get out and find a job," I can hear my mother telling him.

"Get them up a bit later," Jack tells her, "I'm off now, I'll let the dog in when I go."

He goes down the bare stone steps and opens the door. Bunty the dog runs in and straight up the stairs and into my mother's bedroom. I can hear the dog running round and round. Jack shouts up.

"I'm off now Josie."

"No Jack," shouts my mother, "don't go yet, it's the dog – fetch the tongs, fetch the feckin' tongs!"

*

It's nine o'clock. My mother is shouting up the stairs.

"If you two don't get out of that bed, I'm coming up with a bucket of water to throw over you!"

"Is she always like this?" I'm asking Raymin.

"No," he says, "sometimes she's worse. Alright," shouts Raymin, "we're up, we're up!" Then he leans out of the bed and bangs his shoes on the floor boards a couple of times to make it sound like he's up.

At dinner time me and Raymin walk the four and a half miles into Huddersfield. We go to the labour exchange on Queen Street, but there's no jobs going for either of us. There's lots of jobs going in the textile mills, but you have to know how to work the weaving looms. We wait by the police box on Market Place until the *Examiner* newspaper comes out in the late afternoon, but there's no jobs in that either, all the jobs are for skilled workers. We just had enough money to buy the *Examiner*. Now we're walking around the shops looking to see if there's any jobs advertised in the windows. There's only a couple of places looking for waitresses. I'm cold and fed up now. We set off to walk back to Brighouse. We walk through Woolworths and down the steps to the basement to the back door that leads out onto Victoria Lane at the top side of the market hall with the clock tower.

"Come on," I'm telling Raymin, "I'm freezing." I go through the door in front of him. He's waiting back. He's holding the door open for a woman with a pram.

"Come on," I'm telling him, "you're no gentleman!" He holds the door 'til the woman is through. The woman looks at me.

"He's more of a gentleman than you'll ever be!", she says. I don't say anything. I'm just thinking I deserved that. I'm thinking that's not me, I don't usually act like that. Then I'm thinking no one will ever talk to me like that again, I'll never give them cause to. We walk through the market hall, onto King Street, Cross Church Street, Lord Street and on to Bradford Road. By the time we get to Fartown Bar it's getting dark. Raymin tells me to stop.

"Wait here," he says.

"What for?" I'm asking him.

"Just wait," he says. Two minutes later he's running up to me with a bundle of newspapers in his hands.

"Run!" he says, "run, I've nicked some fish and chips!" He's past me and I'm running like hell to catch him. We run out the Bradford Road and don't stop 'til we're near the Ashbrow pub about a mile up the road. We're out of breath, we can hardly talk. He throws me a bundle of newspapers. The papers are warm, they smell lovely. I rip them open. I never knew fish and chips could taste so good. I'm thinking it's not the right thing to do, but that doesn't stop me eating them. We're past the pub, walking slowly up the road eating from the newspapers. A police car speeds past. It slows down and hits its breaks. Now it's reversing back.

"Come on," Raymin shouts, "follow me!"

We drop what's left of the stolen goods and run across the road and jump straight over a wall. I crash through some bushes and land about fifteen foot down on some tree trunks. I hear a splash and a few seconds later, I hear Raymin spluttering my name. He's swimming towards me near the edge of a big pond. I look up and see a policeman looking down over the wall, shining a torch on Raymin.

"Are you alright?" asks the policeman.

"No," says Raymin, "I'm bloody freezing."

"Come out of the water," shouts the policeman.

"Come and get me!" Raymin shouts back.

"Where's your mate?" I hide behind a tree trunk and shout, "I'm in the water too!" The bobby walks along the wall looking for a way down to the pond. Raymin comes out of the water and we make our way around the edge of the pond and away from the two torchlights we can see moving around the pond in our direction. We run like hell across a field and into the woods at the top side of Long Hill Road. From there we cross Bradley Road near the roundabout, go past the farm at Bradley Bar, over the field and across the big excavation that Raymin says some day is going to be part of the M62 motorway, then down towards Birds Royd Lane, keeping on the small roads away from the main Huddersfield Road where the police might still be looking for us.

Raymin tells my mother what he did and she says it's disgraceful. He puts his wet clothes on a chair in front of the fire. Then he hands her the wet *Examiner* paper, so she can see there's no jobs in it, and that we have been looking. When Jack comes in from work, he says that his boss, Jim Kennedy, says there might be a bit of work for me on the demolition site, being tea boy and helping out. He says he'll know in a couple of days. Later, when I'm in bed, I'm thinking that what happened today was disgraceful, and it should never happen again. Next time I'll hold the door open for somebody and be a gentleman, and I'll do it too even when he's not with me, then I won't feel the shame that I felt today when the woman with the pram told me off. And as for those fish and chips, they really were the best fish and chips I've ever tasted.

Jack is up at six o'clock every morning. He lights the coal fire, lets the dog out and brings a cup of tea up to my mother, who then starts shouting at me and Raymin to get up out of the bed and look for work. If we don't get up straight away she's threatening that she'll throw a bucket of water over us. I'm thinking it's hard to want to get up out of a bed that's nearly warm when the bedroom is so cold that your breath turns to steam, and the first job of the morning is to run across the cobble stones outside to empty the galvanised tin pee bucket that's been on the landing all night, into the outside toilet at the end of the street. I run across the cobbles hoping to get the job done before the neighbours see me so I don't get embarrased, even though they will all have pee buckets too. I'm thinking that things aren't any better really since we moved from Belfast to the Devil's Country, where a lot of the houses have 'kitchens' at the top of the cellar steps and no inside toilet. Mind you, we've never actually gone hungry here.

Me and Raymin walk miles every day looking for work, with just enough money that Jack gives us to buy the *Huddersfield Examiner* in the afternoon to see if there's any jobs going. On the Friday night Jack comes home from work and gives my mother most of his wages for the housekeeping. He gives Raymin money for some cigarettes and tells me that Jim Kennedy the demolition boss says that I can go in to work on Monday and be tea boy for the job in Halifax. He says I'll be going to the shop for the men and collecting a tray of tea and coffee from a woman's house beside the site. The men pay her a shilling a day each for the drinks.

On Monday morning Jack gets me up early. Raymin has given me a donkey jacket and lent me a pair of jeans. I've no working boots, so I have to wear my school shoes from Burley in Wharfdale. At a quarter past seven me and Jack leave the house in the rain and the dark, leaving my mother shouting at Raymin and threatening him with water. At the top of Birds Royd Lane where it meets Huddersfield Road, there's a grey Ford tipper wagon waiting for us with two men and a driver in the front cab. Jack says his good mornings and we climb up the back wheels and into the back of the wagon, where there's an old settee to sit on when it's dry but now it's soaking wet with the rain. We squat down behind the wagon headboard on the way into Huddersfield town centre. We stop in the town by the police box and a stone monument where three more men get onto the back of the wagon. They all say hello to Jack. They're Irish: one of them sounds like he's from Dublin, the others sound like Connemara men. They all smell of stale beer. On the way to Halifax the three men who got on the wagon in Huddersfield are dropped off on a site in a place called Elland, where there's a load of houses to be pulled down.

By the time we get to Halifax me and Jack are wet and cold. We jump off the wagon and Jack starts to collect bits of burnt wood from the remains of last week's fire. He finds a piece of rag and dips in into the diesel tank on the wagon then wraps it around a piece of the blackened wood. He lights the rag and pushes it into the pile of timber, and soon the fire is blazing strong. Jack tells me to pick up any old timber, big or small, and keep the fire going.

There's a rattle of noise and a tracked machine with a wide bucket on the front starts knocking down a wall that looks like it's the last bit left of a church that's been pulled down. In between picking the bits of timber from the rubble I go to the sandwich shop at Kings Cross Road junction for some of the men, then they show me which house to go to for the teas. I tell the woman that there's five men on the job today, including me, and I'm the tea boy. She says to tell them that it'll be four shillings today, but she says I can have mine for nowt.

We're all standing around the fire drinking the tea and eating the sandwiches and steaming ourselves dry. I'm sharing sandwiches that my mother made for me and Jack. I'm asking Jack what the big tall tower next to the demolished church is. He says it's called the tower of spite. He says the man who built it made it high so that no one could spoil his view by building a wall around his property. Pat Kennedy is the foreman on the job. I think he's the boss's brother. He's the one who finishes his tea and sandwich first and says back to work lads. I take the tray of cups and the four shillings back to the woman's house on the main road. Pat Kennedy tells me to pick up any pieces of scrap I see and put them into a pile, and also any good pieces of square stone that the other men have missed. Jack shouts over to me that the boss is here. A big white Mercedes car drives over the pavement and onto the site. Jim Kennedy gets out and walks over to me.

"You'll be Jack's lad," he says.

"Yes," I tell him.

"Make sure you pick up all the pieces of scrap," he says, "that's what pays the wages."

I ask him if he has any gloves for me to wear.

"Whaaat," he says, "gloves!?"

Now I'm thinking I know how Oliver Twist must have felt when he asked for more! Come to think of it, Jim Kennedy looks a bit like Mr Bumble.

"Gloves," he says, "no man on my site wears gloves, I'll sack the first man I see wearing gloves! Now head down and arse in the air and get them bits of scrap picked up!"

He's walking over to Pat Kennedy. They're both looking over to see if I'm working hard enough. There's a car stopped by the pavement. A man gets out and walks over to the Kennedy's.

"I'm looking for the boss," he says.

"That'll be me," says Jim Kennedy.

"I've come to complain about the glass in the road from when you pulled the church down," he says. "It could damage my tyres, and if it does, I'll be claiming damages against you."

Kennedy looks at his brother and then back to the complainer.

"And what could you claim for?" he says. "Sure, it's only an old banger you have. Sure, the diesel in my car is worth more than your old banger altogether!"

Kennedy walks back to his Mercedes and drives off, skidding out of the muddy site.

The complainer man looks at Pat Kennedy. Pat shrugs his shoulders. As he passes me, the complainer asks me if the boss is always like that, and I tell him I don't know.

"How long have you worked for that ignorant bastard?" he asks me.

"Two hours," I tell him.

At half past four it's getting dark. The tracked machine stops and we have five minutes around the fire getting warm and steamy before we climb up onto the back of the wagon and go to the Elland site in the cold drizzly rain, where me and jack get off the wagon. We get the bus home to Brighouse to dry our clothes in front of the coal fire and eat a big feast of bacon, cabbage and floury spuds boiled in their jackets.

"How did your first day go?" asks my mother.

"Bloody cold and wet," I tell her.

The next morning I'm on the back of the wagon in donkey jacket, jeans and shoes, all of which are nearly dry from yesterday's rain. It's not raining today, but it's still very cold. When we get to the houses job at Elland, Pat Kennedy gets out of the wagon and tells me that we're on this job today with the other men. Jack climbs off the wagon and gets into the cab and goes off to the Halifax job beside the tower of spite. Pat Kennedy tells two of the men who we've picked up in Huddersfield to carry on stripping the roofs of the houses. He tells me to go with the third man, called Sean O'Conner, and help him strip out the wood inside the houses. Sean shows me how to strip out the windows, doors and floors. All the timber work has to come out. He gives me a pickaxe and we start with the window frames and surrounds. There's dust everywhere. I can hear bits of roof dropping on the bedroom ceilings from the two men taking off the stone slates up there.

At breakfast time Sean gives me some of his sandwich when I tell him that Jack has gone off to the Halifax job with mine. He says he's from Ballyfermot in Dublin. He's good at talking and telling stories. He gives me more of his sandwich and says I'm not to worry because I'll never go hungry with him around. Then he tells me a story about when he took his kids wild camping near Bridlington at the seaside. He says he took his ferret with him to go catching rabbits near the little woods they found to camp in. After two days of catching nothing, he says, he told his kids not to worry about getting hungry: "If we don't catch a rabbit, we'll just have to eat the ferret!

I'm thinking he's not joking. He tells me he can get a job where he gets paid for doing nothing, that it's all to do with his bushy ginger hair and beard. He says that one of the fellas stripping the stone slates on the roof, the big rough one, says he'll pay him just to sit in his front garden and pretend to be a garden gnome. Now I know he's joking … I think.

We carry on pulling off the skirting boards and ripping up the floor boards and throwing them out the windows 'til dinner time. I'm walking out of the front door and I hear someone swearing up on the roof. I look up and see someone hanging onto a heavy ridge stone that he was just going to drop down off the roof.

"Get out of the bloody way!" he shouts down at me, and he holds onto the stone just long enough for Sean to pull me back into the house before the it crashes down onto the garden path and breaks into half a dozen pieces. Sean sticks his head out and shouts up to the fella on the roof.

"Kevin Mullarky! What the feck are you doing, trying to kill my new mate?" The man on the roof shouts back.

"For Jesus sake, will you shout up when you're coming out of the house? Your mate is one lucky bastard that I saw him just in time!"

"What's up over there?" Pat Kennedy shouts over.

"Nothing, we're fine," shouts Sean back to him.

It's dark at half past four and it's starting to rain again. The tipper wagon from Halifax turns up at about a quarter to five. Jack is not on it. The driver says he's gone to another job in Huddersfield. Pat Kennedy comes over to me.

"Don't bother coming in tomorrow, lad," he says.

"OK," I say, "what about the day after?"

"No," he says, "don't bother coming in at all, you're finished."

"Why?"

"Look, lad," he says quietly, "if it was up to me I'd keep you on, but the boss says you're too young and you're no good for this job. I'm sorry, that's it."

He goes over and gets in the wagon. Sean is in the back with Kevin Mullarky and the other big fella who was on the roof.

"See you tomorrow," Sean shouts over.

"Yeah, see you tomorrow," I shout back, knowing I won't.

The rain is getting heavier as I walk down the road, over Elland Bridge and right onto the Brighouse road, under the railway bridge and past some people waiting at the bus stop. Jack had the bus fare and the sandwiches, so I can't even get the bus because I've no money. I'm soaking wet all down my front and just when I think things can't get any worse, a wagon drives past through a big puddle and soaks me all down my right side. Shit, bollix and feck it, feck, feck, feck it!

Four miles in the driving rain and I'm finally home. Jack is home before me. I take my wet clothes off and sit in front of the fire in my vest and underpants. Even my vest is wet. My mother asks me how I got on at work today.

"Not good," I tell her. "Since I started the job I've found out that the boss is an ignorant bastard, who'll sack any man wearing gloves; a man on the roof called Kevin Mullarkey nearly killed me; I've got myself soaked to the skin walking home in the rain; a wagon driver drove through a puddle and soaked me more, and now I've been sacked from the job and I don't know why. Other than that, I'm fine."

"Are you ready for some dinner?" she asks.

"Yes please."

"Right," she says, "there's a big pan of stew on the cooker, and a pan full of spuds. Grab a plate and get yourself some."

"I will in a minute," I tell her, "I want to get warm first."

Raymin says he's got a job to start in the morning with Enrights of Brighouse. He gets the wet jeans from inside the front door and puts them on a chair in front of the fire.

"I'll need them for the morning," he says. "Enrights are paying two pounds ten shillings a day," he tells Jack. Then Jack tells me that he'll see Kennedy on Friday for my two days' wages.

Bunty the dog is lying in front of the fire with steam coming off his wet coat. He smells like the normal wet dog smell, and the steaming jeans don't smell much better. Raymin says he won't need the donkey jacket back 'cos there's one at the top of the cellar steps that Johnny McNiel left when he went back to Belfast. I'm looking at the different shapes in the flames of the coal fire. I'm thinking about getting the job and being sacked on the second day and hoping that it's not compulsary for all bosses to have big cars and be ignorant.

"Don't worry," says my mother to me, "things will get better, for God is good. God is good."

But just now I'm not quite in agreement with her. I'm looking down at the dog, who's looking up at me. I'm thinking Bunty can sense how I'm feeling. I'm hoping he hasn't been eating grass today. Raymin is sat on the settee with Jack smoking a rollup cigarette. There's a radio on the table tuned into a crackling radio Athlone from Ireland. I'm wishing we had a television to watch and not just a radio and a record player. My mother is in the cellar top 'kitchen' banging pans about. Raymin shouts over to her that she won't have to nag at him every day to get a job, and maybe now he'll have a bit of peace and quiet. He looks at Jack and starts to laugh, but he soon stops laughing when my mother comes over from the cooker and hits him over the head with a saucepan. He jumps up.

"What did you do that for?"

"Watch your feckin tongue when you talk to me!"

"Jesus Christ," says Raymin, "you're feckin mad, it was only a joke."

"Well I don't think it was funny," she says, "so sit down and hould your whisht before you get another clatter."

Jack is on his feet and telling her to calm down. The radio is turned off and the record player is turned on. Raymin and Jack are telling her to calm down and turn the music down. She sits at the table by the window smoking her cigarette and staring into the distance, taking no notice of them. Me and Bunty are still by the fire. I'm too damp to bother about anything.

In the morning Jack lets the dog out and brings my mother up her morning cup of tea. Then him and Raymin are off to work with their sandwiches. The dog is back in the house, my mother has finished her cup of tea and the day at home starts.

"Get up out of that bed and get out and look for a job!"

I bang my shoes on the floor boards and tell her I'm up.

"Stop banging your shoes on the floor and get out of that bed before I throw a bucket of water over you!" she shouts up.

At nine o'clock I get my mother to go to the phone box on Mission Street around the corner from the Woodlands Pub to ring up the Children's Department in Shipley to ask whether they have found me yet. Otherwise they will think it's strange if she hasn't been enquiring about me. Mr Mitchell at the office says that he thinks I could be in Keighley with one of my old school friends from St Anne's. He says I've been seen near Marie's house. The money in the phone box runs out and the line goes dead. On the way back to the house my mother says she didn't like doing that. She says it wasn't right. I don't say anything to her. I'm just happy that Mr Mitchell thinks I'm in Keighley.

I run some water into the white pot sink near the window then I boil a kettle of water on the gas cooker to add to it so I can have a wash. I borrow the bus fare to get to Huddersfield and enough money for the Huddersfield paper. It's early afternoon when I get the bus into town, to the square where the police box is. I wait 'til the *Examiner* comes out at about three o'clock. I'm waiting beside the paper seller so I can get the paper as soon as it comes. When the *Examiner* van arrives I'm first in the queue. Cowlings fruit and veg shop on Shambles Lane, part of the old Market Hall, are advertising for a young boy to help with fetching stock from their storeroom and keeping the shelves filled. I apply to Mr Wood and he says I can start work the next day. Five and a half days a week including Saturday with half a day Wednesday, three pounds ten shillings a week.

At teatime at home my mother is happy now that me and Raymin have jobs and she won't have to shout at us every morning, or threaten us with the bucket of water. I'm thinking she'll be feeling a bit like Auntie Mary Murphy in Keighley, with me and Raymin having jobs and us paying her board money every week, as long as we don't get the sack, that is. Raymin says it's hard work at Enrights digging trenches all day for the electric cables and gas and water pipes and things like that. He says the foreman is mad. He spends his day shouting at the men, saying "Rip it up, rip it up, it's not your country you're damaging, rip it up to feck!" Raymin says he's happy with his two pounds ten shillings a day. He says it's hard work but it's good money. I tell him that I'm on three pounds ten shillings a week.

I get my donkey jacket and sew up the cut on the sleeve that must have happened on the ignorant bastard's job the other day. I clean my school shoes and polish them the best I can ready for my new job. In the morning I'm at Cowlings on Shambles Lane for a quarter to nine. The shop is on the outside on the King Street side of the Market Hall that has a big clock tower on top. The boss is called Eric Wood. He's not ignorant and I don't think he has a big white Mercedes, so I'm thinking that's a good start. The salesman is called Paddy Folan and he shows me what to do. There's two other lady assistants who work part-time. Paddy shows me where the storeroom is about 100 yards away down a lane across from the Bull and Mouth pub. I have to bring boxes of fruit and veg from the store on a four-wheeled cart up to the shop and store them behind the front display 'til they're needed. Paddy shouts through a little window in the display and I slide trays of whatever he needs under the display out to the front where he can get them. When he has all he needs, and if he's not busy, he calls me to the front and shows me how to wrap the apples and oranges etc. in coloured paper to make them look fancy. Then he shows me how to cut leaves off the cauliflowers to make them look better. While he's showing me what to do, a woman asks for 2lb of carrots. The woman's watching the needle on the weighing scale and Paddy is doing his best to get the weight right. The nearest he can get is just a tiny bit under the 2lb-mark. He lifts the bag of carrots off the scale, but the woman tells him it's not a full 2lb of carrots. He puts the carrots back on the scales, takes a small penknife out of his pocket and peels one thin slice of carrot into the bag and hands it back to the woman with exactly 2lb of carrots in it. When the woman is gone, Paddy looks at me and says, "You can't please everybody." So now I'm thinking I'm going to need my own penknife for my new job. I ask Paddy if the boss has a big white Mercedes.

"No," he says, "why do you ask that?"

"Oh no reason, I tell him, I was just wondering."

On the Saturday evening Eric, the boss, gives me my wages and says "See you Monday, lad." It looks like he's not going to give me the sack.

It's coming up to Christmas soon. My mother is happy with all of us working and paying her board and lodgings. Jack says we might get a secondhand telly for Christmas and my mother says she's going to get the biggest turkey she's ever had. Raymin says he's going out for a drink with the Enrights men to find himself a different kind of bird for Christmas, and I'm not sure what I'm going to get 'cos after I pay my two pounds ten shillings board to my mother I've only got a pound left and I have to pay my bus fares into Huddersfield every day out of that, and there's the weekly phone call to the Children's Department in Shipley every wednesday afternoon to see if Mr Mitchell has found me yet.

At work I'm getting better at knowing what's needed before Paddy has to ask me. And when it's quiet he lets me serve people and work the till. I'm getting to know the people who work at the other shops on Shambles Lane and some of the shops in the Market Hall, especially the biscuit shop in the middle of the hall, where I go some afternoons and ask for six penn'orth of chocolate biscuits, and the woman always gives me extra biscuits, because of my manners, she says.

At about five o'clock on Christmas Eve the shop is ready for closing after a very busy day. Eric the boss gives me my wages and Paddy gives me a big bag of fruit and vegetables to take home. Then when he knows Eric the boss can't hear, he says, "I've put some cox's apples in too, I know they're you're favourite, I've seen you eating them in the back."

I'm on my way down to Lord Street by the YMCA building to get the number 64 bus home. For twenty minutes on the bus I'm thinking about apples. I'm wondering how long Paddy has known I've been eating the cox's apples. Paddy must have seen me eating them in the little store area behind the display boxes. Now I'm wondering if Eric the boss knows, and if I'm going to be sacked when I go back after Christmas. Maybe he didn't want to spoil my Christmas by sacking me now. Maybe he'll just sack me for the New Year. Maybe, maybe, I'll just have a nice cox's apple while I'm trying to figure it out. And maybe I just worry too much about everything.

Jack is in from work, Raymin is sitting on the settee. Raymin is smoking and grinning a lot. I think he's been drinking. My mother is in the four-foot square kitchen at the top of the cellar steps. There's a lot of banging and grunting and cursing going on at the cooker. It sounds like the trays from the oven are bouncing down the cellar steps. Me and Jack go over to see what's going on. My mother is kneeling with her varicose legs on the cold stone floor. There's a great big turkey on her knees. She's trying her best to shove the turkey into the oven. She's crying. There's tears running down her face. She looks up at Jack.

"It's the turkey," she says, "the feckin turkey, the hoor of a turkey won't fit in the oven!"

So Jack cut the hoor of a turkey in half and my mother calmed down and cooked it in two sessions. By the time the second session of cooking started at about 11pm my mother was on better form, helped along by nearly half a bottle of sherry, and some rebel songs on the record player. And soon the turkey is on the table on two separate plates. One piece has the neck at the top and the other has the parson's nose sticking up in the air.

The secondhand telly didn't arrive 'til two days after Christmas, along with the Christmas tree. One of Jack's friends from work got drunk and forgot all about bringing the telly and the tree. The tree was put up for the New Year. Christmas and the New Year were cold and wet. And all through January, Shambles Lane was mostly draughty cold and wet. I wondered how Alec was doing in Wakefield.

# Chapter 27

## Brighouse – where the police are the bad guys

It's the middle of February and I'm still working at Cowling's shop. Raymin is still working with the Enrights men and getting drunk every weekend and Jack is still working for the ignorant bastard in Huddersfield. Marie, Peter and Boo Boo have moved to Brighouse and are living in the house next door. The council woman has been to this house twice since Christmas looking for me. The first time she came I was at work, and the second time I had to hide down the cellar. I'm getting fed up with being on the run. On the Wednesday afternoon on my half day off, I go around to the phone box on Mission Street with my mother to ring Mr Mitchell at the Children's Department, but this time I'm the one talking to him. I tell him about my job and that I'm staying with my mother and that I want to stay here and keep my job. I tell him that it's no use me going back to the children's home as it's too late to be staying on at school anymore, since I'm just over fifteen and a half now. Mr Mitchell says if I tell him where I am he'll come and fetch me. He says he can't just let me stay at my mother's house because I'm still under the care and control of the West Riding County Council Children's Department. He keeps saying that if I tell him where I am he'll come and collect me, and I tell him I've already said I'm with my mother in Brighouse. I'm thinking that the money in the phone box is lasting longer than usual. The pips should be going for me to put some more money in. Just then there's a police car pulls up outside. I call Mr Mitchell a lousy bastard and put the phone down.

The driver stays in the car and the one in the front passenger seat gets out. He says he's been told to come and pick me up, he doesn't know why, and he's waiting for more instructions to come over his radio. He walks back to the house with us and the driver in the car follows. I'm in the house telling him that all I've done is run away from a children's home. The driver comes into the house and says I've to be taken down to the Brighouse police station, where someone from the council is coming to see me. Now I'm in the car and my mother is telling me not to worry, her and Jack will come to Burley in Wharfdale to see me.

"Don't worry, you'll be OK, God is good, things won't always be like this, God is good."

I'm thinking I've been here before, a few times. They take me to the police station on the Bradford Road, and in through the side door by Wellholme Park and leave me in a big room with a desk at one side and a bench seat on the other. There's a police sergeant at the desk. He's taking my name and details and asking the other policemen why I've been brought into the station. When the two of them leave, there's a plain clothes policeman comes in to join the sergeant at the desk. The plain clothes man has gingery brown hair and some freckles on his face and he's smoking. I'm thinking he must be a CID man. He's stocky in build and his looks are tough and verging on the side of ugliness. The sergeant is tall with dark hair and I'm thinking he looks more like a policeman should look. The CID man tells me to sit on the long bench by the wall. He's standing up looking down at me.

"What have you been brought in for?"

"I ran away from a children's home."

"When?"

"Last October."

"Have you been breaking into places?"

"No."

"Have you been stealing things?"

"No."

"Did you rip the sleeve of your coat when you were breaking in somewhere?"

"No."

"How did you rip your coat then?"

"I did it when I was working on a demolition site."

"Who were you working for?"

"I'm not telling you, in case they get into trouble for employing me."

"How long did you work there?"

Now I'm thinking that I'm not going to tell this ignorant bastard that the other ignorant bastard finished me after two days.

"I worked there for two months," I tell him.

"Where?"

"Halifax and Elland."

"Where did you run away from?"

"Burley in Wharfdale."

"Were you in trouble with the police there?"

"No."

"We can check up!"

"You can check up 'til the cows come home, but I haven't been in trouble with the police ever!"

"What school did you go to?"

"Do you want a list?" I'm asking him.

"Yes," he says.

"All fourteen of them?"

"Are you being clever?"

"No," I tell him, "I went to eleven different schools, fourteen if you count going to some of them twice."

"What's the last one?"

"St Mary's at Menston."

"Did you get into trouble there?"

"Only with the headmaster," I tell him.

"Did your family move around a lot then?"

"Yes."

"Are you a gippo?"

"What's a gippo?"

"You know, a gypsy."

"No, I'm not a bloody gippo."

"So, have you ever stolen anything?"

"Yes. Yes I have."

Now ugly freckle face is looking satisfied with himself.

"So, what did you steal?"

"The first time was in Ilkley and the second time was in Huddersfield," I tell him.

Now freckle face is looking really happy.

"Right then," he says, "out with it, what did you steal?"

"In Ilkley, on the way to school one morning, I stole some apples that were overhanging the footpath on Skipton Road, and in Huddersfield I ate some cox's apples at Cowlings shop without asking, and once in Huddersfield I shared some fish and chips that someone else stole."

The ugly freckle face is going red now. He grabs me by the collar and drags me to my feet. My face is two inches away from his red face and his smokey breath.

"Are you taking the piss?" he shouts at me.

"No!" I tell him.

Just then, I'm remembering about when my father got stopped in Belfast one night when he was drunk. The police asked if he'd been up to anything, like stealing, and he said to them, "No officers, the only things I steal are kisses." He thought it was very funny when he was telling me.

"You must have stolen something more than apples!" the ugly redfaced bastard spits out at me.

I look ugly straight in the eyes. "The only things I've stolen are kisses and that won't include you!"

It doesn't work like it did for my father. I think I might have got my timing wrong. He pushes me hard back onto the bench, where the wall stops my head going through to the next room. I'm half-dazed, wondering what's going on here. There's something very wrong,

I've always thought that the police were supposed to be the good guys. The desk sergeant is looking through the Bradford telephone directory. He's letting the hardfaced ugly bastard knock me about.

I stand up and face them both. I'm shouting at them.

"I didn't come in here to be knocked about! I've been pissed about all my life and I'm not here to be pissed about! I have witnesses to prove that there's no marks on me when I left my mother's house, so knock it off, I haven't done anything wrong!"

Ugly bastard is looking at me, and then at the desk sergeant. The sergeant is still flicking through the telephone directory as he's walking over to me and ugly face. Thank God, I'm thinking, the proper-looking policeman is going to tell the bastard to leave me alone. The sergeant looks at ugly, then at me. Then without any warning, Bradford town hall with six hundred pages behind it hits me like a brick on the side of my head, knocking me back towards the bench seat where, for the second time in five minutes, the wall stops my head from going into the room next door. I slide down the wall and off the bench onto the floor. The sergeant bends over me.

"Shut up you little bastard, that won't leave any marks."

Jesus Christ, I'm thinking, these are supposed to be the good guys. I'm sitting on the floor with my sore head in my hands. The sergeant is back at his desk and the ugly bastard has gone. It's not the sore head that's making me upset, it's the whole situation, and trying to figure out why the good guys are so bad. I'm thinking that they're no better than the cruel bullyboy Christian and De La Salle Brothers that abused and beat the boys in the homes in Ireland.

*

It's an hour 'til the council woman comes for me. It's a different woman than before. It's dark when we're on the Bradford Road leaving Brighouse. I'm thinking about when Jim McGarry in Keighley said that some people who went to Brighouse were never seen again. I'm betting they're buried behind the police station. Now I'm thinking what's the point in complaining to the council woman about the sergeant and ugly face. Who's going to believe me against them two lowsy, domineering, law-upholding bastards? I must have looked really threatening when I stood up to them, sticking out my thirty-four inch chest and looking the freckle-faced, smokey breathed, ugly bastard gobshite straight in the eye. I really didn't like that CID bully. My feckin head is sore. I don't think Mr Watson will be happy to see me when I go back to the home.

We've passed through Bradford and Shipley and are on a straight stretch of road heading towards Menston and Burley in Wharfdale. She turns left off the main road and along the side of a hill. I tell her this is not the way to Burley.

"I know," she says, "Mr Watson doesn't want you back."

She drives into a driveway of a big house that looks a bit like the home in Burley.

"You'll be staying here," she says, "'til we can find somewhere better for you."

"What kind of a place is this?" I ask her.

"It's a remand home for boys waiting to go to court."

"Criminals?" I ask her.

"Yes."

When she pulled off the main road I thought maybe she was calling at home for something. And when she drove onto the big gravel drive I thought she must be really rich if this is where she lives. I ask her if she thinks this is a better place than my mother's house for me to stay, me with a job to go back to in the morning? She doesn't answer. At the front door she rings the bell. There's a key turning at the other side and a clinking noise. A man opens the door and we go inside. He locks the door behind us. I can see through to a big dining room. There's lots of boys having their tea. It's a bit like the home at Burley, except there's lots of male staff with chains and keys on their belts. The council woman says I'll be staying here for a while 'til the Children's Department decide what to do with me.

"Why are the doors kept locked, and why have all the staff got bunches of keys?" I'm asking her.

Again, she doesn't answer me. The man who opened the front door answers for her.

"It's a remand home, lad," he says. "How long have you been remanded for, you know, 'til your next court appearance?"

"I haven't been to court," I tell him. "So when are you going to court?" he asks.

"I'm not going to court for anything."

He looks at the council woman.

"He's not going to court," she tells him. "He's run away from a children's home."

"So why is he here?"

"In case he tries to run away again," she says.

The man is looking puzzled.

"We've nowhere else to put him," she says, as she walks to the front door. "We'll give you all the details tomorrow," she tells him, just before he locks the door behind her.

I don't think I'll be seeing Roger Seamour anytime soon.

The place is called Tong Park House. All the doors to the outside are kept locked and the windows are screwed closed. All the boys here are waiting to go to court. All night there's a member of staff on each corridor upstairs outside the boys' bedrooms. During the day in the playrooms the boys exchange stories about what they've done that has landed them in trouble. House burglary and breaking into shops seem to be the most popular activities. They exchange ideas on the best way to steal things. One of them likes to 'do' C&A shops. He says the louvre glasses above the shop doors come out easily. Another boy is telling all the others the best way to hotwire a car, as long as it doesn't have one of them new steering locks, he says. When I tell them about me stealing apples and sharing the stolen fish and chips, they all laugh at me. I'm thinking I'm not criminal enough to be accepted as a proper crook.

The council leave me locked up in the 'school for criminals' for three weeks, with no contact from them 'til the new council woman comes to take me to a home in Clayton, Bradford. On the way we call at a Council storeroom up Great Horton Road to get me some new clothes. The clothes I have on are a mixture of things from the remand home that resemble something my mother would design. The clothes I get from the council store don't look much better.

The home is second to last on the left at the top of Beaconsfield Road and is run by a Mr and Mrs White. The good news about being here is that my little sister Mandy is in the house next door, that's also run by Mr and Mrs White, in the home for little kids, and I'll be able to see her nearly every day. The bad news is that she is still there. Mr and Mrs White also live in the end house next to their chicken and duck runs. The home for boys where I'll be staying has been made bigger by knocking two houses into one. There's another home at the bottom of the road and that's for girls. The Whites are in charge of all the houses. Mr White is very offhand with me. I don't think he likes me being here. I'm thinking that, like the policemen in Brighouse, he's assuming that I'll be getting into trouble and things like that. When I see

Mandy during the day she's telling me that her and all the other kids get shouted at all the time, and if they're not quiet at night when they go to bed, she says the aunties slap them hard. Mandy tells me about the wallop she got when she first came here, from one of the aunties called Sheila. She says the auntie's ring caught her head and cut it. Mr White called for Dr Black (true, that was his name) and the doctor said she should be taken to the hospital for some stitches. When the doctor left, she heard Mr White telling the auntie to clean her cut and just stick some vaseline on it and that'll do.

After the first week there and seeing little Mandy nearly every day, Mr White tells me that I can only see her once a week, on a Saturday. And he says I have to report to his office in the house first. When I go to his office on Saturday mornings about eleven o'clock, he always makes me wait for ages before I can see her, sometimes twenty minutes, sometimes up to forty-five minutes. One day after waiting about half an hour to see him I knock on his office door. He comes out shouting at me.

"Can't you do as you are told? Did you not learn anything when you were sent to the Remand Home?" "Yes Mr White," I tell him. "I learnt that you can break into C&A stores if you slide out the glass from the louvre windows above the main doors, and how to steal a car by hotwiring it as long as it hasn't got one of those new steering wheel locks on it."

Mr White's face is turning red.

"Get out!" he shouts. "You're not seeing your sister today!"

As I walk out of the house Mandy waves to me from the playroom. There's no logical reason that I can find for the waiting. The first conclusion I come to is that Mr White just wants to show me who is in charge. The second conclusion I come to is that he just doesn't want an older boy here. This was more or less confirmed when, after being there for about two months one of the aunties told me that when Mr White was discussing me with her, he told her that he was surprised that I hadn't run away from the home. Then he said that maybe they're not trying hard enough to get rid of me. Now I'm realising that Mr White is playing the same game as Mr Watson did in the home in Burley in Wharfdale. When he wanted to get rid of the new boy Martin he made his life a misery and encouraged us to stand up to him and even have a fight with him to make him run away, and when he did run away, Mr Watson just said, "Well that bad penny's gone." Now I'm determined that Mr White won't get his way. I'll put up with the shit he gives me, 'til I'm ready to leave, properly. I'm telling Mrs Halligan, the cleaner, about Mr White. She tells me just to stick it out for now, that things will only get better. I'm thinking Mrs Halligan, who is Irish, sounds a bit like my mother.

Mr and Mrs White go away on holiday for a week. It's like a holiday for me too. I get to know the lady across the street and her teenage daughter who look after the chickens and ducks while the Whites are away.

I still get the *Telegraph and Argus* paper every day to see if there's any jobs going. I wish they were on holiday all the time.

There's no sign of my mother coming to see me or Mandy. The home is only about 10 miles from Brighouse.

# *Chapter 28*

## Run away? This time I just walk away

It's mid afternoon and Auntie Karen is in the kitchen cooking the dinner for when the other boys get back from school. She's doing fisherman's pie in the oven, baking the fish in a big white dish with mashed potato on top. I'm in the kitchen with her listening to Beatles songs on her record player. She opens the oven door to check the pie. She screams out and stands back. I look into the oven and see the pie with the top going brown in places, and in the middle of the pie is something like a skinny worm sticking up out of the pie, about two inches long, wiggling around like a miniature snake. Auntie Karen ask's me what it is. I'm telling her it looks like a worm. She runs out of the house to fetch Mr White. When she comes back with him, she's telling him that the fish must be bad and asking if she has to throw it away. Mr White lifts the pie out of the oven and pulls the worm out with the help of the dish cloth. He tells her that nearly all fish have worms in them and it's not harmful to eat them. He puts the dish back in the oven and tells the two of us not to tell the other boys. Then he looks at me.

"Shouldn't you be out looking for a job?"

"The paper isn't out yet," I tell him.

At teatime we are all at the tables having the dinner. Some of the boys are asking why me and Auntie Karen are having sandwiches for tea. We tell them we had some pie at lunchtime.

Contact from the Children's Department comes to me through Mr White. He tells me that they are looking for lodgings for me and that I need to be looking harder for a job. I ask him why I can't just go 'home.' He ignores the question. I see an advert in the *Telegraph and Argus*. Baird Television works in Horton Lane are looking for apprentices to start with them next September. I write them a letter. I check my spelling and do my best writing. I tell them about my father fixing televisions and radios and that I'm very interested in getting a job with Bairds. I'm wanting to tell them about my father fixing his radios on the table and me finding bits of solder in my school sandwiches, but Mrs Halligan the cleaner woman says she doesn't think they'll need to know all that, so I keep the letter short. I finish the letter asking them to:

"Please furnish me with details of the application requirements.

Yours sincerely

Brian O'Donoghue

aged 15 "

I'm thinking 'furnish' sounds better than 'send.' Mrs Halligan agrees with me.

I'm waiting outside Mr White's office to show him my application for his approval. After waiting for about twenty minutes, I knock on his door again. He comes out and says he knows I'm there, but he's still busy and I'm to do as I'm told and wait. Forty minutes leads on to an hour. Then he decides to come out and see me. He reads my letter in the hallway.

"What do you mean by 'furnish me with details'?" he asks me. I'm telling him that it means the same as 'please send me details.'

"So why don't you just write 'send me'?" he says.

"Because 'furnish' sounds better," I tell him.

"OK," he says, "send it off."

Now I'm thinking that he really didn't have to make me wait an hour for him to have a one minute scan of my letter. He really is an awkward bastard, a domineering awkward bastard, as my mother would be saying. I'm now thinking that Mr White is a domineering, awkward AND ignorant bastard. I thank him for looking at my letter. I'm not being sarcastic. I'm just not loosing my manners for him, the lousy feck. Now it makes me wonder if he even knew what furnish meant.

I get an interview at Baird Television and I get the apprenticeship starting in September, but it's still only April. I need a job from now 'til September. Yes it's April and my mother hasn't been in touch since I left Brighouse and no one has been to see Mandy. Louise and Deirdre are still stuck in Belfast with the nuns.

Things really haven't improved much at all since we were dumped in the homes in Limerick all those years ago. When will I let it sink in that my mother was never a mother, my father was never a father, and no one has ever given a shit about any of us! No, that's not exactly right. Grandad in Dublin did his best for us, and Auntie Mary and her family in Keighley were good to us, and others too. I'm just feeling down. I go into the kitchen to listen to Auntie Karen's Beatles songs, and help her make the boys' dinner before getting the early paper for the jobs section. Allied Textiles Ltd are advertising for a young boy to help the overlooker fix the weaving looms and keep the place clean. I go straight down to the mill on Spencer Road and get the job. I can start the next day. Back at the home I tell Mr White that I've got a job. He asks me why I didn't tell him I was going down to the mill to see the overlooker. I tell him I wanted to get there before anyone else. He says I should have come to his office to tell him before I went out. Now I'm thinking there's no pleasing him. I've just had to wait fifteen minutes outside his office to tell him I've got the job. I wasn't going to risk waiting an hour to get permission to go to the mill. Someone might have got there before me. I start at half past seven and finish at half past four. The overlooker is called Jim, but he says I have to call him Mr Crowther in front of the other workers.

I'm at work at twenty-five past seven the next morning. He shows me how to fix the small bits on the looms when they break down. The weaver women write down the faults and breakdown times on a board on the wall. Then when the loom is fixed the overlooker puts the time on the board beside his initials to show the loom has been fixed.

The weaver women communicate to each other across the looms and over the clattering noise by lip-reading. It takes me only two weeks to learn how to do the easy fixing jobs and to learn the lip-reading. Well, some lip-reading. Well, two main things, really. They can understand me if I mouth 'good morning' and 'goodnight.' Anything else I try to mouth to them gets lost in the noise of looms and the haze of the dust in the air that can be seen better if the sunshine is coming through the glass roof. I'm no good at lip-reading, but it gives the weaver women a good laugh when I try. I'm doing really well with the small jobs though. It's good to be able to fix things, like the big, thick leather belts that come off the driveshafts. Or the small leather belts that drive the shuttles across the looms. Some days half the jobs on the wall that have been fixed have my initials beside them. I like learning how to fix things.

Mr and Mrs White are away again for a few days, so I can go to see Mandy more. After seeing her on the Saturday morning, I'm back in the house looking out the front window, listening to the Beatles singing in the background, when I see the teenage girl and her mother who live across the road. The mother is carrying one of Mr White's ducks. She is being followed by her daughter and their big wild-looking cat. I go across to ask them if everything is all right. She shows me the duck. It's dead.

"The bugger of a cat has killed it and if Mr White finds out, he'll want to kill me!" She says she'll have to get rid of it and see if she can find another one the same make and colour. I tell her that she should eat it, as there's nothing much wrong with it, except for being dead of course.

"Oh no," she says, "I couldn't do that," and her daughter looks at the duck and then me and says "Yuk." The mother looks at the cat and says "Shit." The lady did manage to find a 'matching duck' and when the Whites came back, they were none the wiser, and the cat was still alive, lucky cat.

Three weeks after starting work at the mill the council woman (another new one) comes to see me at Beaconsfield Road on a Saturday morning. She says she has found lodging for me near the mill. I bet Mr White will be happy. She takes me to see an Italian woman who has a son just older than me. Mrs Waselena is her name, her husband is Polish. I move into the house and share a bedroom with her son Nicky. I go to work through the week, and I go to see Mandy on a Saturday. I go to Mass with them at the Polish church on Sunday morning, back again later in the afternoon for Benediction, and to the the Italian club in the evening. I get to be friends with a boy called Malcolm Ward who used to be in Mr White's home. Malcolm is lodging with Mrs Halligan, the cleaner woman from the home. He's got a job as an apprentice joiner. We both buy bicycles on hire purchase for five shillings a week each from the local bicycle shop on Horton Lane. On Sundays, when I've been to Mass with Mrs Waselena and her family, I sometimes go out for bike rides with Malcolm. Mrs Waselena's son Nicky sometimes comes with us. One Sunday, me and Malcolm cycle to Brighouse to my mother's house, only to find out that she has moved to a house on Manchester Road in Huddersfield. Marie is still living in the house next door to my mother's old house and she gives me my mother's address and tells me that Peter is out for his regular pint and Boo Boo (Joanna) is nine months old now. She says Peter got a job in the office at Firth Carpets mill at Bailiff Bridge, and my father is still in Keighley with Anna. I ask her about the rest of the family and she says Jack is still working for Kennedy's and Raymin has joined the army. She says Louise and Deirdre are still with the nuns in Belfast, Helen is still in Bury in Lancashire with Uncle Jimmy and his family, and my mother and Jack are trying to get Mandy home.

Mrs Waselena isn't happy when I tell her that we've been to see my mother who wasn't there, but Marie was. I don't know why she doesn't want me to see my family. The next Sunday after Mass when I tell her I want to go to see my mother in Huddersfield, again she isn't happy. In fact, she doesn't want me to go. She wants me to go to Benediction in the afternoon and to the Italian club in the evening with her son Nicky, to the class that teaches the Italian language to the children that have been brought up in England. I go with her to

Benediction, and the club, and the language class. Each Sunday it's the same, Mass at the Polish church, dinner in the afternoon, Benediction later at the Polish church and then Italian lessons at the club. I'm thinking maybe Mrs Waselena is wanting to make me into an Italian priest.

I miss a couple of Saturdays going to see Mandy and when I go on the third week Mr White tells me that she was taken home by my mother two weeks before, "so you won't need to come here anymore will you?" Bastard to the end, I'm thinking as I cycle down Beaconsfield Road, the Beatles in the background agreeing with me, singing 'Yeah, Yeah, Yeah.'

# Chapter 29

## Back home – to live happily ever after?

I'm on the bus from Bradford to Huddersfield. I stuck it out another three months with Mrs Waselena, but I've had enough. I was sixteen last week on the 22nd August. Now it's Sunday again and after Mass this morning when I said I wanted to see my mother and Mandy, Mrs Waselena didn't want me to go. She even reminded me that none of my family sent me a birthday card. I've walked out. I've got my suitcase with me and I've left the bicycle for the cycle shop man to take back. I'm going to have one more go at going 'home' and if the council come to get me back I'll just run off and join the bloody Foreign Legion. Now I'm thinking that I shouldn't really have sworn at Mrs Waselena before I left. She's not a bad person.

I'm on the bus going past the Brighouse police station where the 'good guys' knocked me about when I hadn't done anything wrong. I'm thinking about when Auntie Mary's lodger in Keighley said that Brighouse is down a hole between Halifax, Bradford and Huddersfield. I'm thinking that Brighouse itself is OK. It's just the Brighouse police who were not OK with me. I'm thinking maybe they were just tired and stressed with the job they have to do, and the constant worry about the all the missing people buried at the back of the police station.

I get the Marsden bus from Huddersfield town centre outside Woolworths. The bus driver lets me off the bus a couple of stops after the Junction pub. I knock on the door. My mother opens it and Bunty the dog shows me his teeth for a while.

"Oh it's you. Have you run away again?"

"No," I tell her, "this time I just walked away."

"You better come in then. Do you want a cup of tea?

"Yes please."

"Well get in there and get it yourself," she says, pointing to a small kitchen at the other side of the sitting room. Jack is in the front room. He says hello and I say hello back. I go into the small lean-to kitchen at the back where my mother has directed me. I'm filling the kettle at the cold water tap over the big white pot sink. I look out the window and see the rock cliffs behind the backyard that rise up to about thirty-five or forty feet. At the bottom of the rocks is a small piece of grass garden. Little Mandy is sitting on the grass playing with a scruffy doll. She isn't much bigger than the doll. There's a big tin bath hanging on the wall outside the back door. My mother tells me that Mandy has been home for about three months and that the council woman says she can stay for good now that her and Jack are buying this house. "A five-hundred pound mortgage over twenty-five years," she says, "that's a serious amount of debt to take on." The house has one-and-a-half bedrooms, one sitting room, a lean-to kitchen and an outside toilet. I can't help thinking that my mother, or any of us, haven't progressed much since we left Belfast just over three years ago.

Jack says that Raymin has joined the army and his photo was in the *Huddersfield Examiner* for being the best recruit at Catterick Camp. He says Raymin is on leave soon and will be coming to stay for a while. My mother says that Mandy can sleep in the big bedroom with her and Jack and I can sleep in the small boxroom, and when Raymin comes he'll have to sleep on the fold-down settee in the front room.

On the Monday Morning I'm on St Peter's Street in Huddersfield looking for the Children's Department office. I go in and see the man in charge. His name is Mr Bruce. I tell him that I've left the lodging in Bradford and I'm staying at my mother's house. I tell him why I didn't like being there and that I'm not going back.

"And if you try to send me back, I'll run away again and join the Foreign Legion!"

"I see no point in making you go back to Bradford. So you don't want to be a priest then?"

Now I'm thinking at least he has a sense of humour.

"Mind you look for a job and keep me informed on how you're getting on."

In the afternoon I get the *Huddersfield Examiner* to look at the jobs section. I'm not going back to the job at the mill in Bradford, it's too far to travel by three buses every day. I'm inside the Market Hall, up on the balcony overlooking the stalls, reading the paper. There's a tap on my shoulder. It's Paddy Folan from Cowling's fruit and veg shop. He's asking me how I'm getting on. He says my mother has told him about me being taken back to a home after running away before. I tell him it's all sorted now and I'm living on Manchester Road at my mother's house.

"You know when you worked for us before and you were sent back to the children's home?" he says. "Did you know that Eric, the boss, rang the Children's Department and told them that he would keep your job for you if they let you go home?"

"No, I didn't know that!" I tell him.

"Anyway, what are you doing here?" he asks me.

"I'm looking for a job," I tell him.

"We need someone again," he says. "It's yours if you want it."

"Yes I do, thanks!"

I walk home to tell my mother about what Mr Bruce said and about Paddy giving me my old job back.

"Bejesus" she says, "things are happening quick today. Do you want a cup of tea?"

"Yes," I say to her, "I know where the kettle is."

*

On Sunday mornings me and Jack go for long walks all around Huddersfield and the parks and canals. He shows me the demolition jobs he's worked on, telling me what used to be there. The canal near Manchester Road has no boats on it because it's been abandoned.

All the mills along the canal are busy with day and night shifts, and there's lots of stuff thrown out and dumped at the back of the mills down Stoney Battery Road near home, lots of good stuff. On Wednesday afternoons I go rooting for things. The maintenance man at Stoney Battery Mill says I can have some old oil drums that I want to make a canoe. He says a round drum won't be very stable on the water, but I tell him I'll figure it out.

Jack brings me things home from the demolition jobs, like old tools and a long length of telephone wire that I can use for an aerial for the crystal set radio that I'm making. I've got lots of nails from the rubbish fires at the back of the mills that I can cut down to make rivets for the canoe. And Jack has found me a sledgehammer with a broken handle that I can stick in the ground at the back of the house to use like a blacksmith's anvil. Down the cellar I found a gun, a colt forty-five, wrapped in oil cloth. Jack says he found it on a demolition job at the bottom of King Street in the town. He says he's been told it's an old Nigerian police gun.

"What do you think of it? he asks.

"Not much," I tell him, "I'd rather have some metal working tools."

At the weekend Jack helps me carry the oil drums up the long steep grass slope from Stoney Battery Mill to the back of the house and shows me how to cut them with a hammer and thin chisel, like he does at work in the winter for lighting fires in. Wednesday afternoons are spent working on the canoe, with my mother complaining about the noise. Sunday afternoons Jack helps me and my mother complains about the two of us. She complains more when I climb up to the top of the cliffs to the back of the bowling club to secure the aerial wire for the crystal set radio I've made using an earpiece from a set of headphones and a glass diode I got from Taylor's radio shop on Macauley Street by the bus station.

The canoe has an oil drum at the back for buoyancy and to lean my back against. There's two half drums in the middle to sit in and a half drum at the front with the sides squashed and riveted together to make it streamlined. There's a plywood aerofoil strip at each side to give lift and stability in forward motion. I have a double-ended paddle made out of a brush handle and ply-board from Jack's work. And the cuts on my fingers from the cutting and riveting are nearly healed up.

Sunday Morning is launch time. My mother says we're both feckin mad. Me and Jack carry the canoe across the road and slide it all the way down the side of the hill to the water. I tie on my safety vest, made out of blocks of polystyrene I got from behind the mill. Jack holds the canoe as I get in. It's a bit unsteady. He pushes me out from the towpath. The canoe is quite steady when I'm paddling forward but when I slow down it gets very wobbly. Jack is walking along the towpath level with me shouting "Speed up Lad." I speed up and the wobbling stops. When I slow down and stop the, wobbling is less. I must be getting better at controlling it. It's time to try it in reverse. I start paddling backwards. The aerofoil at the front pulls the pointy end down and I'm in the water. I start to panic, but not for long. My shoes hit the bottom just three-foot down and clouds of black mud are all around me.

"Are you all right lad?" I pull myself and the canoe to the edge and we both pull it onto the towpath and sit down to have a good laugh.

The canoe is at the back of the mill and I'm at home in the backyard with Jack hosing down myself and my muddy trousers and shoes and my mother calling us "two stupid feckers." And Mandy is laughing at us. Bunty the dog is barking at the hosepipe. The water is freezing cold. The cold water is making me think up a new project, a shower. I need to have some system of warm water out here. I'll get a watering can and fill it with hot water from the the heater above the sink and put it on the outside toilet roof where Jack can tilt it over me. And I can tip it over him when he comes in from his demolition job. We'll have to keep our underpants on though in case the neighbours want to go out the communal side gate.

Next Wednesday after work I go across the road to the little building near the bus stop overlooking the valley. On the side there's a sign that says JOHN'S BOOKS - NEW AND SECONDHAND. I need a book with plans in it to get the canoe thing sorted out. There's two men wearing leather jackets and holding helmets talking to the man behind the counter. It doesn't look a bit like the bookshops in town. They all stop talking when I go in, and look straight at me.

"Yes lad?" says the man behind the counter.

"Have you got a secondhand book or magazine on how to make a canoe?" I ask him. He looks at the two other customers and then back at me. He picks up a book from the shelves behind him and puts it on the counter.

"This is the only kind of book I have here, lad."

On the cover is a picture of a lady sitting on a motorbike wearing an apron and not much else.

"No, I want to make a canoe, not a motorbike."

He stands there looking at me. Then the penny finally drops as I leave.

"OK, thanks anyway," I say, remembering to use my manners.

As I cross back over the road I'm thinking, why didn't he just say he only sold motorbike books in the first place?

*

Raymin is back from the army at the weekend. He's telling me all about the training in Catterick Camp at the north side of the town. He's joined the Royal Signals, training to be a radio operator. He says he has a chance later on to join the Parachute Regiment, if he passes the para training, that is. I'm asking him if the basic training at Catterick Camp is hard.

"Naw," he says, "it's a piece of cake after being brought up by the Christian Brothers and the De la Salle Brothers in Ireland."

"What was the best bit of the training?" I'm asking him.

"Being voted the best recruit of the intake and having my photo in the *Examiner* newspaper," he says. "What was the worst bit?"

"When the Huddersfield police saw my photo in the *Examiner* and came up to Catterick to arrest me for not paying a fine I got before I joined up!" He says that his C.O. gave him a good bollicking and told him that if it had been for anything serious he could have been thrown out of the army. I'm asking him if the police knew about him running off with the fish and chips at Fartown Bar on Bradford road last year when he ended up in the mill dam.

"No," he says, "don't be stupid."

Now I'm thinking that maybe it's not always a good thing, having your photo in the paper. Raymin says it's great in the army. He says that when he's done all his radio training that he'll be going abroad and after that he's going to do his best to join the Paras.

"You should join up too."

"I'm too young to join the army."

"You can join the junior soldiers at sixteen."

Raymin is back at Catterick Camp and Helen is still living with Uncle Jimmy in Bury. My mother has been talking to Jack about bringing Louise and Deirdre over from Belfast and shouting at me when I call her Josie. Well, I find it hard to call her Mam or something like that after being in so many homes. I'll just have to keep calling her 'Excuse me' or 'By the way'. I just can't call her Mam. Anyway, I better get on with the bicycle I'm fixing up for getting to work. Yes, the one that Jack got from his work. On Wednesday afternoon I'm fixing the bicycle and thinking about making a trailer for it so I can collect useful things and store them in the backyard. I better make a good job of it so it'll be strong enough to take Mandy out on it too. And I'll need some good strong rope to tie her to the trailer so she won't fall off. Safety is very important. I'm also thinking about what Raymin said about the junior soldiers. I think I'll go to the army recruitment shop and find out more about it.

Josie, with her cigarette, and Mandy and Bunty are looking out the front door after me.

"Where are you rushing off to?" Josie shouts.

"I'm finding out about the junior soldiers," I tell her, as I cross the road to the bus stop. I try thumbing a lift from a wagon and the driver's mate puts two fingers up at me. But I don't let that bother me. I'm thinking about being old enough to be my own boss and make my own decisions. I've got a job, that's a good start. And I've learnt things, like how not to make a canoe. And Marie explained about assets and things. So now I know the difference between good assets and bad assets, and I'm ready to face the world. And from now on I'm in charge of me and I'll make sure everything will go right. It wouldn't matter anyway if I did join the army 'cos the house is a bit small and Josie is expecting a new baby and has been talking about getting married to Jack. Now I'm thinking about the coincidence thing I found out yesterday about Jack being brought up by the not-so-Christian Brothers in Glin where we were in Ireland. This is the start of the rest of my life and everything will be fine. I'm going to walk into town as there's no sign of the bus. Yep, everything is going to work out fine from now on. Nothing will go wrong. I'll keep up with my good manners and cut down with the swearing. I set off in a hurry. I just miss bumping into a man coming out of John's books with his hat pulled down and his collar up. On a warm day? I better turn and wave to Josie and Mandy. Yep! From now on I'm in charge of me. I'll make sure all my future plans will happen. Things are looking good! I turn around quickly. I feel a bump and see a flash of light. I'm on my arse feeling a trickle of blood running down my face. Who put that feckin lamp post there? I'm feeling a bit dazed. My mother and Mandy are out of breath standing over me. Bunty is licking the trickle of blood on the side of my face. Josie asks if I'm alright. I have to think a bit.

"No, I'm not," I tell her, "Raymin still owes me two squares of Cleeves toffee!"

Mine was certainly a different kind of childhood. At times it was very difficult maintaining a child's voice and staying in a child's memory. Thank you for staying with me on this journey.

Little Brian.

We all managed to keep in touch with each other in later life – Most of our glasses are half full!

*Mother and Father in 1950.*

*Limerick City 1954, before the new baby was born. From left to right: Raymin, Marie, Little Brian, Louise, Mammy and Helen.*

*1955 in the People's Park in Limerick – I'm in need of a haircut!*

*1956 in Glin.*

My First Communion, Glin Industrial School, Limerick, 1957.

Raymond, Belfast 1958.

Rubane House, Kircubbin, where we were in 1960. Me and Raymin slept beside the window above the front door.

*Dublin 1959, Dominican Convent. Me, Raymin and Marie visiting Auntie Nuala.*

*Visiting my sisters in Nazereth House, Belfast, back row from right: Deirdre, Helen, me, Louise.*

*Louise, Helen and Deirdre visiting Auntie Peggy and Uncle Declan.*

*Rubane House, Kircubbin 1961, hair growing back after having head shaved – nits!*
*Me – bottom right.*

*1965 – just before I ran away from the Children's Home.*
*Me – bottom row in school blazer.*

*Taking a break from emotional issues during writing.*

Printed in Great Britain
by Amazon

75553429R00285